# What's a Microcontroller?

## Student Guide

VERSION 2.2

## WARRANTY

Parallax Inc. warrants its products against defects in materials and workmanship for a period of 90 days from receipt of product. If you discover a defect, Parallax Inc. will, at its option, repair or replace the merchandise, or refund the purchase price. Before returning the product to Parallax, call for a Return Merchandise Authorization (RMA) number. Write the RMA number on the outside of the box used to return the merchandise to Parallax. Please enclose the following along with the returned merchandise: your name, telephone number, shipping address, and a description of the problem. Parallax will return your product or its replacement using the same shipping method used to ship the product to Parallax.

## 14-DAY MONEY BACK GUARANTEE

If, within 14 days of having received your product, you find that it does not suit your needs, you may return it for a full refund. Parallax Inc. will refund the purchase price of the product, excluding shipping/handling costs. This guarantee is void if the product has been altered or damaged. See the Warranty section above for instructions on returning a product to Parallax.

## COPYRIGHTS AND TRADEMARKS

## ISBN 1-928982-02-6

## DISCLAIMER OF LIABILITY

Parallax Inc. is not responsible for special, incidental, or consequential damages resulting from any breach of warranty, or under any legal theory, including lost profits, downtime, goodwill, damage to or replacement of equipment or property, or any costs of recovering, reprogramming, or reproducing any data stored in or used with

Parallax products. Parallax Inc. is also not responsible for any personal damage, including that to life and health, resulting from use of any of our products. You take full responsibility for your BASIC Stamp application, no matter how life-threatening it may be.

## WEB SITE AND DISCUSSION LISTS

The Parallax Inc. web site (www.parallax.com) has many downloads, products, customer applications and on-line ordering for the components used in this text. We also maintain several e-mail discussion lists for people interested in using Parallax products. These lists are accessible from www.parallax.com via the Support → Discussion Groups menu. These are the lists that we operate:

- <u>BASIC Stamps</u> – With over 4,000 subscribers, this list is widely utilized by engineers, hobbyists and students who share their BASIC Stamp projects and ask questions.
- <u>Stamps in Class</u> – Created for educators *and* students, this list has about 650 subscribers who discuss the use of the Stamps in Class curriculum in their courses. The list provides an opportunity for both students and educators to ask questions and get answers.
- <u>Parallax Educators</u> –Exclusively for educators and those who contribute to the development of Stamps in Class. Parallax created this group to obtain feedback on our curricula and to provide a forum for educators to develop and obtain Teacher's Guides.
- <u>Parallax Translators</u> – Consisting of about 40 people, the purpose of this list is to provide a conduit between Parallax and those who translate our documentation to languages other than English. Parallax provides editable Word documents to our translating partners and attempts to time the translations to coordinate with our publications.
- <u>Toddler Robot</u> – A customer created this discussion list to discuss applications and programming of the Parallax Toddler robot.
- <u>SX Tech</u> – Discussion of programming the SX microcontroller with Parallax assembly language tools and $3^{rd}$ party BASIC and C compilers. Approximately 600 members.
- <u>Javelin Stamp</u> – Discussion of application and design using the Javelin Stamp, a Parallax module that is programmed using a subset of Sun Microsystems' Java® programming language. Approximately 250 members.

## ERRATA

While great effort is made to assure the accuracy of our texts, errors may still exist. If you find an error, please let us know by sending an email to editor@parallax.com. We continually strive to improve all of our educational materials and documentation, and frequently revise our texts. Occasionally, an errata sheet with a list of known errors and corrections for a given text will be posted to our web site, www.parallax.com. Please check the individual product page's free downloads for an errata file.

# Table of Contents

**Preface**......................................................................................................................v
   Audience....................................................................................................................v
   Support and Discussion Groups ...............................................................................v
   Teacher's Guide ......................................................................................................vi
   The Stamps in Class Curriculum .............................................................................vi
   Foreign Translations..............................................................................................viii
   Special Contributors .............................................................................................viii

**Chapter #1: Getting Started**..........................................................................................1
   How Many Microcontrollers Did You Use Today? ......................................................1
   The BASIC Stamp 2 - Your New Microcontroller........................................................1
   Amazing Inventions with BASIC Stamp Microcontrollers ...........................................2
   Hardware and Software ............................................................................................5
   Activity #1: Getting the Software...............................................................................5
   Activity #2: Installing the Software ..........................................................................10
   Activity #3: Setting Up the Hardware and Testing the System ..................................13
   Activity #4: First Program.......................................................................................20
   Activity #5: Looking Up Answers ............................................................................27
   Activity #6: Introducing ASCII Code........................................................................30
   Activity #7: When You're Done ...............................................................................31
   Summary ...............................................................................................................33

**Chapter #2: Lights On – Lights Off**.............................................................................37
   Indicator Lights .....................................................................................................37
   Making a Light Emitting Diode (LED) Emit Light.......................................................37
   Activity #1: Building and Testing the LED Circuit......................................................38
   Activity #2: On/Off Control with the BASIC Stamp....................................................46
   Activity #3: Counting and Repeating.......................................................................52
   Activity #4: Building and Testing a Second LED Circuit ............................................56
   Activity #5: Using Current Direction to Control a Bi-Color LED ..................................60
   Summary ...............................................................................................................67

**Chapter #3: Digital Input - Pushbuttons**....................................................................71
   Found on Calculators, Hand Held Games, and Appliances .......................................71
   Receiving vs. Sending High and Low Signals ..........................................................71
   Activity #1: Testing a Pushbutton with an LED Circuit...............................................71
   Activity #2: Reading a Pushbutton with the BASIC Stamp ........................................75
   Activity #3: Pushbutton Control of an LED Circuit ....................................................80
   Activity #4: Two Pushbuttons Controlling Two LED Circuits.......................................83
   Activity #5: Reaction Timer Test .............................................................................88
   Summary ...............................................................................................................97

**Chapter #4: Controlling Motion** ................................................................. **103**
Microcontrolled Motion ....................................................................... 103
On/Off Signals and Motor Motion ....................................................... 103
Activity #1: Connecting and Testing the Servo ................................... 103
Activity #2: Controlling Position with Your Computer ......................... 119
Activity #3: Converting Position to Motion .......................................... 125
Activity #4: Pushbutton Controlled Servo ........................................... 128
Summary ............................................................................................. 134

**Chapter #5: Measuring Rotation** ................................................................. **139**
Adjusting Dials and Monitoring Machines ........................................... 139
The Variable Resistor under the Dial – A Potentiometer ..................... 139
Activity #1: Building and Testing the Potentiometer Circuit ................ 141
Activity #2: Measuring Resistance by Measuring Time ....................... 143
Activity #3: Reading the Dial with the BASIC Stamp .......................... 149
Activity #4: Controlling a Servo with a Potentiometer ........................ 152
Summary ............................................................................................. 160

**Chapter #6: Digital Display** ........................................................................ **165**
The Every-Day Digital Display ............................................................. 165
What's a 7-Segment Display? .............................................................. 165
Activity #1: Building and Testing the 7-Segment LED Display ............ 167
Activity #2: Controlling the 7-Segment LED Display ........................... 171
Activity #3: Displaying Digits .............................................................. 174
Activity #4: Displaying the Position of a Dial ...................................... 181
Summary ............................................................................................. 186

**Chapter #7: Measuring Light** ...................................................................... **189**
Devices that Contain Light Sensors .................................................... 189
Introducing the Photoresistor .............................................................. 189
Activity #1: Building and Testing the Light Meter ............................... 190
Activity #2: Graphing Light Measurements ......................................... 193
Activity #3: Tracking Light Events ....................................................... 197
Activity #4: Simple Light Meter ........................................................... 203
Summary ............................................................................................. 215

**Chapter #8: Frequency and Sound** ............................................................ **219**
Your Day and Electronic Beeps ........................................................... 219
Microcontrollers, Speakers, Beeps and On/Off Signals ...................... 219
Activity #1: Building and Testing the Speaker ..................................... 220
Activity #2: Action Sounds .................................................................. 222
Activity #3: Musical Notes and Simple Songs ..................................... 227
Activity #4: Microcontroller Music ....................................................... 232
Activity #5: Cell Phone RingTones ...................................................... 245

Summary ............................................................................................................257

**Chapter #9: Electronic Building Blocks** ...........................................................**261**
Those Little Black Chips ....................................................................................261
Expand Your Projects with Peripheral Integrated Circuits .........................................262
Activity #1: Control Current Flow with a Transistor.................................................263
Activity #2: Introducing the Digital Potentiometer ...................................................265
Summary ............................................................................................................276

**Chapter #10: Running the Whole Show** ...........................................................**279**
Subsystem Integration ........................................................................................279
Activity #1: Building and Testing Each Pushbutton Circuit .........................................280
Activity #2: Building and Testing Each RC-Time Circuit .............................................283
Activity #3: Subsystem Integration Example.............................................................285
Activity #4: Developing and Adding a Software Subsystem ........................................289
Summary ............................................................................................................295

**Appendix A: USB to Serial Adapter**....................................................................**299**

**Appendix B: Equipment and Parts Lists**.............................................................**301**

**Appendix C: BASIC Stamp and Carrier Board Components and Functions**....**305**

**Appendix D: Batteries and Power Supplies**........................................................**309**

**Appendix E: Trouble-Shooting**............................................................................**313**

**Appendix F: More about Electricity** ....................................................................**317**

**Appendix G: RTTTL Format Summary** .................................................................**325**

**Index** ......................................................................................................................**327**

# Preface

This text answers the question "What's a microcontroller?" by showing students how they can design their own customized, intelligent inventions with Parallax, Inc.'s BASIC Stamp® microcontroller module. The activities in this text incorporate a variety of fun and interesting experiments designed to appeal to a student's imagination by using motion, light, sound, and tactile feedback to introduce new concepts. These activities introduce students to a variety of basic principles in the fields of computer programming, electricity and electronics, mathematics and physics. Many of the activities facilitate hands-on presentation of design practices used by engineers and technicians in the creation of modern machines and appliances, using common inexpensive parts.

## AUDIENCE

This text is organized so that it can be used by the widest possible variety of students as well as independent learners. Middle school students can try the examples in this text in a guided tour fashion by simply following the check-marked instructions and instructor supervision. At the other end of the spectrum, pre-engineering students' comprehension and problem-solving skills can be tested with the questions, exercises and projects (with solutions) in each chapter summary. The independent learner can work at his or her own pace, and obtain assistance through the Stamps in Class® Yahoo Group forum cited below.

## SUPPORT AND DISCUSSION GROUPS

The following two Yahoo! Discussion Groups are available for those who would like support in using this text. These groups are accessible from www.parallax.com under Discussion Groups on the Support menu.

Stamps In Class Group: Open to students, educators, and independent learners, this forum allows members to ask each other questions and share answers as they work through the activities, exercises and projects in this text.

Parallax Educator's Group: This moderated forum provides support for educators and welcomes feedback as we continue to develop our Stamps in Class curriculum. To join this group you must have proof of your status as an educator verified by Parallax. The Teacher's Guide for this text is available as a free download through this forum.

Educational Support: stampsinclass@parallax.com Contact the Parallax Stamps in Class Team directly if you are having difficulty subscribing to either of these Yahoo! Groups, or have questions about the material in this text, our Stamps in Class Curriculum, our Educator's Courses, or any of our educational services.

Educational Sales: sales@parallax.com Contact our Sales Team for information about educational discount pricing and classroom packs for our Stamps in Class kits and other selected products.

Technical Support: support@parallax.com Contact our Tech Support Team for general questions regarding the set-up and use of any of our hardware or software products.

## TEACHER'S GUIDE

Each chapter summary contains a set of questions, exercises and projects with solutions provided. A Teacher's Guide is also available for this text. It contains an additional set of solved questions, exercises and projects, as well as some expanded and alternative solutions to the material in the text. The Teacher's Guide is available free in both Word and PDF file formats by joining the Parallax Educators Yahoo Group or by emailing stampsinclass@parallax.com. To obtain these files, you must provide proof of your status as an educator.

## THE STAMPS IN CLASS CURRICULUM

*What's a Microcontroller?* is the gateway text to our Stamps in Class curriculum. After completing this text, you can continue your studies with any of the Student Guides listed below. All of the books listed are available for free download from www.parallax.com. The versions cited below were current at the time of this printing. Please check our web sites www.parallax.com or www.stampsinclass.com for the latest revisions; we continually strive to improve our educational program.

### Stamps in Class Student Guides:

For a well-rounded introduction to the design practices that go into modern devices and machinery, working through the activities and projects in the following Student Guides is highly recommended.

> "*Applied Sensors*", Student Guide, Version 1.3, Parallax Inc., 2003
> "*Basic Analog and Digital*", Student Guide, Version 1.3, Parallax Inc., 2004
> "*Industrial Control*", Student Guide, Version 1.1, Parallax Inc., 1999
> "*Robotics with the Boe-Bot*", Student Guide, Version 2.0, Parallax Inc., 2003

## More Robotics Kits:

Some enter the Stamps in Class curriculum through the *Robotics with the Boe-Bot* Student Guide. After completing it, you will be ready for either or both of these more advanced robotics texts and kits:

> "*Advanced Robotics: with the Toddler*", Student Guide, Version 1.2, Parallax Inc., 2003
> "*SumoBot*", Manual, Version 2.0, Parallax Inc., 2004

## Educational Project Kits:

*Elements of Digital Logic, Understanding Signals* and *Experiments with Renewable Energy* focus more closely on topics in electronics, while *StampWorks* provides a variety of projects that are useful to hobbyists, inventors and product designers interested in trying a variety of projects.

> "*Elements of Digital Logic*", Student Guide, Version 1.0, Parallax Inc., 2003
> "*Experiments with Renewable Energy*", Student Guide, Version 1.0, Parallax Inc., 2004
> "*StampWorks*", Manual, Version 1.2, Parallax Inc., 2001
> "*Understanding Signals*", Student Guide, Version 1.0, Parallax Inc., 2003

## Reference

This book is an essential reference for all Stamps in Class Student Guides. It is packed with information on the BASIC Stamp series of microcontroller modules, our BASIC Stamp Editor, and our PBASIC programming language.

> "*BASIC Stamp Manual*", Version 2.0c, Parallax Inc., 2000

## FOREIGN TRANSLATIONS

Parallax educational texts may be translated to other languages with our permission (e-mail stampsinclass@parallax.com). If you plan on doing any translations please contact us so we can provide the correctly-formatted MS Word documents, images, etc. We also maintain a discussion group for Parallax translators that you may join. It's called the Parallax Translators Yahoo-group, and directions for finding it are included on the inside cover of this text. See section entitled: WEB SITE AND DISCUSSION LISTS after the Title page.

## SPECIAL CONTRIBUTORS

The Parallax team assembled to write this text includes: curriculum design and technical writing by Andy Lindsay, illustration by Rich Allred, cover design by Jen Jacobs and Larissa Crittenden, general consulting by Aristides Alvarez and Jeff Martin, electromechanical consulting by John Barrowman, technical review and solutions by Kris Magri, technical editing by Stephanie Lindsay, and committee review by Rich Allred, Gabe Duran, Stephanie Lindsay, and Kris Magri.

*What's a Microcontroller?* Student Guide Version 2.2 was written by Andy Lindsay after collecting observations and educator feedback while traveling the nation teaching Parallax Educators Courses. Andy studied Electrical and Electronic Engineering at California State University, Sacramento, and this is his third Stamps in Class Student Guide. He is also a contributing author of several papers that address the topic of microcontrollers in pre-engineering curricula. When he's not writing educational material, Andy does product engineering for Parallax.

Parallax wishes to thank StampsInClass Yahoo Group member Robert Ang for his thorough draft review and detailed input, and veteran engineer and esteemed customer Sid Weaver for his insightful review. Thanks also to Stamps in Class authors Tracy Allen (*Applied Sensors*), and Martin Hebel (*Industrial Control*) for their review and recommendations. Andy Lindsay wishes to thank his father Marshall and brother-in-law Kubilay for their expert musical advice and suggestions. Stamps in Class was founded by Ken Gracey, and Ken wishes to thank the Parallax staff for the great job they do. Each and every Parallaxian has made contributions to this and every Stamps in Class text.

1

# Chapter #1: Getting Started

## HOW MANY MICROCONTROLLERS DID YOU USE TODAY?

A microcontroller is a kind of miniature computer that you can find in all kinds of gizmos. Some examples of common, every-day products that have microcontrollers built-in are shown in Figure 1-1. If it has buttons and a digital display, chances are it also has a programmable microcontroller brain.

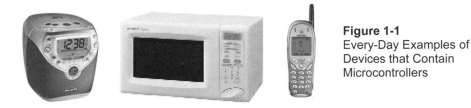

**Figure 1-1**
Every-Day Examples of Devices that Contain Microcontrollers

Try making a list and counting how many devices with microcontrollers you use in a typical day. Here are some examples: if your clock radio goes off, and you hit the snooze button a few times in the morning, the first thing you do in your day is interact with a microcontroller. Heating up some food in the microwave oven and making a call on a cell phone also involve operating microcontrollers. That's just the beginning. Here are a few more examples: turning on the television with a handheld remote, playing a handheld game, using a calculator, and checking your digital wristwatch. All those devices have microcontrollers inside them that interact with you.

## THE BASIC STAMP 2 - YOUR NEW MICROCONTROLLER

Parallax, Inc.'s BASIC Stamp® 2 module shown in Figure 1-2 has a microcontroller built onto it. It's the black chip with lettering on it that reads "PIC16C57". The rest of the components on the BASIC Stamp module are also found in consumer appliances you use every day. All together, they are correctly called an embedded computer system. This name is almost always shortened to just "embedded system". Frequently, such modules are commonly just called "microcontrollers."

The activities in this text will guide you through building circuits similar to the ones found in consumer appliances and high-tech gizmos. You will also write computer programs that the BASIC Stamp module will run. These programs will make the BASIC Stamp module monitor and control these circuits so that they perform useful functions.

**Figure 1-2**
The BASIC Stamp® 2
Microcontroller Module

*BASIC Stamp 2
modules are the most
popular
microcontrollers made
by Parallax, Inc.*

In this text, "BASIC Stamp" refers to Parallax Inc.'s BASIC Stamp® 2 microcontroller
module. There are other BASIC Stamp modules, some of which are shown in Figure 1-3.
Each BASIC Stamp module is color coded. The BASIC Stamp 2 is green. The BASIC
Stamp 2e is red. The BASIC Stamp 2SX is blue, and the BASIC Stamp 2p is gold. Each
variation on the BASIC Stamp 2 is slightly different, featuring higher speed, more memory,
additional functionality, or some combination of these extra features.

**Figure 1-3**
BASIC Stamp®
Modules

From Left to Right:
BASIC Stamp® 2, 2e,
2SX, and 2p

## AMAZING INVENTIONS WITH BASIC STAMP MICROCONTROLLERS

Consumer appliances aren't the only things that contain microcontrollers. Robots,
machinery, aerospace designs and other high-tech devices are also built with
microcontrollers. Let's take a look at some examples that were created with BASIC
Stamp modules.

Robots have been designed to do everything from helping students learn more about
microcontrollers, to mowing the lawn, to solving complex mechanical problems. Figure
1-4 shows two example robots. On each of these robots, students use the BASIC Stamp 2
to read sensors, control motors, and communicate with other computers. The robot on

1

the left is Parallax Inc.'s Boe-Bot™. The projects in the *Robotics with the Boe-Bot* text can be tackled using the Boe-Bot after you've worked through the activities in this one. The robot on the right was built by a group of students and entered into a First Robotics competition. The goal of the contest is different each year. In the example shown, the goal was to see which group's robot could sort colored hoops the fastest.

**Figure 1-4**
Educational Robots

*Parallax Boe-Bot™ (left)*
*First Competition Robot*
*(right)*

Other robots solve complex problems, such as the autonomous remote flight robot shown at the left of Figure 1-5. This robot was built and tested by mechanical engineering students at the University of California, Irvine. They used a BASIC Stamp module to help it communicate with a satellite global positioning system (GPS) so that the robot could know its position and altitude. The BASIC Stamp also read level sensors and controlled the motor settings to keep the robot flying properly. The mechanical millipede robot on the right was developed by a professor at Nanyang Technical University, Singapore. It has more than 50 BASIC Stamp modules, and they all communicate with each other in an elaborate network that helped control and orchestrate the motion of each set of legs. Robots like this not only help us better understand designs in nature, but they may eventually be used to explore remote locations, or even other planets.

**Figure 1-5**
Examples of Research
Robots that Contain
Microcontrollers

*Autonomous flying*
*robot at UC Irvine (left)*
*and Millipede Project at*
*Nanyang University*
*(right)*

With the help of microcontrollers, robots will also take on day-to-day tasks, such as mowing the lawn. The BASIC Stamp module inside the robotic lawn mower shown in Figure 1-6 helps it stay inside the boundaries of the lawn, and it also reads sensors that detect obstacles and controls the motors that make it move.

**Figure 1-6**
Robotic Lawn Mower

*Prototype by the Robot Shop*

Microcontrollers are also used in scientific, high technology, and aerospace projects. The weather station shown on the left of Figure 1-7 is used to collect environmental data related to coral reef decay. The BASIC Stamp module inside it gathers this data from a variety of sensors and stores it for later retrieval by scientists. The submarine in the center is an undersea exploration vehicle, and its thrusters, cameras and lights are all controlled by BASIC Stamp microcontrollers. The rocket shown on the right is one that was part of a competition to launch a privately owned rocket into space. Nobody won the competition, but this rocket almost made it! The BASIC Stamp controlled just about every aspect of the launch sequence.

**Figure 1-7**
High-tech and Aerospace
Microcontroller Examples

*Ecological data collection by EME Systems (left), undersea research by Harbor Branch Institute (center), and JP Aerospace test launch (right)*

From common household appliances all the way through scientific and aerospace applications, the microcontroller basics you will need to get started on projects like these are introduced here. By working through the activities in this book, you will get to

1

experiment with and learn how to use a variety of building blocks found in all these high-tech inventions. You will build circuits for displays, sensors, and motion controllers. You will learn how to connect these circuits to the BASIC Stamp 2 module, and then write computer programs that make it control displays, collect data from the sensors, and control motion. Along the way, you will learn many important electronic and computer programming concepts and techniques. By the time you're done, you might find yourself well on the way to inventing a gizmo of your own design.

## HARDWARE AND SOFTWARE

Getting started with BASIC Stamp microcontroller modules is similar to getting started with a brand-new PC or laptop. The first things that most people have to do when they get a new PC or laptop is take it out of the box, plug it in, install and test some software, and maybe even write some software of their own using a programming language. If this is your first time using a BASIC Stamp module, you will be doing all these same activities. If you are in a class, your hardware may already be all set up for you. If this is the case, your teacher may have other instructions. If not, this chapter will take you through all the steps of getting your new BASIC Stamp microcontroller up and running.

## ACTIVITY #1: GETTING THE SOFTWARE

The BASIC Stamp Editor (version 2.0 or higher) is the software you will use in most of the activities and projects in this text. You will use this software to write programs that the BASIC Stamp module will run. You can also use this software to display messages sent by the BASIC Stamp that help you understand what it senses.

> **The BASIC Stamp Editor is free software**, and the two easiest ways to get it are:
>
> - **Download from the Internet:** Look for "BASIC Stamp Windows Editor version 2.0…" on the www.parallax.com → Downloads → BASIC Stamp Software page.
>
> - **Included on the Parallax CD:** Follow the Software link on the Welcome page. Make sure the date printed on the CD is May 2003 or newer.
>
> **In a Hurry?** Get your copy of the BASIC Stamp Windows Editor version 2.0 (or higher) and install it on your PC or laptop. Then, skip to: Activity #3: Setting Up the Hardware and Testing the System.
>
> **If you have questions along the way,** Activity #1 can be used as a step-by-step reference for getting the software, and Activity #2 can be used as a reference for the installation procedure.

## Computer System Requirements

You will need either a PC or laptop computer to run the BASIC Stamp Editor software. Getting started with BASIC Stamp programming is easiest if your PC or laptop has the following features:

- Microsoft Windows 95® or newer operating system
- A serial or USB port
- A CD-ROM drive, World Wide Web access, or both

 **USB Port Adapter** If your computer only has USB ports, you will need a USB to Serial Adapter. See Appendix A: USB to Serial Adapter for details and installation instructions.

## Downloading the Software from the Internet

It's easy to download the BASIC Stamp Editor software from the Parallax web site. The web page shown in Figure 1-8 may look different from the web page you see when you visit the site. Nonetheless, the steps for downloading the software should still be similar to these:

√ Using a web browser, go to www.parallax.com (shown in Figure 1-8).
√ Point at the *Downloads* menu to display the options.
√ Point at the *BASIC Stamp Software* link and click to select it.

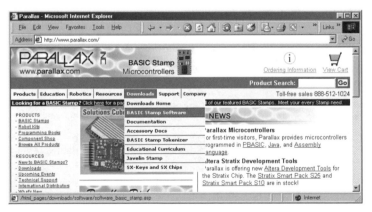

**Figure 1-8**
The Parallax Web Site:

*www.parallax.com*

√ When you get to the BASIC Stamp Software page, find the most recent version of the BASIC Stamp Windows Editor download, with a version number of 2.0 or higher.

√ Click the *Download* icon. In Figure 1-9, the download icon looks like a file folder to the right of the description: "BASIC Stamp Windows Editor version 2.0 Beta 1 (6MB)".

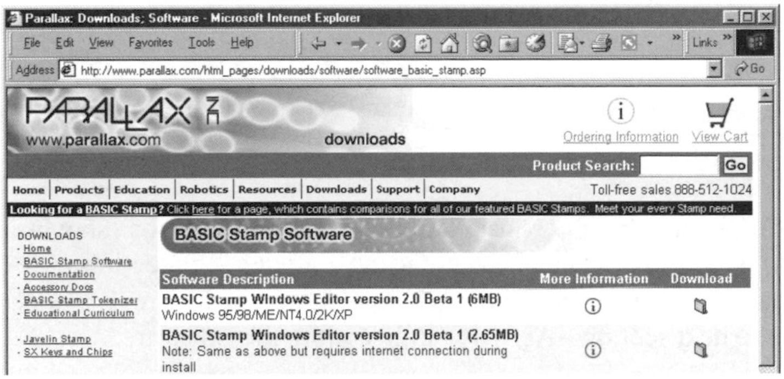

**Figure 1-9**
The Parallax Web Site Downloads Page

√ When the File Download window shown in Figure 1-10 appears, select: *Save this program to disk.*

√ Click the *OK* button.

**Figure 1-10**
File Download Window

Figure 1-11 shows the Save As window that appears next. You can use the *Save in* field to browse your computer's hard drives to find a convenient place to save the file.

√ After choosing where to save the file you are downloading, click the *Save* Button.

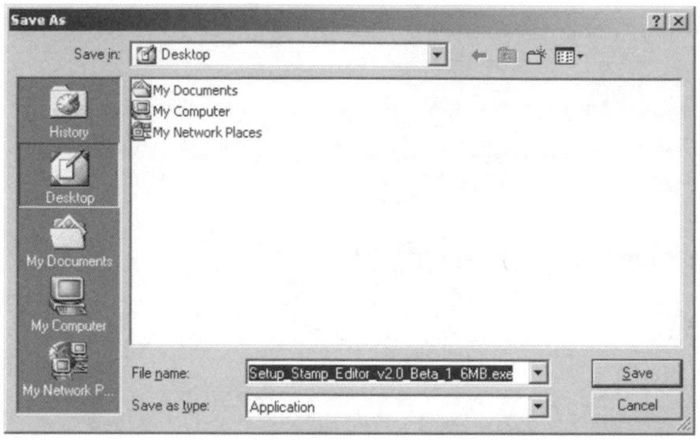

**Figure 1-11**
Save As Window

*Selecting a place to
save the file*

√ Wait while the BASIC Stamp Editor installation program downloads (shown in Figure 1-12). This may take a while if you are using a modem connection.

√ When the download is complete, leave the window shown in Figure 1-13 open while you skip to the next section - Activity #2: Installing the Software.

**Figure 1-12:** Download Progress Window

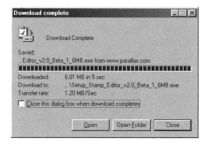

**Figure 1-13:** Download Complete

### Finding the Software on the Parallax CD

You can also install the BASIC Stamp Editor from the Parallax CD, but it has to be May 2003 or newer so that you can get the version of the BASIC Stamp Editor that is compatible with the examples in this text. You can find the Parallax CD's Year and Month by examining the labeling on the front of the CD.

√ Place the Parallax CD into your computer's CD drive. The Parallax CD Welcome application shown in Figure 1-14 should run as soon as you load the CD into your computer's CD drive.

√ If the Welcome application does not automatically run, double-click *My Compute*r, then double-click your CD drive, then double-click *Welcome*.

**Figure 1-14**
The Parallax CD Browser

√ Click the *Software* link shown in Figure 1-14.
√ Click the + next to the BASIC Stamps folder shown in Figure 1-15.
√ Click the + next to the Windows folder.
√ Click the floppy diskette icon labeled "Stamp 2/2e/2sx/2p/2pe (stampw.exe)".
√ Move on to Activity #2: Installing the Software.

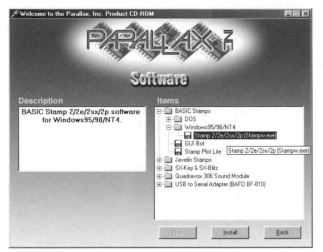

**Figure 1-15**
The Parallax CD Browser

*Select the BASIC Stamp Editor installation program from the Software page.*

> **Free downloads** at the Parallax web site are included in the Parallax CD, but only up to the date the CD was created. The date on the front of the CD indicates when it was created. If the CD is just a few months old, you will probably have the most up-to-date material. If it's an older CD, consider requesting a new one from Parallax or downloading the files you need from the Parallax web site.

## ACTIVITY #2: INSTALLING THE SOFTWARE

By now, you have either downloaded the BASIC Stamp Editor Installer from the Parallax web site or located it on the Parallax CD. Now let's run the BASIC Stamp Editor Installer.

### Installing the Software Step by Step

√   If you downloaded the BASIC Stamp Editor Installer from the Internet, click the *Open* button on the Download Complete window shown in Figure 1-16.

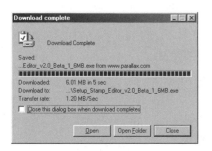

**Figure 1-16**
Download Complete Window

*If you skipped here from the "Downloading the Software from the Internet" section, click the Open button.*

√ If you located the software on the Parallax CD, click the *Install* button shown in Figure 1-17.

**Figure 1-17**
The Parallax CD Browser

*Install button located near bottom of window.*

√ When the BASIC Stamp Editor InstallShield Wizard window opens, click the *Next* button shown in Figure 1-18.

**Figure 1-18**
InstallShield Wizard for the BASIC Stamp Editor

*Click Next.*

√ Select *Typical* for your setup type as shown in Figure 1-19.
√ Click the *Next* button.

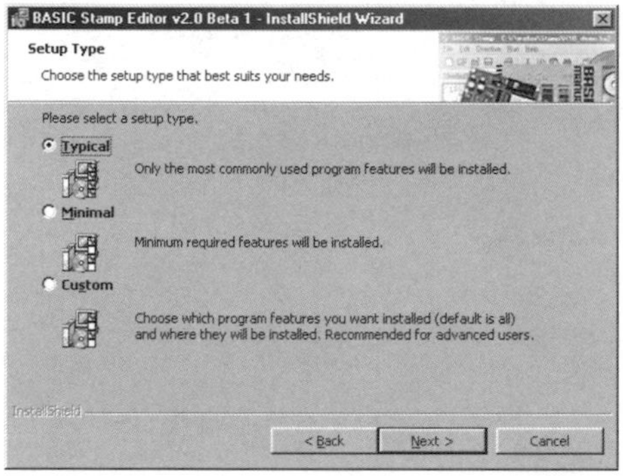

**Figure 1-19**
Setup Type

*Click Typical, then click the Next button.*

√ When the InstallShield Wizard tells you it is "Ready to Install the Program", click the *Install* button shown in Figure 1-20.

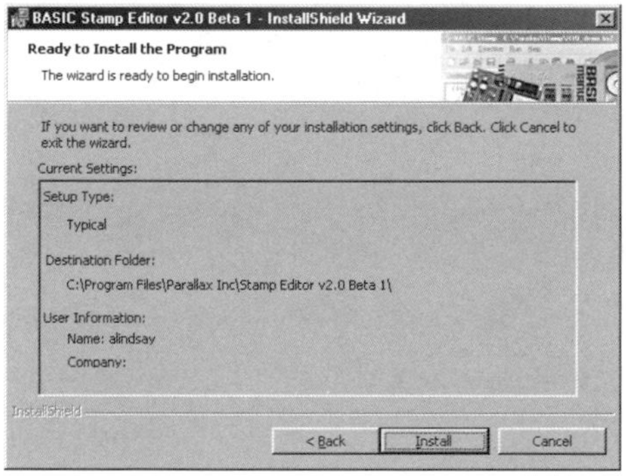

**Figure 1-20**
Ready to Install.

*Click the Install button.*

√ When the InstallShield Wizard window tells you "InstallShield Wizard Completed", as shown in Figure 1-21, click *Finish*.

**Figure 1-21**
InstallShield Wizard
Completed:

*Click the Finish button.*

## ACTIVITY #3: SETTING UP THE HARDWARE AND TESTING THE SYSTEM

The BASIC Stamp module needs to be connected to power for it to run. It also needs to be connected to a PC so it can be programmed. After making these connections, you can use the BASIC Stamp Editor to test the system. This activity will show you how.

### Introducing the BASIC Stamp®, Board of Education®, and HomeWork Board™

Parallax Inc.'s Board of Education® carrier board shown in Figure 1-22 next to a BASIC Stamp module. As mentioned earlier, the BASIC Stamp is a type of very small computer. This very small computer plugs into the Board of Education carrier board. As you will soon see, the Board of Education makes it easy to connect a power supply and serial cable to the BASIC Stamp module. In later activities, you will also see how the Board of Education makes it easy to build circuits and connect them to your BASIC Stamp module.

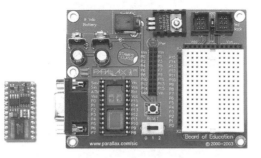

**Figure 1-22**
BASIC Stamp® 2
Microcontroller Module (left)
and Board of Education ®
Carrier Board (right)

Parallax, Inc.'s BASIC Stamp HomeWork Board™ is shown in Figure 1-23. This board is like a Board of Education with the BASIC Stamp 2 module built-in. Its surface-mounted components are visible to the left of the white breadboard area. You can use either the Board of Education with a BASIC Stamp module or the BASIC Stamp HomeWork Board as your project platform for the activities in this text.

**Figure 1-23**
BASIC
Stamp®
HomeWork
Board™
Project
Platform.

> ℹ️ **Learn more** about the features, parts and functions of BASIC Stamp modules, Board of Education carrier boards, and the HomeWork Board project platform. See Appendix C: BASIC Stamp and Carrier Board Components and Functions on page 305.

### Required Hardware

(1) BASIC Stamp 2 module  AND
(1) Board of Education
      - or -
(1) BASIC Stamp HomeWork Board

(1) 9 V battery
(1) strip of 4 adhesive rubber feet
(1) Serial cable

> ℹ️ **Start with a new or fully charged 9 V battery.** Avoid all the confusion a dead battery can cause. Start with a new alkaline battery or a rechargeable battery that has recently been fully recharged.

>  **CAUTION! Before using an AC adapter, "battery replacer", or DC supply:**
>
> √ Consult Appendix D: Batteries and Power Supplies on page 309 to make sure the supply you use is appropriate for the activities in this text.

### Connecting the Hardware

Both the Board of Education and the BASIC Stamp HomeWork Board come with a strip that has four adhesive rubber feet. These rubber feet are shown in Figure 1-24, and they should be affixed to the underside of your Board of Education or BASIC Stamp HomeWork Board.

**Figure 1-24**
Rubber Feet

√ Remove each rubber foot from the adhesive strip and affix it to the underside of your board as shown in Figure 1-25. If you are using the Board of Education, it has circles on its underside that show where each rubber foot should be attached. For the HomeWork Board, just place a rubber foot next to each plated hole at each corner.

**Figure 1-25**
Rubber Foot
Affixed to
Underside of Board
of Education (left)
and HomeWork
Board (right)

Next, the Board of Education or BASIC Stamp HomeWork Board should be connected to your PC or laptop by a serial cable.

√ Connect your serial cable to an available COM port on the back of your computer as shown in Figure 1-26.

**USB Port Adapter** If you are using a USB to Serial Adapter:

√ Connect the USB end to your PC's USB port.

√ Connect the COM port adapter either directly to your Board of Education or HomeWork Board, or connect it to the serial cable as shown in Figure 1-26.

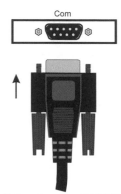

**Figure 1-26:** PC or Laptop COM Port

*Plug the serial cable into an available COM port on your PC or laptop.*

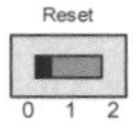

**Figure 1-27:** 3-position Switch

*Set to the 0 position to turn off the power.*

If you are using the BASIC Stamp 2 module and Board of Education:

√ Set the 3-position switch on the Board of Education to position-0 as shown in Figure 1-27.

**Only the Board of Education Rev C** has a 3-position switch. To turn off power on a Board of Education Rev B, simply disconnect the power source by either unplugging the DC supply or the battery These are shown in Figure 1-28, step 3 or 4.

√ If your BASIC Stamp module is not already plugged into your Board of Education, insert it into the socket, oriented as shown in Figure 1-28, step-1. Make sure the pins are lined up properly with the holes in the socket and not folded under, then press down firmly.

√ Plug the serial cable into the Board of Education as shown in step-2.

√ Plug a DC power supply into the 6-9 VDC jack as shown in step-3, or plug a 9-V battery into the 9 VDC battery jack as shown in step-4.

√ Move the 3-position switch from position-0 to position-1. The green light labeled Pwr on the Board of Education should now be on.

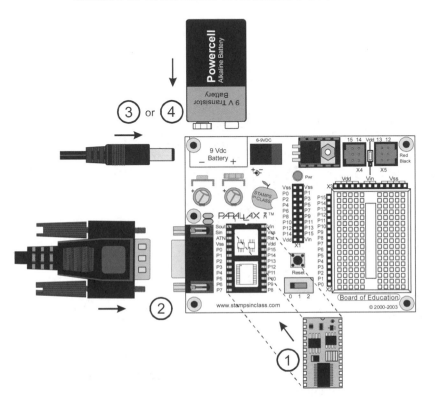

**Figure 1-28**
Board of Education, BASIC Stamp Module, Battery and Serial Cable.

*Connect components in the order shown in the diagram. Make sure to properly orient your BASIC Stamp module right side up, matching the notch on its top edge to notch on the socket.*

If you are using the BASIC Stamp HomeWork Board:

√ Connect the serial cable to the HomeWork Board  (Figure 1-29, step-1).
√ Connect a 9 V battery to the battery clip as shown in step-2.

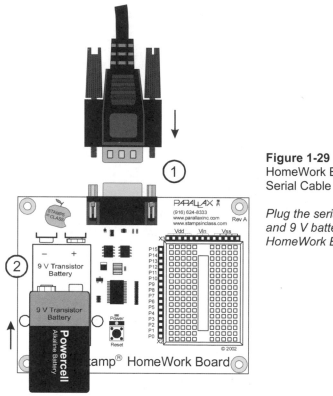

**Figure 1-29**
HomeWork Board and
Serial Cable

*Plug the serial cable
and 9 V battery into the
HomeWork Board.*

## Testing for Communication

The BASIC Stamp Editor has a feature for testing to make sure your PC or laptop can communicate with your BASIC Stamp module.

√   Double-click the BASIC Stamp Editor shortcut on your desktop. It should look similar to the one shown in Figure 1-30.

**Figure 1-30**
BASIC Stamp Editor Shortcut

*Look for a shortcut similar to
this one on your computer's
desktop.*

1

 **The Windows Start Menu** can also be used to run the BASIC Stamp Editor. Click your Windows *Start* button, then select *Programs → Parallax, Inc. → BASIC Stamp Editor 2...*, then click the *BASIC Stamp Editor* icon.

Your BASIC Stamp Editor window should look similar to the one shown in Figure 1-31.

 **The first time you run your BASIC Stamp Editor,** it may display some messages and a list of your COM ports found by the software.

√ To make sure your BASIC Stamp module is communicating with your computer, click the *Run* menu, then select *Identify*.

**Figure 1-31**
BASIC Stamp
Editor

*Select Identify
from the Run
menu.*

An Identification window similar to the one shown in Figure 1-32 will appear. The example in the figure shows that a BASIC Stamp 2 has been detected on COM2.

√ Check the Identification window to make sure a BASIC Stamp 2 module has been detected on one of the COM ports. If it has been detected, then you are ready for Activity #4: First Program.
√ If the Identification window does not detect a BASIC Stamp 2 module on any of the COM ports, go to Appendix E: Trouble-Shooting on page 313.

**Figure 1-32**
Identification Window

*Example: BASIC Stamp
2 found on COM2.*

## ACTIVITY #4: FIRST PROGRAM

The first program you will write and test will tell the BASIC Stamp to send a message to your PC or laptop. Figure 1-33 shows how it sends a stream of ones and zeros to communicate the text characters displayed by the PC or laptop. These ones and zeros are called binary numbers. The BASIC Stamp Editor software has the ability to detect and display these messages as you will soon see.

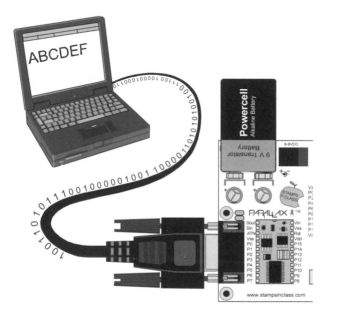

**Figure 1-33**
Messages from the BASIC Stamp module to your Computer

*The BASIC Stamp module sends characters to your PC or laptop by transmitting a stream of binary ones and zeros. The BASIC Stamp Editor can detect and convert these binary codes to characters and display them.*

### First Program

The program listings that you will type into the BASIC Stamp Editor and download to the BASIC Stamp module will always be shown with a gray background like this:

### Example Program: FirstProgram.bs2

```
' What's a Microcontroller - FirstProgram.bs2
' BASIC Stamp sends message to Debug Terminal.

' {$STAMP BS2}
' {$PBASIC 2.5}

DEBUG "Hello, it's me, your BASIC Stamp!"
END
```

You will enter this program into the BASIC Stamp Editor. Some lines of the program are made automatically by clicking buttons on the toolbar. Other lines are made by typing them in from the keyboard.

√ Begin by clicking the BS2 icon (the green diagonal chip) on the toolbar, shown highlighted in Figure 1-34. If you hold your cursor over this button, its flyover help description "Stamp Mode: BS2" will appear.

√ Next, click on the gear icon labeled "2.5" shown highlighted in Figure 1-35. It's flyover help description is "PBASIC Language: 2.5".

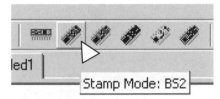

**Figure 1-34**
BS2 Icon

*Clicking on this button will automatically place " ' {$STAMP BS2}" at the beginning of your program.*

**Figure 1-35**
PBASIC 2.5 Icon

*Clicking on this button will automatically place " ' {$PBASIC 2.5}" at the beginning of your program.*

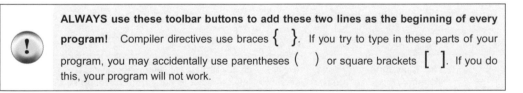

**ALWAYS use these toolbar buttons to add these two lines as the beginning of every program!** Compiler directives use braces { }. If you try to type in these parts of your program, you may accidentally use parentheses ( ) or square brackets [ ]. If you do this, your program will not work.

√ Type in the remaining 4 lines of the program exactly as shown in Figure 1-36.

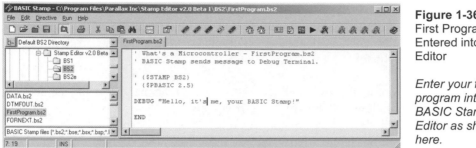

**Figure 1-36**
First Program
Entered into
Editor

*Enter your first
program into the
BASIC Stamp
Editor as shown
here.*

√ Save your work by clicking *File* and selecting *Save* as shown in Figure 1-37.
√ Enter the name FirstProgram into the *File name* field near the bottom of the *Save As* window as shown in Figure 1-38.
√ Click the *Save* button.

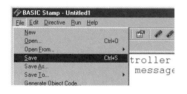

**Figure 1-37:** Saving the First Program

**Figure 1-38:** Entering the File Name

**The next time you save,** the BASIC Stamp Editor will automatically save to the same filename (FirstProgram.bs2) unless you tell it to save to a different filename by clicking *File* and selecting *Save As* (instead of just Save).

√ Click *Run*, and select *Run* from the menu that appears (by clicking it) as shown in Figure 1-39.

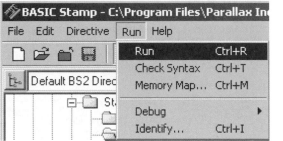

**Figure 1-39**
Running Your First
Program

A Download Progress window will appear briefly as the program is transmitted from the PC or laptop to your BASIC Stamp module. Figure 1-40 shows the Debug Terminal that should appear when the download is complete. You can prove to yourself that this is a message from the BASIC Stamp by pressing and releasing the *Reset* button on your board. Every time you press and release it, the program will re-run, and you will see another copy of the message displayed in the Debug Terminal.

√  Press and release the Reset button. Did you see a second "Hello…" message appear in the Debug Terminal?

**Figure 1-40**
Debug Terminal

*The Debug Terminal displays messages sent to the PC/laptop by the BASIC Stamp module.*

> **The BASIC Stamp Editor has shortcuts** for most common tasks. For example, to run a program, you can press the 'Ctrl' and 'R' keys at the same time. You can also click the *Run* button. It's the blue triangle shown in Figure 1-41 that looks like a CD player's Play button. The flyover help (the Run hint) will appear if you point at the *Run* button with your mouse. You can get similar hints to find out what the other buttons do by pointing at them too. 
>
> **Figure 1-41**
>
> BASIC Stamp Editor Shortcut Buttons

### How FirstProgram.bs2 Works

The first two lines in the example are called comments. A comment is a line of text that gets ignored by the BASIC Stamp Editor, because it's meant for a human reading the program, not for the BASIC Stamp module. In PBASIC, everything to the right of an apostrophe is normally considered to be a comment by the BASIC Stamp Editor. The first comment tells which book the example program is from, and the program's filename. The second comment contains a handy, one-line description that explains what the program does.

```
' What's a Microcontroller - FirstProgram.bs2
' BASIC Stamp sends message to Debug Terminal.
```

Although comments are ignored most of the time, the BASIC Stamp Editor does search through comments for special directives. Every program in this text will use these two directives:

```
' {$STAMP BS2}
' {$PBASIC 2.5}
```

The first directive is called the $STAMP Directive, and it tells the BASIC Stamp Editor that you will be downloading the program specifically to a BASIC Stamp 2 module. The second directive is called the $PBASIC directive, and it tells the BASIC Stamp Editor that you are using version 2.5 of the PBASIC programming language. Note that these compiler directives are enclosed in braces { } not parentheses ( ). You should always use the toolbar icons to place these compiler directives in your program to avoid typing errors. Also, entering the compiler directives by hand may not activate the syntax highlighting in the BASIC Stamp Editor. That function is what causes various letters, characters and words in your program to appear in different colors and capitalizations. Syntax highlighting makes your programs easier to read, understand, and correct if there are any bugs in them.

1

A command is a word you can use to tell the BASIC Stamp do a certain job. The first of the two commands in this program is called the **DEBUG** command:

```
DEBUG "Hello, it's me, your BASIC Stamp!"
```

This is the command that tells the BASIC Stamp to send a message to the PC using the serial cable.

The second command is called the **END** command:

```
END
```

This command is handy because it puts the BASIC Stamp into low power mode when it's done running the program. In low power mode, the BASIC Stamp waits for either the Reset button to be pressed (and released), or for a new program to be loaded into it by the BASIC Stamp Editor. If the Reset button on your board is pressed, the BASIC Stamp will re-run the program you loaded into it. If a new program is loaded into it, the old one is erased, and the new program begins to run.

### Your Turn – DEBUG Formatters and Control Characters

A **DEBUG** formatter is a code-word you can use to make the message the BASIC Stamp sends look a certain way in the Debug Terminal. **DEC** is an example of a formatter that makes the Debug Terminal display a decimal value. An example of a control character is **CR**, which is used to send a carriage return to the Debug Terminal. The text or numbers that come after a **CR** will appear on the line below characters that came before it. You can modify your program so that it contains more **DEBUG** commands along with some formatters and control characters. Here's an example of how to do it:

√ First, save the program under a new name by clicking *File* and selecting *Save As*. A good new name for the file would be FirstProgramYourTurn.bs2

√ Modify the comments at the beginning of the program so that they read:

```
' What's a Microcontroller - FirstProgramYourTurn.bs2
' BASIC Stamp sends messages to Debug Terminal.
```

√ Add these three lines between the first **DEBUG** command and the **END** command:

```
DEBUG CR, "What's 7 X 11?"
DEBUG CR, "The answer is: "
DEBUG DEC 7 * 11
```

√ Save the changes you made by clicking *File* and selecting *Save*.

Your program should now look like the one shown in Figure 1-42.

√ Run your modified program. You will have to either select *Run* from the Run menu again, like in Figure 1-39 or click the *Run* button, like in Figure 1-41.

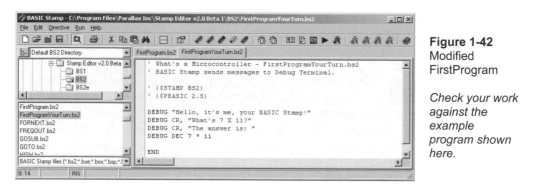

**Figure 1-42**
Modified
FirstProgram

*Check your work
against the
example
program shown
here.*

**Where did my Debug Terminal go?** Sometimes the Debug Terminal gets hidden behind the BASIC Stamp Editor window. You can bring it back to the front by using the *Run* menu as shown at the left of Figure 1-43, the *Debug Terminal 1* shortcut button shown at the right of the figure, or the F12 key on your keyboard.

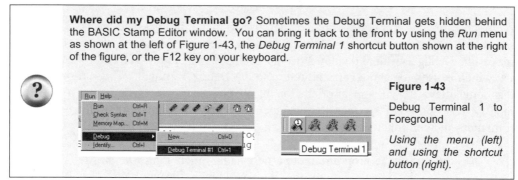

**Figure 1-43**

Debug Terminal 1 to Foreground

*Using the menu (left) and using the shortcut button (right).*

Your Debug Terminal should now resemble Figure 1-44.

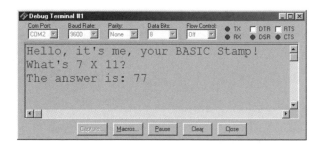

**Figure 1-44**
Modified
FirstProgram.bs2
Debug Terminal Output

*Make sure that when
you re-run your
program, you get the
results you expect.*

## ACTIVITY #5: LOOKING UP ANSWERS

The two activities you just finished introduced two PBASIC commands: DEBUG and END. You can find out more about these commands and how they are used by looking them up, either in the BASIC Stamp Editor's Help or in the BASIC Stamp Manual. This activity guides you through an example of looking up DEBUG using the BASIC Stamp Editor's Help and the BASIC Stamp Manual.

### Using the BASIC Stamp Editor's Help

√ In the BASIC Stamp Editor, Click *Help*, then select *Index* (Figure 1-45).

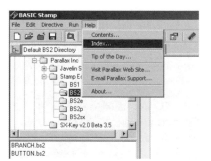

**Figure 1-45**
Selecting Index
from the Help
Menu

√ Type DEBUG in the field labeled *Type in the keyword to find:* ( Figure 1-46).
√ When the word DEBUG appears in the list below where you are typing, click it, then click the *Display* button.

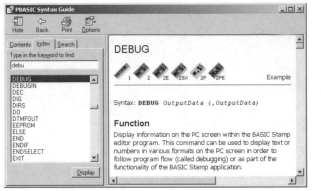

**Figure 1-46**
Looking up
the DEBUG
Command
Using Help.

## Your Turn

√   Use the scrollbar to review the **DEBUG** command's write-up. Notice that it has lots of explanations and example programs you can try.

√   Click the *Contents* tab, and find DEBUG there.

√   Click the *Search* tab, and run a search for the word DEBUG.

√   Repeat this process for the **END** command.

### Getting and Using the BASIC Stamp Manual

The BASIC Stamp Manual is available for free download from the Parallax web site, and it's also included on the Parallax CD. It can also be purchased as a printed book.

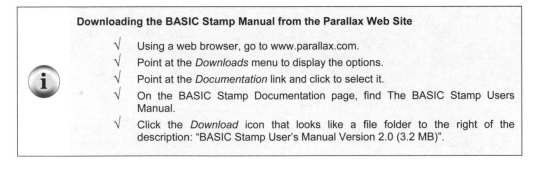

**Downloading the BASIC Stamp Manual from the Parallax Web Site**

√   Using a web browser, go to www.parallax.com.

√   Point at the *Downloads* menu to display the options.

√   Point at the *Documentation* link and click to select it.

√   On the BASIC Stamp Documentation page, find The BASIC Stamp Users Manual.

√   Click the *Download* icon that looks like a file folder to the right of the description: "BASIC Stamp User's Manual Version 2.0 (3.2 MB)".

**Viewing the BASIC Stamp Manual on the Parallax CD**

√   Click the *Documentation* link.
√   Click the + next to the BASIC Stamps folder.
√   Click the BASIC Stamp Manual book icon.
√   Click the *View* button.

√   Figure 1-47 shows an excerpt from the *BASIC Stamp Manual* v2.0 Contents section, showing that information on the DEBUG command is found on page 97.

**BASIC STAMP COMMAND REFERENCE** ........................................................... 77
   AUXIO .............................................................................................................. 81
   BRANCH .......................................................................................................... 83
   BUTTON .......................................................................................................... 85
   COUNT ............................................................................................................ 89
   DATA ................................................................................................................ 91
   DEBUG ............................................................................................................ 97

**Figure 1-47**
Finding the
DEBUG
Command in
the Table of
Contents

Figure 1-48 shows an excerpt from page 97 in the BASIC Stamp Manual v2.0. The DEBUG command is explained in detail here along with example programs to demonstrate how the DEBUG command can be used.

√   Look over the *BASIC Stamp Manual's* explanation of the DEBUG command.
√   Count the number of example programs in the DEBUG section. How many are there?

## 5: BASIC Stamp Command Reference - DEBUG

| DEBUG | BS1 | BS2 | BS2e | BS2sx | BS2p |
|-------|-----|-----|------|-------|------|

DEBUG *OutputData {, OutputData}*

**Figure 1-48**
Reviewing
the DEBUG
Command
in the
BASIC
Stamp
Manual

### Function
Display information on the PC screen within the BASIC Stamp editor program. This command can be used to display text or numbers in various formats on the PC screen in order to follow program flow (called debugging) or as part of the functionality of the BASIC Stamp application.

## Your Turn

√   Use the BASIC Stamp Manual's Index to look up the DEBUG command.
√   Look up the END command in the BASIC Stamp Manual.

## ACTIVITY #6: INTRODUCING ASCII CODE

In Activity #4, you used the DEC formatter with the DEBUG command to display a decimal number in the Debug Terminal. But what happens if you don't use the DEC formatter with a number? If you use the DEBUG command followed by a number with no formatter, the BASIC Stamp will read that number as an ASCII code.

### Programming with ASCII Code

ASCII is short for American Standard Code for Information Interchange. Most microcontrollers and PC computers use this code to assign a number to each keyboard function. Some numbers correspond to keyboard actions, such as cursor up, cursor down, space, and delete. Other numbers correspond to printed characters and symbols. The numbers 32 through 126 correspond to those characters and symbols that the BASIC Stamp can display in the Debug Terminal. The following program will use ACSII code to display the words "BASIC Stamp 2" in the Debug Terminal.

### Example Program – ASCIIName.bs2

√   Enter and run ASCIIName.bs2.

> **Remember to use the toolbar icons to place Compiler Directives into your programs!**
> '{$STAMP BS2}  –  Use the diagonal green electronic chip icon.
> '{$PBASIC 2.5}  –  Use the gear icon labeled 2.5.
>
> You can see a picture of these icons again on page 21.

```
'What's a Microcontroller - ASCIIName.bs2
'Use ASCII code in a DEBUG command to display the words BASIC Stamp 2.

'{$STAMP BS2}
'{$PBASIC 2.5}

DEBUG 66,65,83,73,67,32,83,116,97,109,112,32,50

END
```

1

### How ASCIIName.bs2 Works

Each letter in the **DEBUG** command corresponds to one ASCII code symbol that appeared in the Debug Terminal.

```
DEBUG 66,65,83,73,67,32,83,116,97,109,112,32,50
```

66 is the ASCII code for capital "B", 65 is the code for capital "A" and so on. 32 is the code for a space between characters. Notice that each code number was separated with a comma. The commas allow the one instance of **DEBUG** to execute each symbol as a separate command. This is much easier to type than 12 separate **DEBUG** commands.

### Your Turn – Exploring ASCII Code

√   Save ASCIIName.bs2 as ASCIIRandom.bs2
√   Pick 12 random numbers between 32 and 127.
√   Replace the ASCII code numbers in the program with the numbers you chose.
√   Run your modified program to see what you get!

The *BASIC Stamp Manual* Appendix A has a chart of ASCII code numbers and their corresponding symbols. You can look up the corresponding code numbers to spell your own name.

√   Save ASCIIRandom.bs2 as YourASCIIName.bs2
√   Look up the ASCII Chart in the BASIC Stamp Manual.
√   Modify the program to spell your own name.
√   Run the program to see if you spelled your name correctly.
√   If you did, good job, and save your program!

### ACTIVITY #7: WHEN YOU'RE DONE

It's important to disconnect the power from your BASIC Stamp and Board of Education (or HomeWork Board). First, your batteries will last longer if the system is not drawing power when you're not using it. Second, soon you will build circuits on the Board of Education or HomeWork Board prototyping area.

 **Circuit prototypes** should never be left unattended with a battery or power supply connected. **Always disconnect the power** from your Board of Education or HomeWork Board before you walk away, even if you only plan on leaving it alone for a minute or two.

## Disconnecting Power

With the Board of Education Rev C, disconnecting power is easy. If you are using the Board of Education Rev C, power is disconnected by moving the 3-position switch to position-0 by pushing it to the left as shown in Figure 1-49.

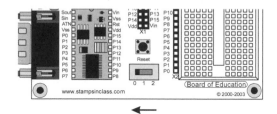

**Figure 1-49**
Turning the Power off

*Board of Education
Rev C*

 **Do not remove the BASIC Stamp module from its socket in the Board of Education!** Every time the BASIC Stamp is removed and re-inserted into the socket on the Board of Education, you risk damaging it. You do not need to remove it for storage.

Disconnecting the BASIC Stamp HomeWork Board's power is easy too. If you are using the BASIC Stamp HomeWork Board, disconnect the battery as shown in Figure 1-50.

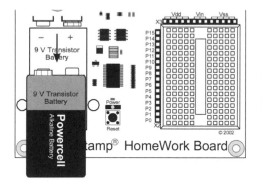

**Figure 1-50**
Disconnecting the power to the HomeWork Board

If you are using a Board of Education Rev B, you will not have a 3-position switch. Either unplug power supply, or remove the 9 V battery, whichever you are using.

## Your Turn

√   Disconnect the power to your board now.

1

## SUMMARY

This chapter guided you through the following:

- An introduction to some devices that contain microcontrollers
- An introduction to the BASIC Stamp module
- A tour of some interesting inventions made with BASIC Stamp modules.
- Where to get the free BASIC Stamp Editor software you will use in just about all of the experiments in this text
- How to install the BASIC Stamp Editor software
- An introduction to the BASIC Stamp module, Board of Education, and HomeWork Board
- How to set up your BASIC Stamp hardware
- How to test your software and hardware
- How to write and run a PBASIC program
- Using the DEBUG and END commands
- Using the CR control character and DEC formatter
- How to use the BASIC Stamp Editor's Help and the BASIC Stamp Manual
- A brief introduction to ASCII code
- How to disconnect the power to your Board of Education or HomeWork Board when you're done.

### Questions

1. What is a microcontroller?
2. Is the BASIC Stamp module a microcontroller, or does it contain one?
3. What clues would you look for to figure out whether or not an appliance like a clock radio or a cell phone contains a microcontroller?
4. What does an apostrophe at the beginning of a line of PBASIC program code signify?
5. What PBASIC commands did you learn in this chapter?
6. Let's say you want to take a break from your BASIC Stamp project to go get a snack, or maybe you want to take a longer break and return to the project in a couple days. What should you always do before you take your break?

### Exercises

1. Explain what the asterisk does in this command:

```
DEBUG DEC 7 * 11
```

2. Guess what the Debug Terminal would display if you ran this command:

```
DEBUG DEC 7 + 11
```

3. There is a problem with these two commands. When you run the code, the numbers they display are stuck together so that it looks like one large number instead of two small ones. Modify these two commands so that the answers appear on different lines in the Debug Terminal.

```
DEBUG DEC 7 * 11
DEBUG DEC 7 + 11
```

## Projects

1. Use **DEBUG** to display the solution to the math problem: $1 + 2 + 3 + 4$.
2. Which lines can you delete in FirstProgramYourTurn.bs2 if you place the command shown below on the line just before the **END** command in the program? Test your hypothesis (your prediction of what will happen). Make sure to save FirstProgramYourTurn.bs2 with a new name, like FirstProgramCh01Project05.bs2. Then make your modification, save and run your program.

```
DEBUG "What's 7 X 11?", CR, "The answer is: ", DEC 7 * 11
```

## Solutions

Q1. A microcontroller is a kind of miniature computer found in electronic products.

Q2. The BASIC Stamp module contains a microcontroller called the PIC16C57.

Q3. If the appliance has buttons and a digital display, these are good clues that it has a microcontroller inside.

Q4. A comment.

Q5. **DEBUG** and **END**

Q6. Disconnect the power from the BASIC Stamp project.

E1. It multiplies the two operands 7 and 11, resulting in a product of 77. The asterisk is the multiply operator.

E2. The Debug Terminal would display: 18

E3. To fix the problem, add a carriage return, the **CR,** control character.

```
DEBUG DEC 7 * 11
DEBUG CR, DEC 7 + 11
```

P1. Here is a program to display a solution to the math problem: 1+2+3+4

```
'{$STAMP BS2}
'{$PBASIC 2.5}
```

```
DEBUG "What's 1+2+3+4?"
DEBUG CR, "The answer is: "
DEBUG DEC 1+2+3+4

END
```

P2. The last three **DEBUG** lines can be deleted. An additional **CR** is needed after the "Hello" message.

```
' What's a Microcontroller - FirstProgramYourTurn.bs2
' BASIC Stamp sends message to Debug Terminal.

' {$STAMP BS2}
' {$PBASIC 2.5}

DEBUG "Hello, it's me, your BASIC Stamp!", CR

DEBUG "What's 7 X 11?", CR, "The answer is: ", DEC 7 * 11

END
```

The output from the Debug Terminal is:
```
Hello, it's me, your BASIC Stamp!
What's 7 X 11?
The answer is: 77
```
This output is the same as it was with the previous code. This is an example of using commas to output a lot of information, using only one **DEBUG** statement.

## Further Investigation

In this chapter, you visited the Software section of either the Parallax web site or the Parallax CD to get a copy of the BASIC Stamp Editor. You can go to the Documentation sections of either the Parallax web site or the Parallax CD to get a free copy of this text and of the *BASIC Stamp Manual*. Printed copies can also be purchased from Parallax.

**"*BASIC Stamp Manual*", Users Manual, Version 2.0c, Parallax Inc., 2000**

You can learn much more about the **DEBUG** and **END** commands by looking them up in the *BASIC Stamp Manual*. You can find them using the Table of Contents. The *BASIC Stamp Manual* has many more examples you can try, along with lessons similar to those in the Projects section you just completed.

# Chapter #2: Lights On – Lights Off

## INDICATOR LIGHTS

Indicator lights are so common that most people tend not to give them much thought. Figure 2-1 shows three indicator lights on a laser printer. Depending on which light is on, the person using the printer knows if it is running properly or needs attention. Here are just a few examples of devices with indicator lights: car stereos, televisions, VCRs, disk drives, printers, and alarm system control panels.

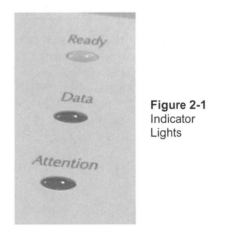

**Figure 2-1**
Indicator
Lights

Turning an indicator light on and off is a simple matter of connecting and disconnecting it from a power source. In some cases, the indicator light is connected directly to the battery or power supply, like the power indicator light on the Board of Education. Other indicator lights are switched on and off by a microcontroller inside the device. These are usually status indicator lights that tell you what the device is up to.

## MAKING A LIGHT EMITTING DIODE (LED) EMIT LIGHT

Most of the indicator lights you see on devices are called light emitting diodes. You will often see a light emitting diode referred to in books and circuit diagrams by the letters LED. The name is usually pronounced as three letters: "L-E-D". You can build an LED circuit and connect power to it, and the LED emits light. You can disconnect the power from an LED circuit, and the LED stops emitting light.

An LED circuit can be connected to the BASIC Stamp, and the BASIC Stamp can be programmed to connect and disconnect the LED circuit's power. This is much easier than manually changing the circuit's wiring or connecting and disconnecting the battery. The BASIC Stamp can also be programmed to do the following:

- Turn an LED circuit on and off at different rates
- Turn an LED circuit on and off a certain number of times
- Control more than one LED circuit
- Control the color of a bi-color (two color) LED circuit

## ACTIVITY #1: BUILDING AND TESTING THE LED CIRCUIT

It's important to test components individually before building them into a larger system. This activity focuses on building and testing two different LED circuits. The first circuit is the one that makes the LED emit light. The second circuit is the one that makes it not emit light. In the activity that comes after this one, you will build the LED circuit into a larger system by connecting it to the BASIC Stamp. You will then write programs that make the BASIC Stamp cause the LED to emit light, then not emit light. By first testing each LED circuit to make sure it works, you can be more confident that it will work when you connect it to a BASIC Stamp.

### Introducing the Resistor

A resistor is a component that 'resists' the flow of electricity. This flow of electricity is called current. Each resistor has a value that tells how strongly it resists current flow. This resistance value is called the ohm, and the sign for the ohm is the Greek letter omega: $\Omega$. The resistor you will be working with in this activity is the 470 $\Omega$ resistor shown in Figure 2-2. The resistor has two wires (called leads and pronounced "leeds"), one coming out of each end. There is a ceramic case between the two leads, and it's the part that resists current flow. Most circuit diagrams that show resistors use the jagged line symbol on the left to tell the person building the circuit that he or she must use a 470 $\Omega$ resistor. This is called a schematic symbol. The drawing on the right is a part drawing used in some beginner level Stamps in Class texts to help you identify the resistor in your kit.

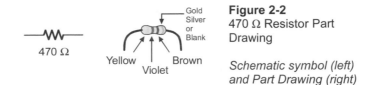

**Figure 2-2**
470 Ω Resistor Part
Drawing

*Schematic symbol (left)*
*and Part Drawing (right)*

2

Resistors like the ones we are using in this activity have colored stripes that tell you what their resistance values are. There is a different color combination for each resistance value. For example, the color code for the 470 Ω resistor is yellow-violet-brown.

There may be a fourth stripe that indicates the resistor's tolerance. Tolerance is measured in percent, and it tells how far off the part's true resistance might be from the labeled resistance. The fourth stripe could be gold (5%), silver (10%) or no stripe (20%). For the activities in this book, a resistor's tolerance does not matter, but its value does.

Each color bar that tells you the resistor's value corresponds to a digit, and these colors/digits are listed in Table 2-1. Figure 2-3 shows how to use each color bar with the table to determine the value of a resistor.

| Table 2-1: Resistor Color Code Values | |
| --- | --- |
| **Digit** | **Color** |
| 0 | Black |
| 1 | Brown |
| 2 | Red |
| 3 | Orange |
| 4 | Yellow |
| 5 | Green |
| 6 | Blue |
| 7 | Violet |
| 8 | Gray |
| 9 | White |

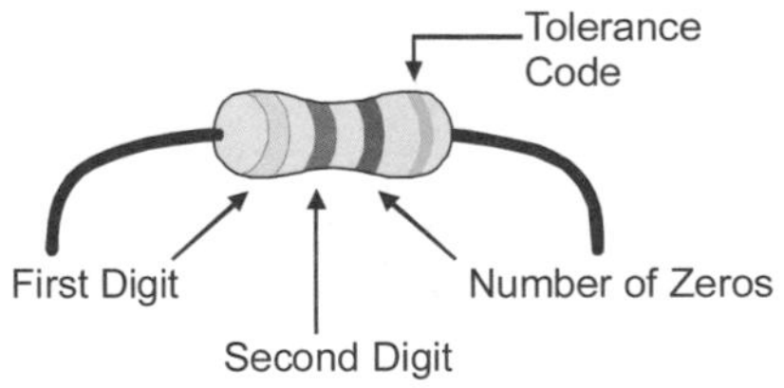

**Figure 2-3**
Resistor Color Codes

Here is an example that shows how Table 2-1 and Figure 2-3 can be used to figure out a resistor value by proving that yellow-violet-brown is really 470 Ω:

- The first stripe is yellow, which means the leftmost digit is a 4.
- The second stripe is violet, which means the next digit is a 7.
- The third stripe is brown. Since brown is 1, it means add one zero to the right of the first two digits.

Yellow-Violet-Brown = 4-7-0.

## Introducing the LED

A diode is a one-way current valve, and a light emitting diode (LED) emits light when current passes through it. Unlike the color codes on a resistor, the color of the LED usually just tells you what color it will glow when current passes through it. The important markings on an LED are contained in its shape. Since an LED is a one-way current valve, you have to make sure to connect it the right way, or it won't work as intended.

Figure 2-4 shows an LED's schematic symbol and part drawing. An LED has two terminals. One is called the anode, and the other is called the cathode. In this activity, you will have to build the LED into a circuit, paying attention to make sure the leads connected to the anode and cathode are connected to the circuit properly. On the part drawing, the anode lead is labeled with the plus-sign (+). On the schematic symbol, the anode is the wide part of the triangle. In the part drawing, the cathode lead is the unlabeled pin, and on the schematic symbol, the cathode is the line across the point of the triangle.

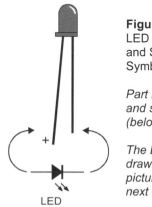

LED

**Figure 2-4**
LED Part Drawing
and Schematic
Symbol

*Part Drawing (above)
and schematic symbol
(below).*

*The LED's part
drawings in later
pictures will have a +
next to the anode leg.*

When you start building your circuit, make sure to check it against the schematic symbol and part drawing.  For the part drawing, note that the LED's leads are different lengths. The longer lead is connected to the LED's anode, and the shorter lead is connected to its cathode.  Also, if you look closely at the LED's plastic case, it's mostly round, but there is a small flat spot right near the shorter lead that that tells you it's the cathode.  This really comes in handy if the leads have been clipped to the same length.

### LED Test Circuit Parts

(1) LED – Green
(1) Resistor – 470 Ω (yellow-violet-brown)

 **Identifying the parts:**  In addition to the part drawings in Figure 2-2 and Figure 2-4, you can use the photo on the last page of the book to help identify the parts in the kit needed for this and all other activities.  For more information on the parts in this photo, see Appendix B: Equipment and Parts Lists.

### Building the LED Test Circuit

You will build a circuit by plugging the LED and resistor leads into small holes called sockets on the prototyping area shown in Figure 2-5.  This prototyping area has black sockets along the top and along the left.  The black sockets along the top have labels above them: Vdd, Vin, and Vss.  These are called the power terminals, and they will be used to supply your circuits with electricity.  The black sockets on the left have labels like P0, P1, up through P15.  These are sockets that you can use to connect your circuit to the BASIC Stamp module's input/output pins.  The white board with lots of holes in it is called a solderless breadboard.  You will use this breadboard to connect components to each other and build circuits.

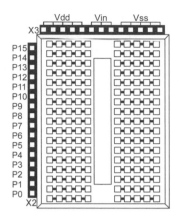

**Figure 2-5**
Prototyping Area

*Power terminals (black sockets along top), I/O pin access (black sockets along the side), and solderless breadboard (white sockets)*

**Input/output pins** are usually called I/O pins, and after connecting your circuit to one or more of these I/O pins, you can program your BASIC Stamp to monitor the circuit (input) or send on or off signals to the circuit (output). You will try this in the next activity.

Figure 2-6 shows a circuit schematic, and a picture of how that circuit will look when it is built on the prototyping area. The breadboard is separated into rows of five sockets. Each row can connect up to five leads, or wires, to each other. For this circuit, the resistor and the LED are connected because each one has a lead plugged into the same 5-socket row. Note that one lead of the resistor is plugged into Vdd so the circuit can draw power. The other resistor lead connects to the LED's anode lead. The LED's cathode lead is connected to Vss, or ground, completing the circuit.

You are now ready to build the circuit shown in Figure 2-6 (below) by plugging the LED and resistor leads into sockets on the prototyping area. Follow these steps:

√ Disconnect power from your Board of Education or HomeWork Board.
√ Use Figure 2-4 to decide which lead is connected to the LED's cathode. Look for the shorter lead and the flat spot on the plastic part of the LED.
√ Plug the LED's cathode into one of the black sockets labeled Vss on the prototyping area.
√ Plug the LED's anode (the other, longer lead) into the socket shown on the breadboard portion of the prototyping area.
√ Plug one of the resistor's leads into the same breadboard row as the LED's anode. This will connect those two leads together.

√ Plug the resistor's other lead into one of the sockets labeled Vdd.

> **Direction does matter for the LED, but not for the resistor.** If you plug the LED in backward, the LED will not emit light when you connect power. The resistor just resists the flow of current. There is no backwards or forwards for a resistor.

√ Reconnect power to your Board of Education or HomeWork Board.
√ Check to make sure your green LED is emitting light. It should glow green.

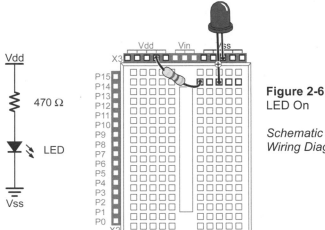

**Figure 2-6**
LED On

*Schematic (left) and
Wiring Diagram (right)*

If your green LED does not emit light when you connect power to the board:

√ Some LEDs are brightest when viewed from above. Try looking straight down onto the dome part of the LED's plastic case from above.
√ If the room is bright, try turning off some of the lights, or use your hands to cast a shadow on the LED.

If you still do not see any green glow, try these steps:

√ Double check to make sure your cathode and anode are connected properly. If not, simply remove the LED, give it a half-turn, and plug it back in. It will not hurt the LED if you plug it in backwards, it just doesn't emit light. When you have it plugged in the right direction, it should emit light.

√ Double check to make sure you built your circuit exactly as shown in Figure 2-6.
√ If you are using a What's a Microcontroller kit that somebody used before you, the LED may be damaged, so try a different one.
√ If you are in a lab class, check with your instructor.

**Still stuck?** If you don't have an instructor or friend who can help, you can always check with the Stamps in Class discussion group. The first pages of this book has Internet Access information on where to find the Stamps in Class discussion group. If the group is unable to help you solve the problem, you can contact the Parallax Technical Support department by following the Support link at www.parallax.com.

### How the LED Test Circuit Works

The Vdd and Vss terminals supply electrical pressure in the same way that a battery would. The Vdd sockets are like the battery's positive terminal, and the Vss sockets are like the battery's negative terminal. Figure 2-7 shows how applying electrical pressure to a circuit using a battery causes electrons to flow through it. This flow of electrons is called electric current, or often just current. Electric current is limited by the resistor. This current is what causes the diode to emit light.

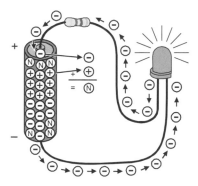

**Figure 2-7**
LED On Circuit Electron Flow

*The minus signs with the circles around them are used to show electrons flowing from the battery's negative terminal to its positive terminal.*

2

> **Chemical reactions** inside the battery supply the circuit with current. The battery's negative terminal contains a compound that has molecules with extra electrons (shown in Figure 2-7 by minus-signs). The battery's positive terminal has a chemical compound with molecules that are missing electrons (shown by plus-signs). When an electron leaves a molecule in the negative terminal and travels through the wire, it is called a free electron (also shown by minus-signs). The molecule that lost that extra electron no longer has an extra negative charge; it is now called neutral (shown by an N). When an electron gets to the positive terminal, it joins a molecule that was missing an electron, and now that molecule is neutral too.

Figure 2-8 shows how the flow of electricity through the LED circuit is described using schematic notation. The electric pressure across the circuit is called voltage. The + and – signs are used to show the voltage applied to a circuit. The arrow shows the current flowing through the circuit. This arrow is almost always shown pointing the opposite direction of the actual flow of electrons. Benjamin Franklin is credited with not having been aware of electrons when he decided to represent current flow as charge passing from the positive to negative terminal of a circuit. By the time physicists discovered the true nature of electric current, the convention was already well established.

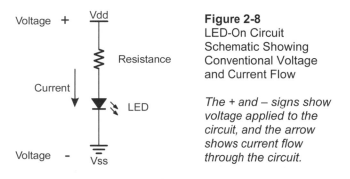

**Figure 2-8**
LED-On Circuit
Schematic Showing
Conventional Voltage
and Current Flow

*The + and – signs show voltage applied to the circuit, and the arrow shows current flow through the circuit.*

> **A schematic drawing** (like Figure 2-8) is a picture that explains how one or more circuits are connected. Schematics are used by students, electronics hobbyists, electricians, engineers, and just about everybody else who works with circuits.
>
> **Appendix F: More about Electricity:** This appendix contains some glossary terms and an activity you can try to get more familiar with measurements of voltage, current and resistance.

### Your Turn – Modifying the LED Test Circuit

In the next activity, you will program the BASIC Stamp to turn the LED on, then off, then on again. The BASIC Stamp will do this by switching the LED circuit between two different connections, Vdd and Vss. You just finished working with the circuit where the resistor is connected to Vdd, and the LED emits light. Make the changes shown in Figure 2-9 to verify that the LED will turn off (not emit light) when the resistor's lead is disconnected from Vdd and connected to Vss.

√   Disconnect power from your Board of Education or HomeWork Board.
√   Unplug the resistor lead that's plugged into the Vdd socket, and plug it into a socket labeled Vss as shown in Figure 2-9.
√   Reconnect power to your Board of Education or HomeWork Board.
√   Check to make sure your green LED is **not emitting light**. It should not glow green.

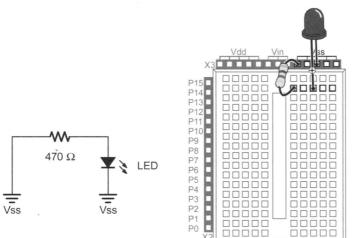

**Figure 2-9**
LED Off Circuit

*Schematic (left) and wiring diagram (right).*

## ACTIVITY #2: ON/OFF CONTROL WITH THE BASIC STAMP

In Activity #1, two different circuits were built and tested. One circuit made the LED emit light while the other did not. Figure 2-10 shows how the BASIC Stamp can do the same thing if you connect an LED circuit to one if its I/O pins. In this activity, you will connect the LED circuit to the BASIC Stamp and program it to turn the LED on and off.

You will also experiment with programs that make the BASIC Stamp do this at different speeds.

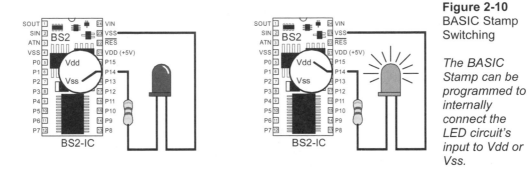

**Figure 2-10**
BASIC Stamp Switching

*The BASIC Stamp can be programmed to internally connect the LED circuit's input to Vdd or Vss.*

There are two big differences between changing the connection manually and having the BASIC Stamp do it. First, the BASIC Stamp doesn't have to cut the power when it changes the LED circuit's supply from Vdd to Vss. Second, while a human can make that change several times a minute, the BASIC Stamp can do it thousands of times per second!

### LED Test Circuit Parts

Same as Activity #1.

### Connecting the LED Circuit to the BASIC Stamp

The LED circuit shown in Figure 2-11 is wired almost the same as the circuit in the previous exercise. The difference is that the resistor's lead that was manually switched between Vdd and Vss is now plugged into a BASIC Stamp I/O pin.

√ Disconnect power from your Board of Education or HomeWork Board.
√ Modify the circuit you were working with in Activity #1 so that it matches Figure 2-11.

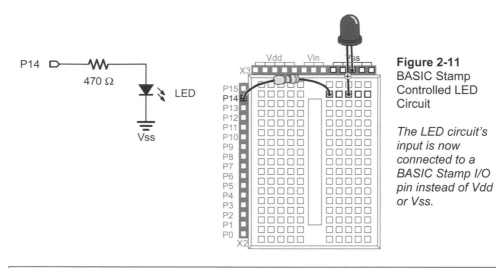

**Figure 2-11**
BASIC Stamp
Controlled LED
Circuit

*The LED circuit's
input is now
connected to a
BASIC Stamp I/O
pin instead of Vdd
or Vss.*

> **Resistors are essential.** Always remember to use a resistor. Without it, too much current will flow through the circuit, and it could damage any number of parts in your circuit, BASIC Stamp, or Board of Education or HomeWork Board.

### Turning the LED On/Off with a Program

The example program makes the LED blink on and off one time per second. It introduces several new programming techniques at once. After running it, you will experiment with different parts of the program to better understand how it works.

### Example Program: LedOnOff.bs2

√ Enter the LedOnOff.bs2 code into the BASIC Stamp Editor.
√ Reconnect power to your Board of Education or HomeWork Board.
√ Run the program.
√ Verify that the LED flashes on and off once per second.
√ Disconnect power when you are done with the program.

```
'What's a Microcontroller - LedOnOff.bs2
'Turn an LED on and off.  Repeat 1 time per second indefinitely.

'{$STAMP BS2}
'{$PBASIC 2.5}

DEBUG "The LED connected to Pin 14 is blinking!"
```

2

```
DO

  HIGH 14
  PAUSE 500
  LOW 14
  PAUSE 500

LOOP
```

## How LedOnOff.bs2 Works

The command **DEBUG "The LED connected to Pin 14 is blinking!"** makes this statement appear in the Debug Terminal. The command **HIGH 14** causes the BASIC Stamp to internally connect I/O pin P14 to Vdd. This turns the LED on.

The command **PAUSE 500** causes the BASIC Stamp to do nothing for ½ a second while the LED stays on. The number 500 tells the **PAUSE** command to wait for 500/1000 of a second. The number that follows **PAUSE** is called an argument. If you look up **PAUSE** in the BASIC Stamp Manual, you will discover that it calls this number the *Duration* argument. The name duration was chosen for this argument to show that the **PAUSE** command pauses for a certain 'duration' of time, in milliseconds.

 **What's a Millisecond?** A millisecond is 1/1000 of a second. It is abbreviated as ms. It takes 1000 ms to equal one second.

The command **LOW 14** causes the BASIC Stamp to internally connect I/O pin P14 to Vss. This turns the LED off. Since **LOW 14** is followed by another **PAUSE 500**, the LED stays off for half a second.

The reason the code repeats itself over and over again is because it is nested between the PBASIC keywords **DO** and **LOOP**. Figure 2-12 shows how a **DO...LOOP** works. By placing the code segment that turns the LED on and off with pauses between **DO** and **LOOP**, it tells the BASIC Stamp to execute those four commands over and over again. The result is that the LED flashes on and off, over and over again. It will keep flashing until you disconnect power, press and hold the Reset button, or until the battery runs out.

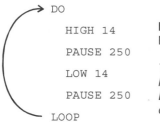

```
  DO

      HIGH 14

      PAUSE 250

      LOW 14

      PAUSE 250

  LOOP
```

**Figure 2-12**
DO...LOOP

*The code between the keywords DO and LOOP get executed over and over again.*

## A Diagnostic Test for your Computer

A very few computers, such as some laptops, will halt the PBASIC program after the first time through a `DO...LOOP` loop. These computers have a non-standard serial port design. By placing a `DEBUG` command the program LedOnOff.bs2, the open Debug Terminal prevents this from possibly happening. You will next re-run this program without the `DEBUG` command to see if your computer has this non-standard serial port problem. It is not likely, but it would be important for you to know.

√   Open LedOnOff.bs2.
√   Delete the entire `DEBUG` instruction.
√   Run the modified program while you observe your LED.

If the LED blinks on and off continuously, just as it did when you ran the original program with the `DEBUG` command, your computer will not have this problem.

If the LED blinked on and off only once and then stopped, you have a computer with a non-standard serial port design. If you disconnect the serial cable from your board and press the Reset button, the BASIC Stamp will run the program properly without freezing. In programs you write yourself, you should add a single command:

```
DEBUG "Program Running!"
```

right after the compiler directives. This will open the Debug Terminal and keep the COM port open. This will prevent your programs from freezing after one pass through the `DO...LOOP`, or any of the other looping commands you will be learning in later chapters. You will see this command in some of the example programs that would not otherwise need a DEBUG instruction. So, you should be able to run all of the remaining programs in this book even if your computer failed the diagnostic test.

**2**

### Your Turn – Timing and Repetitions

By changing the PAUSE command's *Duration* argument you can change the amount of time the LED stays on and off. For example, by changing both the *Duration* arguments to 250, it will cause the LED to flash on and off twice per second. The DO...LOOP in your program will now look like this:

```
DO

  HIGH 14
  PAUSE 250
  LOW 14
  PAUSE 250

LOOP
```

√   Open LedOnOff.bs2
√   Change the PAUSE command's *Duration* arguments from 500 to 250, and re-run the program.

If you want to make the LED blink on and off once every three seconds, with the low time twice as long as the high time, you can program the PAUSE command after the HIGH 14 command so that it takes one second using PAUSE 1000. The PAUSE command after the LOW 14 command will have to be PAUSE 2000.

```
DO

  HIGH 14
  PAUSE 1000
  LOW 14
  PAUSE 2000

LOOP
```

√   Modify and re-run the program using the code snippet above.

A fun experiment is to see how short you can make the pauses and still see that the LED is flashing. When the LED is flashing very fast, but it looks like it's just on, it's called persistence of vision. Here is how to test to see what your persistence of vision threshold is:

√    Try modifying both of your **PAUSE** command's *Duration* arguments so that they are 100.

√    Re-run your program and check for flicker.

√    Reduce both *Duration* arguments by 5 and try again.

√    Keep reducing the *Duration* arguments until the LED appears to be on all the time with no flicker. It will be dimmer than normal, but it should not appear to flicker.

One last thing to try is to create a one-shot LED flasher. When the program runs, the LED flashes only once. This is a way to look at the functionality of the **DO...LOOP**. You can temporarily remove the **DO...LOOP** from the program by placing an apostrophe to the left of both the **DO** and **LOOP** keywords as shown below.

```
' DO

  HIGH 14
  PAUSE 1000
  LOW 14
  PAUSE 2000

' LOOP
```

√    Modify and re-run the program using the code snippet above.

√    Explain what happened, why did the LED only flash once?

> **Commenting a line of code:** Placing an apostrophe to the left of a command changes it into a comment. This is a useful tool because you don't actually have to delete the command to see what happens if you remove it from the program. It is much easier to add and remove an apostrophe than it is to delete and re-type the commands.

## ACTIVITY #3: COUNTING AND REPEATING

In the previous activity, the LED circuit either flashed on and off all the time, or it flashed once and then stopped. What if you only want the LED to flash on and off ten times? Computers (including the BASIC Stamp) are great at keeping running totals of how many times something happens. Computers can also be programmed to make decisions based on a variety of conditions.  In this activity, you will program the BASIC Stamp to stop flashing the LED on and off after ten repetitions.

### Counting Parts and Test Circuit

Use the example circuit shown in Figure 2-11 on page 48.

### How Many Times?

There are many ways to make the LED blink on and off ten times.  The simplest way is to use a **FOR...NEXT** loop.  The **FOR...NEXT** loop is similar to the **DO...LOOP**.  Although either loop can be used to repeat commands a fixed number of times, **FOR...NEXT** is easier to use.

The **FOR...NEXT** loop depends on a variable to track how many times the LED has blinked on and off.  A variable is a word of your choosing that is used to store a value.  The next example program uses the word **counter** to 'count' how many times the LED has been turned on and off.

---

**Picking words for variable names has several rules:**

1.  The name cannot be a word that is already used by PBASIC.  These words are called reserved words, and some examples that you should already be familiar with are: **DEBUG**, **PAUSE**, **HIGH**, **LOW**, **DO**, and **LOOP**.

2.  The name cannot contain a space.

3.  Even though the name can contain letters, numbers, or underscores, it must begin with a character.

4.  The name must be less than 33 characters long.

---

### Example Program: LedOnOffTenTimes.bs2

The program LedOnOffTenTimes.bs2 demonstrates how to use a **FOR...NEXT** loop to blink an LED on and off ten times.

- √   Your test circuit from Activity #2 should be built (or rebuilt) and ready to use.
- √   Enter the LedOnOffTenTimes.bs2 code into the BASIC Stamp Editor.
- √   Connect power to your Board of Education or HomeWork Board.
- √   Run the program.
- √   Verify that the LED flashes on and off ten times.

√  Run the program a second time, and verify that the value of **counter** shown in the Debug Terminal accurately tracks how many times the LED blinked. Hint: instead of clicking *Run* a second time, you can press and release the Reset button on your Board of Education or HomeWork Board.

```
' What's a Microcontroller - LedOnOffTenTimes.bs2
' Turn an LED on and off.  Repeat 10 times.

' {$STAMP BS2}
' {$PBASIC 2.5}

counter VAR Byte

FOR counter = 1 TO 10

  DEBUG ? counter

  HIGH 14
  PAUSE 500
  LOW 14
  PAUSE 500

NEXT

DEBUG "All done!"

END
```

## How LedOnOffTenTimes.bs2 Works

This PBASIC statement

```
counter VAR Byte
```

tells the BASIC Stamp Editor that your program will use the word **counter** as a variable that can store a byte's worth of information.

**What's a Byte?** A byte is enough memory to store a number between 0 and 255. The BASIC Stamp has four different types of variables, and each can store a different range of numbers:

**Table 2-2:** Variable Types and Values They Can Store

| Variable type | Range of Values |
|---|---|
| Bit | 0 to 1 |
| Nib | 0 to 15 |
| Byte | 0 to 255 |
| Word | 0 to 65535 |

The question mark formatter before a variable in a **DEBUG** command tells the Debug Terminal to display the name of the variable and its value. This is how the command

```
DEBUG ? counter
```

displays both the name and the value of the **counter** variable in the Debug Terminal.

The **FOR...NEXT** loop and all the commands inside it are shown below. The statement **FOR counter = 1 to 10** tells the BASIC Stamp that it will have to set the **counter** variable to 1, then keep executing commands until it gets to the **NEXT** statement. When the BASIC Stamp gets to the **NEXT** statement, it jumps back to the **FOR** statement. The **FOR** statement adds one to the value of **counter**. Then, it checks to see if **counter** is greater than ten yet. If not, it repeats the process. When the value of counter finally reaches eleven, the program skips the commands between the **FOR** and **NEXT** statements and moves on to the command that comes after the **NEXT** statement.

```
FOR counter = 1 to 10

  DEBUG ? counter, CR

  HIGH 14
  PAUSE 500
  LOW 14
  PAUSE 500

NEXT
```

The command that comes after the **NEXT** statement is:

```
DEBUG "All done!"
```

This command is included just to show what the program does after ten times through the FOR...NEXT loop. It moves on to the command that comes after the NEXT statement.

### Your Turn – Other Ways to Count

√    Replace the statement

```
FOR counter = 1 to 10     with this:    FOR counter = 1 to 20
```

in LedOnOffTenTimes.bs2 and re-run the program. What did the program do differently, and was this expected?

√    Try a second modification to the FOR statement. This time, change it to

```
FOR counter = 20 to 120 STEP 10
```

How many times did the LED flash? What values displayed in the Debug Terminal?

## ACTIVITY #4: BUILDING AND TESTING A SECOND LED CIRCUIT

Indicator LEDs can be used to tell the machine's user many things. Many devices need two, three, or more LEDs to tell the user if the machine is ready or not, if there is a malfunction, if it's done with a task, and so on.

In this activity, you will repeat the LED circuit test in Activity #1 for a second LED circuit. Then you will adjust the example program from Activity #2 to make sure the LED circuit is properly connected to the BASIC Stamp. After that, you will modify the example program from Activity #2 to make the LEDs operate in tandem.

### Extra Parts

In addition to the parts you used in Activities 1 and 2, you will need these parts:

(1) LED - yellow
(1) Resistor – 470 Ω (yellow-violet-brown)

## Building and Testing the Second LED Circuit

In Activity #1, you manually tested the first LED circuit to make sure it worked before connecting it to the BASIC Stamp. Before connecting the second LED circuit to the BASIC Stamp, it's important to test it too.

√ Disconnect power from your Board of Education or HomeWork Board.
√ Construct the second LED circuit as shown in Figure 2-13.
√ Reconnect power to your Board of Education or HomeWork Board.
√ Did the LED circuit you just added turn on? If yes, then continue. If no, Activity #1 has some trouble-shooting suggestions that you can repeat for this circuit.

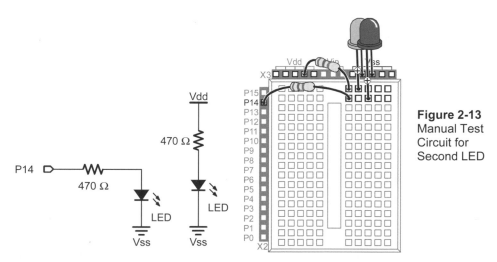

**Figure 2-13**
Manual Test Circuit for Second LED

√ Disconnect power to your Board of Education or HomeWork Board.
√ Modify the second LED circuit you just tested by connecting the LED circuit's resistor lead (input) to P15 as shown in Figure 2-14.

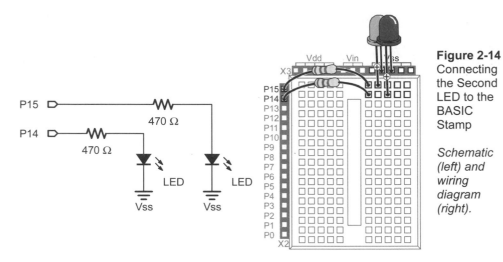

**Figure 2-14**
Connecting the Second LED to the BASIC Stamp

*Schematic (left) and wiring diagram (right).*

## Using a Program to Test the Second LED Circuit

In Activity #2, you used an example program and the **HIGH** and **LOW** commands to control the LED circuit connected to P14. These commands will have to be modified to control the LED circuit connected to P15. Instead of using **HIGH 14** and **LOW 14**, you will use **HIGH 15** and **LOW 15**.

### Example Program: TestSecondLed.bs2

√ Enter TestSecondLed.bs2 into the BASIC Stamp Editor.
√ Connect power to your Board of Education or HomeWork Board.
√ Run TestSecondLED.bs2.
√ Make sure the LED circuit connected to P15 is flashing. If the LED connected to P15 flashes, move on to the next example (Controlling Both LEDs). If the LED circuit connected to P15 is not flashing, check your circuit for wiring errors and your program for typing errors and try again.

```
' What's a Microcontroller - TestSecondLed.bs2
' Turn LED connected to P15 on and off.
' Repeat 1 time per second indefinitely.

' {$STAMP BS2}
' {$PBASIC 2.5}

DEBUG "Program Running!"
```

```
DO

  HIGH 15
  PAUSE 500
  LOW 15
  PAUSE 500

LOOP
```

### Controlling Both LEDs

Yes, you can flash both LEDs at once. One way you can do this is to use two **HIGH** commands before the first **PAUSE** command. One **HIGH** command sets P14 high, and the next **HIGH** command sets P15 high. You will also need two **LOW** commands to turn both LEDs off. It's true that both LEDs will not turn on and off at exactly the same time because one is turned on or off after the other. However, there is no more than a millisecond's difference between the two changes, and the human eye will not detect it.

### Example Program: FlashBothLeds.bs2

    √    Enter the FlashBothLeds.bs2 code into the BASIC Stamp Editor.
    √    Run the program.
    √    Verify that both LEDs appear to flash on and off at the same time.

```
' What's a Microcontroller - FlashBothLeds.bs2
' Turn LEDs connected to P14 and P15 on and off.

' {$STAMP BS2}
' {$PBASIC 2.5}

DEBUG "Program Running!"

DO

  HIGH 14
  HIGH 15
  PAUSE 500
  LOW 14
  LOW 15
  PAUSE 500

LOOP
```

## Your Turn – Alternate LEDs

You can cause the LEDs to alternate by swapping the **HIGH** and **LOW** commands that control one of the I/O pins. This means that while one LED is on, the other will be off.

√ Modify FlashBothLeds.bs2 so that the commands between the **DO** and **LOOP** keywords look like this:

```
HIGH 14
LOW 15
PAUSE 500
LOW 14
HIGH 15
PAUSE 500
```

√ Run the modified version of FlashBothLeds.bs2 and verify that the LEDs flash alternately on and off.

## ACTIVITY #5: USING CURRENT DIRECTION TO CONTROL A BI-COLOR LED

The device shown in Figure 2-15 is a security monitor for electronic keys. When an electronic key with the right code is used, the LED changes color, and a door opens. This kind of LED is called a bi-color LED. This activity answers two questions:

1. How does the LED change color?
2. How can you run one with the BASIC Stamp?

**Figure 2-15**
Bi-color LED in a
Security Device

*When the door is
locked, this bi-color
LED glows red.
When the door is
unlocked by an
electronic key with
the right code, the
LED turns green.*

### Introducing the Bi-Color LED

The bi-color LED's schematic symbol and part drawing are shown in Figure 2-16.

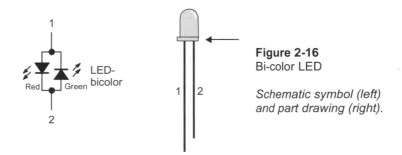

**Figure 2-16**
Bi-color LED

*Schematic symbol (left)
and part drawing (right).*

The bi-color LED is really just two LEDs in one package. Figure 2-17 shows how you can apply voltage in one direction and the LED will glow red. By disconnecting the LED and plugging it back in reversed, the LED will then glow green. As with the other LEDs, if you connect both terminals of the circuit to Vss, the LED will not emit light.

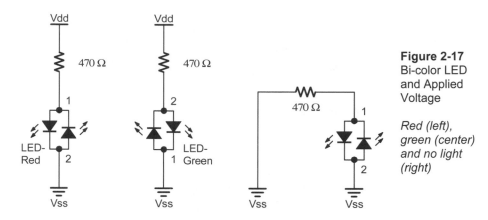

**Figure 2-17**
Bi-color LED
and Applied
Voltage

*Red (left),
green (center)
and no light
(right)*

## Bi-Color LED Circuit Parts

(1) LED – bi-color
(1) Resistor 470 Ω (yellow-violet-brown)
(1) Jumper wire

## Building and Testing the Bi-Color LED Circuit

Figure 2-18 shows the manual test for the bi-color LED.

> √   Disconnect power from your Board of Education or HomeWork Board.
> √   Build the circuit shown on the left side of Figure 2-18.
> √   Reconnect power and verify that the bi-color LED is emitting red light.
> √   Disconnect power again.
> √   Modify your circuit so that it matches the right side of Figure 2-18.
> √   Reconnect power.
> √   Verify that the bi-color LED is now emitting green light.
> √   Disconnect power.

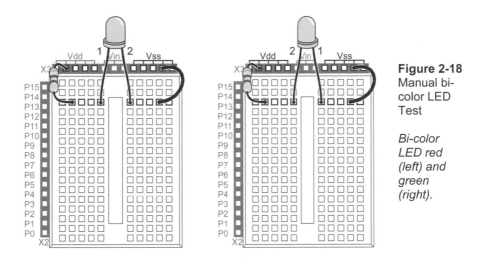

**Figure 2-18**
Manual bi-color LED Test

*Bi-color LED red (left) and green (right).*

Controlling a bi-color LED with the BASIC Stamp requires two I/O pins. After you have manually verified that the bi-color LED works using the manual test, you can connect the circuit to the BASIC Stamp as shown in Figure 2-19.

√    Connect the bi-color LED circuit to the BASIC Stamp as shown in Figure 2-19.

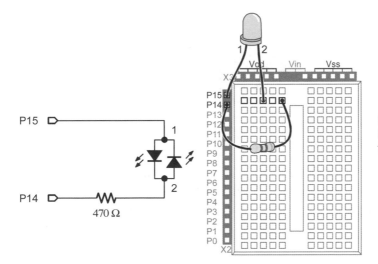

**Figure 2-19**
Bi-color LED Connected to BASIC Stamp

### BASIC Stamp Bi-Color LED Control

Figure 2-20 shows how you can use P15 and P14 to control the current flow in the bi-color LED circuit. The upper schematic shows how current flows through the red LED when P15 is set to Vdd and P14 is set to Vss. This is because the red LED will let current flow through it when electrical pressure is applied as shown, but the green LED acts like a closed valve and does not let current through it. The bi-color LED glows red.

The lower schematic shows what happens when P15 is set to Vss and P14 is set to Vdd. The electrical pressure is now reversed. The red LED shuts off and does not allow current through. Meanwhile, the green LED turns on, and current passes through the circuit in the opposite direction.

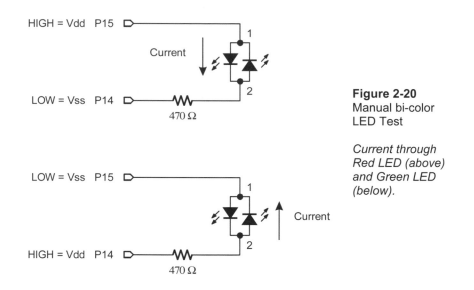

**Figure 2-20**
Manual bi-color
LED Test

*Current through
Red LED (above)
and Green LED
(below).*

Figure 2-20 also shows the key to programming the BASIC Stamp to make the bi-color LED glow two different colors. The upper schematic shows how to make the bi-color LED red using **HIGH 15** and **LOW 14**. The lower schematic shows how to make the bi-color LED glow green by using **LOW 15** and **HIGH 14**. To turn the LED off, send low signals to both P14 and P15 using **LOW 15** and **LOW 14**. In other words, use **LOW** on both pins.

**The bi-color LED will also turn off** if you send high signals to both P14 and P15. Why? Because the electrical pressure is the same at P14 and P15 regardless of whether you set both I/O pins high or low.

### Example Program: TestBiColorLED.bs2

√  Reconnect power.
√  Enter the TestBiColorLed.bs2 code into the BASIC Stamp Editor.
√  Run the program.
√  Verify that the LED cycles through the red, green, and off states.

```
' What's a Microcontroller - TestBiColorLed.bs2
' Turn bi-color LED red, then green, then off in a loop.

' {$STAMP BS2}
' {$PBASIC 2.5}

DEBUG "Program Running!"

DO

  HIGH 15          ' Red
  LOW 14
  PAUSE 500

  LOW 15           ' Green
  HIGH 14
  PAUSE 500

  LOW 15           ' Off
  LOW 14
  PAUSE 500

LOOP
```

### Your Turn – Lights Display

In Activity #3, a variable named `counter` was used to control how many times the LED blinked. What happens if you use the value `counter` to control the **PAUSE** command's *Duration* argument?

√  Rename and save TestBiColorLed.bs2 as TestBiColorLedYourTurn.bs2.
√  Add a counter variable declaration before the **DO** statement:

```
counter VAR BYTE
```

√  Nest the **FOR...NEXT** loop below within the **DO...LOOP**.

```
FOR counter = 1 to 50

   HIGH 15
   LOW 14
   PAUSE counter

   LOW 15
   HIGH 14
   PAUSE counter

NEXT
```

When you are done, your code should look like this:

```
counter VAR BYTE

DO

   FOR counter = 1 to 50

      HIGH 15
      LOW 14
      PAUSE counter

      LOW 15
      HIGH 14
      PAUSE counter

   NEXT

LOOP
```

At the beginning of each pass through the **FOR...NEXT** loop, the **PAUSE** value (*Duration* argument) is only one millisecond.  Each time through the **FOR...NEXT** loop, the pause gets longer by one millisecond at a time until it gets to 50 milliseconds.  The **DO...LOOP** causes the **FOR...NEXT** loop to execute over and over again.

√  Run the modified program and observe the effect.

## SUMMARY

The BASIC Stamp can be programmed to switch a circuit with a light emitting diode (LED) indicator light on and off. LED indicators are useful in a variety of places including many computer monitors, disk drives, and other devices. The LED was introduced along with a technique to identify its anode and cathode terminals. An LED circuit must have a resistor to limit the current passing through it. Resistors were introduced along with one of the more common coding schemes you can use to figure out a resistor's value.

The BASIC Stamp switches an LED circuit on and off by internally connecting an I/O pin to either Vdd or Vss. The **HIGH** command can be used to make the BASIC Stamp internally connect one of its I/O pins to Vdd, and the **LOW** command can be used to internally connect an I/O pin to Vss. The **PAUSE** command is used to cause the BASIC Stamp to not execute commands for an amount of time. This was used to make LEDs stay on and/or off for certain amounts of time. This amount of time is determined by the number used in the **PAUSE** command's *Duration* argument.

The **DO...LOOP** can be used to create an infinite loop. The commands between the **DO** and **LOOP** keywords will execute over and over again. Even though this is called an infinite loop, the program can still be re-started by disconnecting and reconnecting power or pressing and releasing the Reset button. A new program can also be downloaded to the BASIC Stamp, and this will erase the program with the infinite loop.

Current direction and voltage polarity were introduced using a bi-color LED. If voltage is applied across the LED circuit, current will pass through it in one direction, and it glows a particular color. If the voltage polarity is reversed, current travels through the circuit in the opposite direction and it glows a different color.

### Questions

1. What is the name of this Greek letter: $\Omega$, and what measurement does $\Omega$ refer to?
2. Which resistor would allow more current through the circuit, a 470 $\Omega$ resistor or a 1000 $\Omega$ resistor?
3. How do you connect two wires using a breadboard? Can you use a breadboard to connect four wires together?

4. What do you always have to do before modifying a circuit that you built on a breadboard?
5. How long would **PAUSE 10000** last?
6. How would you cause the BASIC Stamp to do nothing for an entire minute?
7. What are the different types of variables?
8. Can a byte hold the value 500?
9. What will the command **HIGH 7** do?

## Exercises

1. Draw the schematic of an LED circuit like the one you worked with in Activity #2, but connect the circuit to P13 instead of P14. Explain how you would modify LedOnOff.bs2 on Page 48 so that it will make your LED circuit flash on and off four times per second.
2. Explain how to modify LedOnOffTenTimes.bs2 so that it makes the LED circuit flash on and off 5000 times before it stops. Hint: you will need to modify just two lines of code.

## Project

1. Make a 10-second countdown using one yellow LED and one bi-color LED. Make the bi-color LED start out red for 3 seconds. After 3 seconds, change the bi-color LED to green. When the bi-color LED changes to green, flash the yellow LED on and off once every second for ten seconds. When the yellow LED is done flashing, the bi-color LED should switch back to red and stay that way.

## Solutions

Q1. Omega refers to the ohm which measures how strongly something resists current flow.
Q2. A 470 Ω resistor: higher values resist more strongly than lower values, therefore lower values allow more current to flow.
Q3. To connect 2 wires, plug the 2 wires into the same row of 5 sockets. You can connect 4 wires by plugging all 4 wires into the same row of 5 sockets.
Q4. Disconnect the power.
Q5. 10 seconds.
Q6.  PAUSE 60000
Q7. Bit, Nib, Byte, and Word

2

Q8. No. The largest value a byte can hold is 255. The value 500 is out of range for a byte.

Q9. **HIGH 7** will cause the BASIC Stamp to internally connect I/O pin P7 to Vdd.

E1. The **PAUSE** *Duration* must be reduced to 500ms / 4 = 125ms. To use I/O pin P13, **HIGH 14** and **LOW 14** have been replaced with **HIGH 13** and **LOW 13**.

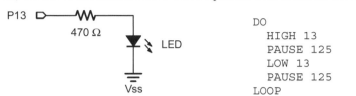

```
DO
   HIGH 13
   PAUSE 125
   LOW 13
   PAUSE 125
LOOP
```

E2. The **counter** variable has to be changed to **word** size, and the **FOR** statement has to be modified to count from 1 to 5000).

```
counter VAR Word
FOR counter = 1 to 5000
   DEBUG ? counter, CR
   HIGH 14
   PAUSE 500
   LOW 14
   PAUSE 500
NEXT
```

P1. The bi-color LED schematic, on the left, is unchanged from Figure 2-20 on page 64. The yellow LED schematic is based on Figure 2-11 on page 48. For this project P14 was changed to P13.

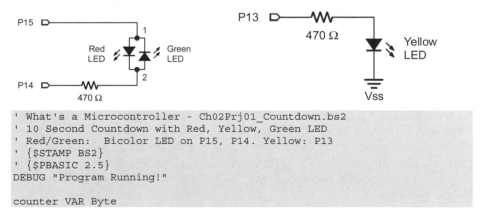

```
' What's a Microcontroller - Ch02Prj01_Countdown.bs2
' 10 Second Countdown with Red, Yellow, Green LED
' Red/Green:  Bicolor LED on P15, P14. Yellow: P13
' {$STAMP BS2}
' {$PBASIC 2.5}
DEBUG "Program Running!"

counter VAR Byte
```

```
' Red for three seconds                  ' Bi-color LED Red
  HIGH 15
  LOW 14
  PAUSE 3000

' Green for 10 seconds...
  LOW 15                                  ' Bi-color LED Green
  HIGH 14

' ...while the yellow LED is flashing
  FOR counter = 1 TO 10
     HIGH 13                              ' Yellow LED on
     PAUSE 500
     LOW 13                               ' Yellow LED off
     PAUSE 500
  NEXT

' Red stays on                           ' Bi Color LED Red
  HIGH 15
  LOW 14
```

## Further Investigation

The resources listed here are available for free download from the Parallax web site and are also included on the Parallax CD.

**"*BASIC Stamp Manual*", Users Manual, Version 2.0c, Parallax Inc., 2000**
> The *BASIC Stamp Manual* has more examples you can try and information that further explains the following commands: `HIGH`, `LOW`, `PAUSE`, the `DEBUG ?` formatter, and `FOR...NEXT`.

**"*Basic Analog and Digital*", Student Guide, Version 2.0, Parallax Inc., 2003**
> *Basic Analog and Digital* uses LEDs to describe counting in binary, describes analog conditions, and it introduces new ways to adjust an LED's brightness.

**"*BASIC Stamp Editor Help File*", PBASIC 2.5 Version 2.0 Parallax Inc., 2003**
> The PBASIC 2.5 Help File has information on `DO...LOOP`, which is new to PBASIC 2.5 and not included in the BASIC Stamp Manual. You can find this information by clicking the book icon on your BASIC Stamp Editor task bar, then selecting PBASIC Reference from the menu in the left sidebar window. This will open the PBASIC Command Reference alphabetical listing in the main window. Detailed information can be found by clicking on each command.

# Chapter #3: Digital Input - Pushbuttons

## FOUND ON CALCULATORS, HAND HELD GAMES, AND APPLIANCES

How many devices with pushbuttons do you use on a daily basis? Here are a few examples that might appear in your list: computer, mouse, calculator, microwave oven, handheld remote, handheld games, and VCR. In each device, there is a microcontroller scanning the pushbuttons and waiting for the circuit to change. When the circuit changes, the microcontroller detects the change and takes action. By the end of this chapter, you will have experience with designing pushbutton circuits and programming the BASIC Stamp to monitor them and take action when changes occur.

## RECEIVING VS. SENDING HIGH AND LOW SIGNALS

In Chapter #2, you programmed the BASIC Stamp to send high and low signals, and you used LED circuits to display these signals. Sending high and low signals means you used a BASIC Stamp I/O pin as an output. In this chapter, you will use a BASIC Stamp I/O pin as an input. As an input, an I/O pin listens for high/low signals instead of sending them. You will send these signals to the BASIC Stamp using a pushbutton circuit, and you will program the BASIC Stamp to recognize whether the pushbutton is pressed or not pressed.

 **Other terms that mean send, high/low, and receive:** Sending high/low signals is described in different ways. You may see sending referred to as transmitting, controlling, or switching. Instead of high/low, you might see it referred to as binary, TTL, CMOS, or Boolean signals. Another term for receiving is sensing.

## ACTIVITY #1: TESTING A PUSHBUTTON WITH AN LED CIRCUIT

If you can use a pushbutton to send a high or low signal to the BASIC Stamp, can you also control an LED with a pushbutton? The answer is yes, and you will use it to test a pushbutton in this activity.

### Introducing the Pushbutton

Figure 3-1 shows the schematic symbol and the part drawing of a normally open pushbutton. Two of the pushbutton's pins are connected to each terminal. This means that connecting a wire or part lead to pin 1 of the pushbutton is the same as connecting it to pin 4. The same rule applies with pins 2 and 3. The reason the pushbutton doesn't just have two pins is because it needs stability. If the pushbutton only had two pins, those pins would eventually bend and break from all the pressure that the pushbutton receives when people press it.

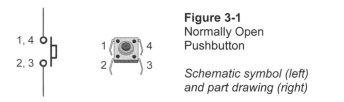

**Figure 3-1**
Normally Open
Pushbutton

*Schematic symbol (left)
and part drawing (right)*

The left side of Figure 3-2 shows how a normally open pushbutton looks when it's not pressed. When the button is not pressed, there is a gap between the 1,4 and 2,3 terminals. This gap makes it so that the 1,4 terminal can not conduct current to the 2,3 terminal. This is called an open circuit. The name "normally open" means that the pushbutton's normal state (not pressed) forms an open circuit. When the button is pressed, the gap between the 1,4 and 2,3 terminals is bridged by a conductive metal. This is called closed, and current can flow through the pushbutton.

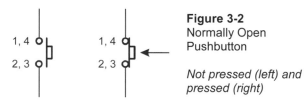

**Figure 3-2**
Normally Open
Pushbutton

*Not pressed (left) and
pressed (right)*

### Test Parts for the Pushbutton

(1) LED – pick a color
(1) Resistor - 470 Ω (yellow-violet-brown)
(1) Pushbutton - normally open
(1) Jumper wire

### Building the Pushbutton Test Circuit

Figure 3-3 shows a circuit you can build to manually test the pushbutton.

**Always disconnect power** from your Board of Education or BASIC Stamp HomeWork Board before making any changes to your test circuit. From here onward, the instructions will no longer say "Disconnect power…" between each circuit modification. It is up to you to remember to do this.

**Always reconnect power** to your Board of Education or BASIC Stamp HomeWork Board before downloading a program to the BASIC Stamp.

√  Build the circuit shown in Figure 3-3.

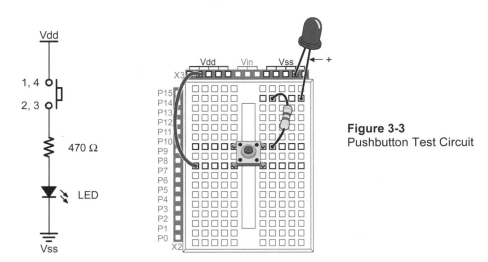

**Figure 3-3**
Pushbutton Test Circuit

## Testing the Pushbutton

When the pushbutton is not pressed, the LED will be off. If the wiring is correct, when the pushbutton is pressed, the LED should be on (emitting light).

**Warning signs:** If the Pwr LED on the Board of Education flickers, goes dim, or goes out completely when you plug the power supply back in, it means you have a short circuit. If this happens to you, disconnect power immediately and find and correct the mistake in your circuit.

The Power LED on the HomeWork Board is different. It glows only while a program is running. If a program ends (using the **END** command), the Power LED will also turn off.

√  Verify that the LED in your test circuit is off.

√  Press and hold the pushbutton, and verify that the LED emits light while you are holding the pushbutton down.

### How the Pushbutton Circuit Works

The left side of Figure 3-4 shows what happens when the pushbutton is not pressed. The LED circuit is not connected to Vdd. It is an open circuit that cannot conduct current. By pressing the pushbutton, you close the connection between the terminals with conductive metal making a pathway for electrons to flow through the circuit.

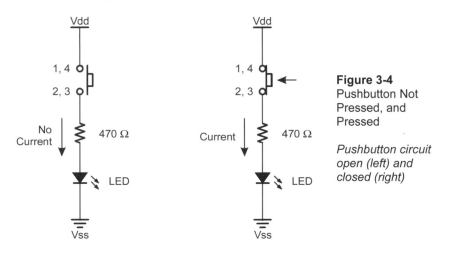

**Figure 3-4**
Pushbutton Not Pressed, and Pressed

*Pushbutton circuit open (left) and closed (right)*

### Your Turn – A Short-Circuit

Figure 3-5 shows a different circuit that will cause the LED to behave differently. When the button is not pressed, the LED stays on. When the button is pressed, the LED turns off. The reason the LED turns off when the pushbutton is pressed is because current always follows the path of least resistance. When the pushbutton is pressed, terminals 1,4 and 2,3, have almost no resistance between them, so all the current passes through the pushbutton (short circuit) instead of the LED.

√  Build the circuit shown in Figure 3-5.
√  Repeat the tests you performed on the first pushbutton circuit you built with this new circuit.

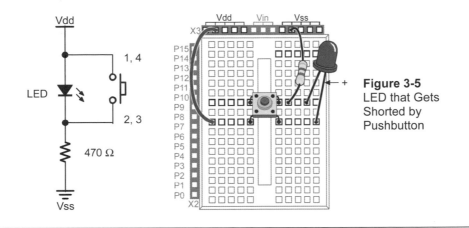

**3**

**Figure 3-5**
LED that Gets
Shorted by
Pushbutton

> **Can you really do that with the LED?** Up until now, the LED's cathode has always been connected to Vss. Now, the LED is in a different place in the circuit, with its anode connected to Vdd. People often ask if this breaks any circuit rules, and the answer is no. The electrical pressure supplied by Vdd and Vss is 5 volts. The diode will always use 1.6 volts, and the resistor will always use 3.4 volts, regardless of their order.

## ACTIVITY #2: READING A PUSHBUTTON WITH THE BASIC STAMP

In this activity, you will connect a pushbutton circuit to the BASIC Stamp and display whether or not the pushbutton is pressed. You will do this by writing a PBASIC program that checks the state of the pushbutton and displays it in the Debug Terminal.

### Parts for a Pushbutton Circuit

(1) Pushbutton - normally open
(1) Resistor – 220 Ω (red-red-brown)
(1) Resistor – 10 kΩ (brown-black-orange)
(2) Jumper wires

### Building a Pushbutton Circuit for the BASIC Stamp

Figure 3-6 shows a pushbutton circuit that is connected to BASIC Stamp I/O pin P3.

√ Build the circuit shown in Figure 3-6.

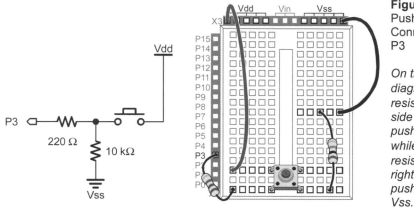

**Figure 3-6**
Pushbutton Circuit
Connected to I/O Pin
P3

*On the wiring
diagram, the 220 Ω
resistor is on the left
side connecting the
pushbutton to P3
while the 10 kΩ
resistor is on the
right, connecting the
pushbutton circuit to
Vss.*

Figure 3-7 shows what the BASIC Stamp sees when the button is pressed, and when it's not pressed. When the pushbutton is pressed, the BASIC Stamp senses that Vdd is connected to P3. Inside the BASIC Stamp, this causes it to place the number 1 in a part of its memory that stores information about its I/O pins. When the pushbutton is not pressed, the BASIC Stamp cannot sense Vdd, but it can sense Vss through the 10 kΩ and 220 Ω resistors. This causes it to store the number 0 in that same memory location that stored a 1 when the pushbutton was pressed.

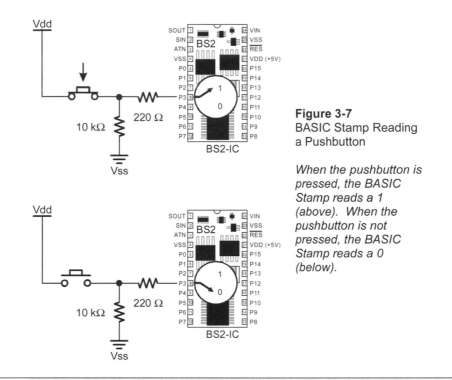

**Figure 3-7**
BASIC Stamp Reading
a Pushbutton

*When the pushbutton is
pressed, the BASIC
Stamp reads a 1
(above). When the
pushbutton is not
pressed, the BASIC
Stamp reads a 0
(below).*

> **Binary and Circuits:** The base-2 number system uses only the digits 1 and 0 to make numbers, and these binary values can be transmitted from one device to another. The BASIC Stamp interprets Vdd (5 V) as binary-1 and Vss (0 V) as binary-0. Likewise, when the BASIC Stamp sets an I/O pin to Vdd using **HIGH**, it sends a binary-1. When it sets an I/O pin to Vss using **LOW**, it sends a binary-0. This is a very common way of communicating binary numbers used by many computer chips and other devices.

## Programming the BASIC Stamp to Monitor the Pushbutton

The BASIC Stamp stores the one or zero it senses at I/O pin P3 in a memory location called **IN3**. Here is an example program that shows how this works:

### Example Program: ReadPushbuttonState.bs2

This program makes the BASIC Stamp check the pushbutton every ¼ second and send the value of **IN3** to the Debug Terminal. Figure 3-8 shows the Debug Terminal while the program is running. When the pushbutton is pressed, the Debug Terminal displays the number 1, and when the pushbutton is not pressed, the Debug Terminal displays the number 0.

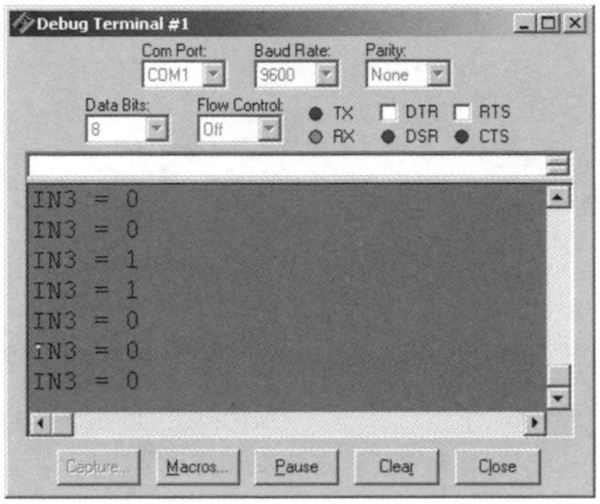

**Figure 3-8**
Debug Terminal
Displaying
Pushbutton States

*The Debug Terminal
displays 1 when the
pushbutton is pressed
and 0 when it is not
pressed.*

√   Enter the ReadPushbuttonState.bs2 program into the BASIC Stamp Editor.
√   Run the program.
√   Verify that the Debug Terminal displays the value 0 when the pushbutton is not pressed.
√   Verify that the Debug Terminal displays the value 1 when the pushbutton is pressed and held.

```
' What's a Microcontroller - ReadPushbuttonState.bs2
' Check and send pushbutton state to Debug Terminal every 1/4 second.

' {$STAMP BS2}
' {$PBASIC 2.5}

DO

  DEBUG ? IN3
  PAUSE 250

LOOP
```

## How ReadPushbuttonState.bs2 Works

The **DO…LOOP** in the program repeats every ¼ second because of the command **PAUSE 250**. Each time through the **DO…LOOP**, the command **DEBUG ? IN3** sends the value of **IN3** to the Debug Terminal. The value of **IN3** is the state that I/O pin P3 senses at the instant the **DEBUG** command is executed.

### Your Turn – A Pushbutton with a Pull-up Resistor

The circuit you just finished working with has a resistor connected to Vss. This resistor is called a pull-down resistor because it pulls the voltage at P3 down to Vss (0 volts) when the button is not pressed. Figure 3-9 shows a pushbutton circuit that uses a pull-up resistor. This resistor pulls the voltage up to Vdd (5 volts) when the button is not pressed. The rules are now reversed. When the button is not pressed, IN3 stores the number 1, and when the button is pressed, IN3 stores the number 0.

 **The 220 Ω resistor** is used in the pushbutton example circuits to protect the BASIC Stamp I/O pin. Although it's a good practice for prototyping, in most products, this resistor is replaced with a wire (since wires cost less than resistors).

√ Modify your circuit as shown in Figure 3-9.
√ Re-run ReadPushbuttonState.bs2.
√ Using the Debug Terminal, verify that IN3 is 1 when the button is not pressed and 0 when the button is pressed.

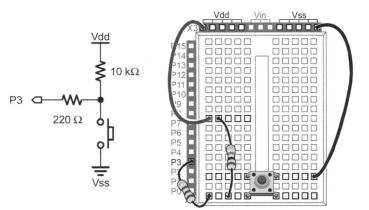

**Figure 3-9**
Modified Pushbutton
Circuit

 **Active-low vs. Active-high:** This pushbutton Figure 3-9 is called active-low because it sends the BASIC Stamp a low signal (Vss) when the button is active (pressed). The pushbutton circuit in Figure 3-6 the main activity is active-high because it sends a high signal (Vdd) when the button is active (pressed).

## ACTIVITY #3: PUSHBUTTON CONTROL OF AN LED CIRCUIT

Figure 3-10 shows a zoomed in view of a pushbutton and LED used to adjust the settings on a computer monitor. This is just one of many devices that have a pushbutton that you can press to adjust the device and an LED to show you the device's status.

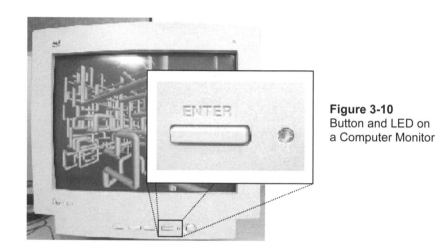

**Figure 3-10**
Button and LED on
a Computer Monitor

The BASIC Stamp can be programmed to make decisions based on what it senses. For example, it can be programmed to decide to flash the LED on/off ten times per second when the button is pressed.

### Pushbutton and LED Circuit Parts

(1) Pushbutton – normally open
(1) Resistor - 10 kΩ (brown-black-orange)
(1) LED – any color
(1) Resistor – 220 Ω (red-red-brown)
(1) Resistor – 470 Ω (yellow-violet-brown)
(2) Jumper wires

### Building the Pushbutton and LED Circuits

Figure 3-11 shows the pushbutton circuit used in the activity you just finished along with the LED circuit used in Chapter #2, Activity #2.

√ Build the circuit shown in Figure 3-11.

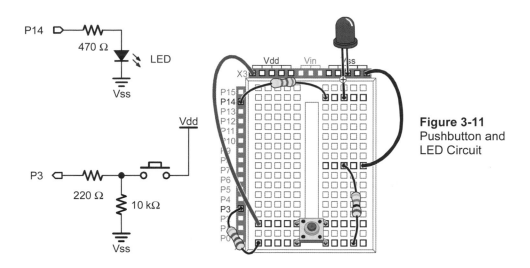

**Figure 3-11**
Pushbutton and
LED Circuit

### Programming Pushbutton Control

The BASIC Stamp can be programmed to make decisions using an **IF...THEN...ELSE**
statement. The example program you are about to run will flash the LED on and off
when the pushbutton is pressed using an **IF...THEN...ELSE** statement. Each time through
the **DO...LOOP**, the **IF...THEN...ELSE** statement checks the state of the pushbutton and
decides whether or not to flash the LED.

### Example Program: PushbuttonControlledLed.bs2

√ Enter PushbuttonControlledLed.bs2 into the BASIC Stamp Editor and run it.
√ Verify that the LED flashes on and off while the pushbutton is pressed and
held down.
√ Verify that the LED does not flash when the pushbutton is not pressed down.

```
' What's a Microcontroller - PushbuttonControlledLed.bs2
' Check pushbutton state 10 times per second and blink LED when pressed.

' {$STAMP BS2}
' {$PBASIC 2.5}

DO
```

```
DEBUG ? IN3

IF (IN3 = 1) THEN
   HIGH 14
   PAUSE 50
   LOW 14
   PAUSE 50

ELSE
   PAUSE 100

ENDIF

LOOP
```

### How PushbuttonControlledLed.bs2 Works

This program is a modified version of ReadPushbuttonState.bs2 from the previous activity. The **DO...LOOP** and **DEBUG ? IN3** commands are the same. The **PAUSE 250** was replaced with an **IF...THEN...ELSE** statement. When the condition after the **IF** is true (**IN3 = 1**), the commands that come after the **THEN** statement are executed. They will be executed until the **ELSE** statement is reached, at which point the program skips to the **ENDIF** and moves on. When the condition after the **IF** is not true (**IN3 = 0**), the commands after the **ELSE** statement are executed until the **ENDIF** is reached.

You can make a detailed list of what a program should do, to either help you plan the program or to describe what it does. This kind of list is called pseudo code, and the example below uses pseudo code to describe how PushbuttonControlledLed.bs2 works.

- *Do the commands between here and the Loop statement over and over again*
  - o *Display the value of IN3 in the Debug Terminal*
  - o *If the value of IN3 is 1, Then*
    - ▪ *Turn the LED on*
    - ▪ *Wait for 1/20 of a second*
    - ▪ *Turn the LED off*
    - ▪ *Wait for 1/20 of a second*
  - o *Else, (if the value of IN3 is 0)*
    - ▪ *do nothing, but wait for the same amount of time it would have taken to briefly flash the LED (1/10 of a second).*
- *Loop*

### Your Turn – Faster/Slower

√  Save the example program under a different name.
√  Modify the program so that the LED flashes twice as fast when you press and hold the pushbutton.
√  Modify the program so that the LED flashes half as fast when you press and hold the pushbutton.

## ACTIVITY #4: TWO PUSHBUTTONS CONTROLLING TWO LED CIRCUITS

Let's add a second pushbutton into the project and see how it works. To make things a little more interesting, let's also add a second LED circuit and use the second pushbutton to control it.

### Pushbutton and LED Circuit Parts

(2) Pushbuttons – normally open
(2) Resistors - 10 kΩ  (brown-black-orange)
(2) Resistors – 470 Ω (yellow-violet-brown)
(2) Resistors – 220 Ω (red-red-brown)
(2) LEDs – any color

### Adding a Pushbutton and LED Circuit

Figure 3-12 shows a second LED and pushbutton circuit added to the circuit you tested in the previous activity.

√  Build the circuit shown in Figure 3-12. If you need help building the circuit shown in the schematic, use the wiring diagram in Figure 3-13 as a guide.
√  Modify ReadPushbuttonState.bs2 so that it reads **IN4** instead of **IN3**, and use it to test your second pushbutton circuit.

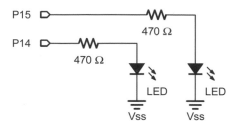

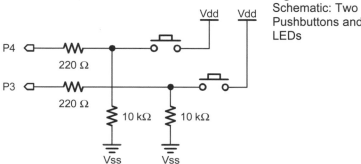

**Figure 3-12**
Schematic: Two
Pushbuttons and
LEDs

 **Connecting wires with dots:** There are three places where wires intersect in Figure 3-12, but only two dots. Wires only connect if there is a dot at the intersection. The wire that connects the P4 pushbutton to the 10 kΩ resistor does not connect to the P3 pushbutton circuit because there is no dot.

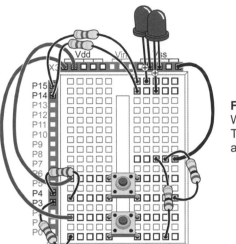

**Figure 3-13**
Wiring Diagram:
Two Pushbuttons
and LEDs

### Programming Pushbutton Control

In the previous activity, you experimented with making decisions using an
**IF...THEN...ELSE** statement. There is also such a thing as an **IF...ELSEIF...ELSE** statement.
It works great for deciding which LED to flash on and off. The next example program
shows how it works.

### Example Program: PushbuttonControlOfTwoLeds.bs2

√ Enter PushbuttonControlOfTwoLeds.bs2 into the BASIC Stamp Editor and
run it.
√ Verify that the LED in the circuit connected to P14 flashes on and off while
the pushbutton in the circuit connected to P3 is held down.
√ Also check to make sure the LED in the circuit connected to P15 flashes while
the pushbutton in the circuit connected to P4 is held down

```
' What's a Microcontroller - PushbuttonControlOfTwoLeds.bs2
' Blink P14 LED if P3 pushbutton is pressed, and blink P15 LED if
' P4 pushbutton is pressed.

' {$STAMP BS2}
' {$PBASIC 2.5}

DO
```

```
   DEBUG HOME
   DEBUG ? IN4
   DEBUG ? IN3

   IF (IN3 = 1) THEN
     HIGH 14
     PAUSE 50

   ELSEIF (IN4 = 1) THEN
     HIGH 15
     PAUSE 50

   ELSE
     PAUSE 50

   ENDIF

   LOW 14
   LOW 15

   PAUSE 50

LOOP
```

### How PushbuttonControlOfTwoLeds.bs2 Works

If the display of **IN3** and **IN4** scrolled down the Debug Terminal as they did in the previous example, it would be difficult to read. One way to fix this is to always send the cursor to the top-left position in the Debug Terminal using the **HOME** formatter:

```
       DEBUG HOME
```

By sending the cursor to the home position each time through the **DO…LOOP**, the commands:

```
       DEBUG ? IN4
       DEBUG ? IN3
```

display the values of **IN4** and **IN3** in the same part of the Debug Terminal each time.

The **DO** keyword begins the loop in this program:

```
       DO
```

These commands in the **IF** statement are the same as the ones in the example program from the previous activity:

```
         IF (IN3 = 1) THEN
           HIGH 14
```

```
      PAUSE 50
```

This is where the **ELSEIF** keyword helps. If **IN3** is not 1, but **IN4** is 1, we want to turn the LED connected to P15 on instead of the one connected to P14.

```
ELSEIF (IN4 = 1) THEN
   HIGH 15
   PAUSE 50
```

If neither statement is true, we still want to pause for 50 ms without changing the state of any LED circuits.

```
ELSE
   PAUSE 50
```

When you're finished with all the decisions, don't forget the **ENDIF**.

```
ENDIF
```

It's time to turn the LEDs off and pause again. You could try to decide which LED you turned on and turn it back off. PBASIC commands execute pretty quickly, so why not just turn them both off and forget about more decision making?

```
LOW 14
LOW 15

PAUSE 50
```

The **LOOP** statement sends the program back up to the **DO** statement, and the process of checking the pushbuttons and changing the states of the LEDs starts all over again.

```
LOOP
```

### Your Turn – What about Pressing Both Pushbuttons?

The example program has a flaw. Try pressing both pushbuttons at once, and you'll see the flaw. You would expect both LEDs to flash on and off, but they don't because only one code block in an **IF...ELSEIF...ELSE** statement gets executed before it skips to the **ENDIF**.

Here is how you can fix this problem:

√ Save PushbuttonControlOfTwoLeds.bs2 under a new name.
√ Replace this **IF** statement and code block:

```
IF (IN3 = 1) THEN
```

```
      HIGH 14
      PAUSE 50
```

with this **IF...ELSEIF** statement:

```
  IF (IN3 = 1) AND (IN4 = 1) THEN
      HIGH 14
      HIGH 15
      PAUSE 50

  ELSEIF (IN3 = 1) THEN
      HIGH 14
      PAUSE 50
```

> **A code block** is a group of commands. The **IF** statement above has a code block with three commands (**HIGH**, **HIGH**, and **PAUSE**). The **ELSEIF** statement has a code block with two commands (**HIGH**, **PAUSE**).

√ Run your modified program and see if it handles both pushbutton and LED circuits as you would expect.

> **The AND keyword** can be used in an **IF...THEN** statement to check if more than one condition is true. All conditions with **AND** have to be true for the **IF** statement to be true.
>
> **The OR keyword** can also be used to check if at least one of the conditions are true.

You can also modify the program so that the LED that's flashing stays on for different amounts of time. For example, you can reduce the *Duration* of the **PAUSE** for both pushbuttons to 10, increase the **PAUSE** for the P14 LED to 100, and increase the **PAUSE** for the P15 LED to 200.

√ Modify the **PAUSE** commands in the **IF** and the two **ELSEIF** statements as discussed.
√ Run the modified program.
√ Observe the difference in the behavior of each light.

## ACTIVITY #5: REACTION TIMER TEST

You are the embedded systems engineer at a video game company. The marketing department recommends that a circuit to test the player's reaction time be added to the next hand held game controller. Your next task is to develop a proof of concept for the reaction timer test.

The solution you will build and test in this activity is an example of how to solve this problem, but it's definitely not the only solution. Before continuing, take a moment to think about how you would design this reaction timer.

### Reaction Timer Game Parts

(1) LED – bi-color
(1) Resistor – 470 Ω (yellow-violet-brown)

(1) Pushbutton – normally open
(1) Resistor – 10 kΩ (brown-black-orange)
(1) Resistor – 220 Ω (red-red-brown)
(2) Jumper wires

### Building the Reaction Timer Circuit

Figure 3-14 shows a schematic and wiring diagram for a circuit that can be used with the BASIC Stamp to make a reaction timer game.

√ Build the circuit shown in Figure 3-14.
√ Run TestBiColorLED.bs2 from Chapter #2, Activity #5 to test the bi-color LED circuit and make sure your wiring is correct.
√ If you re-built the pushbutton circuit for this activity, run ReadPushbuttonState.bs2 from Activity #2 in this chapter to make sure your pushbutton is working properly.

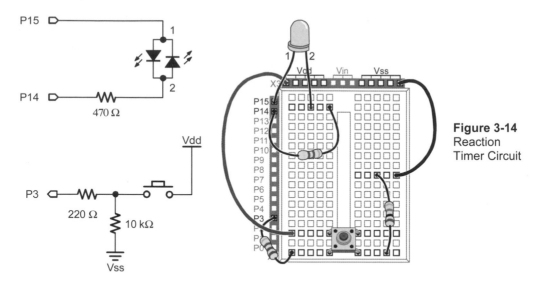

**Figure 3-14**
Reaction
Timer Circuit

## Programming the Reaction Timer

This next example program will leave the bi-color LED off until the game player presses and holds the pushbutton. When the pushbutton is held down, the LED will turn red for a short period of time. When it turns green, the player has to let go of the pushbutton as fast as he or she can. The time between when the LED turns green and when the pushbutton is tracked by the program is used as a measure of reaction time.

The example program also demonstrates how polling and counting work. Polling is the process of checking something over and over again very quickly to see if it has changed. Counting is the process of adding a number to a variable each time something does (or does not) happen. In this program, the BASIC Stamp will poll from the time the bi-color LED turns green until the pushbutton is released. It will wait 1/1000 of a second by using the command **PAUSE 1**. Each time it polls and the pushbutton is not yet released, it will add 1 to the counting variable named **timeCounter**. When the pushbutton is released, the program stops polling and sends a message to the Debug Terminal that displays the value of the **timeCounter** variable.

### Example Program: ReactionTimer.bs2

√   Enter and run ReactionTimer.bs2.
√   Follow the prompts on the Debug Terminal (see Figure 3-15).

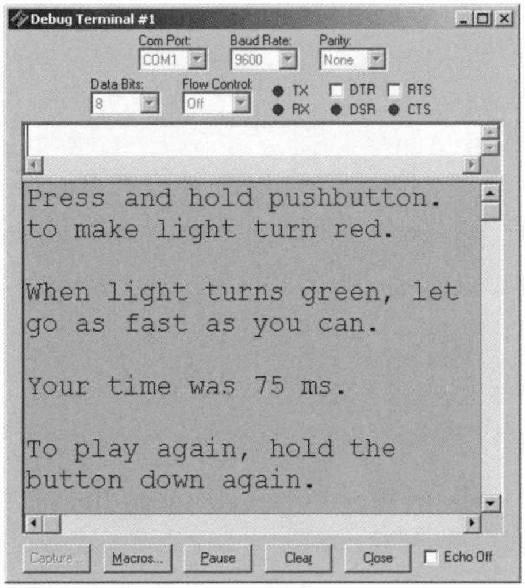

**Figure 3-15**
Debug Terminal
Reaction Timer Game
Instructions

```
' What's a Microcontroller - ReactionTimer.bs2
' Test reaction time with a pushbutton and a bi-color LED.

' {$STAMP BS2}
' {$PBASIC 2.5}

timeCounter     VAR     Word                    ' Declare variable to store time.

DEBUG "Press and hold pushbutton.", CR,         ' Display reaction instructions.
      "to make light turn red.", CR, CR,
      "When light turns green, let", CR,
      "go as fast as you can.", CR, CR

DO                                              ' Begin main loop.

  DO                                            ' Nested loop repeats...
  LOOP UNTIL IN3 = 1                            ' until pushbutton press.

  LOW 14                                        ' Bi-color LED red.
  HIGH 15

  PAUSE 1000                                    ' Delay 1 second.

  HIGH 14                                       ' Bi-color LED green.
  LOW 15

  timeCounter = 0                               ' Set timeCounter to zero.
```

```
DO                                         ' Nested loop, count time...

  PAUSE 1
  timeCounter = timeCounter + 1

LOOP UNTIL IN3 = 0                         ' until pushbutton is released.

LOW 14                                     ' Bi-color LED off.

DEBUG "Your time was ", DEC timeCounter,   ' Display time measurement.
      " ms.", CR, CR,
      "To play again, hold the ", CR,      ' Play again instructions.
      "button down again.", CR, CR

LOOP                                       ' Back to "Begin main loop".
```

## How ReactionTimer.bs2 Works

Since the program will have to keep track of the number of times the pushbutton was polled, a variable called **timeCounter** is declared.

```
timeCounter VAR Word          ' Declare variable to store time.
```

 **Variables initialize to zero:** When a variable is declared in PBASIC, its value is automatically zero until a command sets it to a new value.

The **DEBUG** commands contain instructions for the player of the game.

```
DEBUG "Press and hold pushbutton.", CR,
      "to make light turn red.", CR, CR,
      "When light turns green, let", CR,
      "go as fast as you can.", CR, CR
```

**DO...LOOP** statements can be nested. In other words, you can put one **DO...LOOP** inside another.

```
DO                              ' Begin main loop.

  DO                            ' Nested loop repeats...
  LOOP UNTIL IN3 = 1            ' until pushbutton press.

  ' Rest of program was here.

LOOP                            ' Back to "Begin main loop".
```

The inner DO...LOOP deserves a closer look. A DO...LOOP can use a condition to decide whether or not to break out of the loop and move on to more commands that come afterwards. This DO...LOOP will repeat itself as long as the button is not pressed (IN3 = 0). The DO...LOOP will execute over and over again, until IN3 = 1. Then, the program moves on to the next command after the LOOP UNTIL statement. This is an example of polling. The DO...LOOP UNTIL polls until the pushbutton is pressed.

```
DO                          ' Nested loop repeats...
LOOP UNTIL IN3 = 1          ' until pushbutton press.
```

The commands that come immediately after the LOOP UNTIL statement turn the bi-color LED red, delay for one second, then turn it green.

```
LOW 14                      ' Bi-color LED red.
HIGH 15

PAUSE 1000                  ' Delay 1 second.

HIGH 14                     ' Bi-color LED green.
LOW 15
```

As soon as the bi-color LED turns green, it's time to start counting to track how long until the player releases the button. The timeCounter variable is set to zero, then another DO...LOOP with an UNTIL condition starts repeating itself. It repeats itself until the player releases the button (IN3 = 0). Each time through the loop, the BASIC Stamp delays for 1 ms using PAUSE 1, and it also adds 1 to the value of the timeCounter variable.

```
timeCounter = 0             ' Set timeCounter to zero.

DO                          ' Nested loop, count time...

   PAUSE 1
   timeCounter = timeCounter + 1

LOOP UNTIL IN3 = 0          ' until pushbutton is released.
```

The bi-color LED is turned off.

```
LOW 14
```

The results are displayed in the Debug Terminal.

```
DEBUG "Your time was ", DEC timeCounter,
      " ms.", CR, CR,
      "To play again, hold the ", CR,
```

```
                  "button down again.", CR, CR
```

The last statement in the program is LOOP, which sends the program back to the very first DO statement.

### Your Turn – Revising the Design

The marketing department gave your prototype to some game testers. When the game testers were done, the marketing department came back to you with an itemized list of three problems that have to be fixed before your prototype can be built into the game controller.

√   Save ReactionTimer.bs2 under a new name (like ReactionTimerYourTurn.bs2).

The "itemized list" of problems and their solutions are discussed below.

Item-1

**When a player holds the button for 30 seconds, his score is actually 14000 ms, a measurement of 14 seconds. This has to be fixed!**

It turns out that executing the loop itself along with adding one to the timeCounter variable takes about 1 ms without the PAUSE 1 command. This is called code overhead, and it's the amount of time it takes for the BASIC Stamp to execute the commands. A quick fix that will improve the accuracy is to simply comment out the PAUSE 1 command by deleting it or adding an apostrophe to the left of it.

```
    ' PAUSE 1
```

√   Try commenting PAUSE 1 and test to see how accurate the program is.

Instead of commenting the delay, another way you can fix the program is to multiply your result by two. For example, just before the DEBUG command that displays the number of ms, you can insert a command that multiplies the result by two:

```
    timeCounter = timeCounter * 2          ' <- Add this
    DEBUG "Your time was ", DEC timeCounter, " ms.", CR, CR
```

√   Uncomment the PAUSE command by deleting the apostrophe, and try the multiply by two solution instead.

**3**

> **For precision,** you can use the */ operator to multiply by a value with a fraction to make your answer more precise. The */ operator is not hard to use; here's how:
>
> 1)  Place the value or variable you want to multiply by a fractional value before the */ operator.
>
> 2)  Take the fractional value that you want to use and multiply it by 256.
>
> 3)  Round off to get rid of anything to the right of the decimal point.
>
> 4)  Place that value after the */ operator.
>
> **Example:** Let's say you want to multiply the timeCounter variable by 3.69.
>
> 1)  Start by placing timeCounter to the left of the */ operator:
>
>     timeCounter = timeCounter */
>
> 2)  Multiply your fractional value by 256: 3.69 X 256 = 944.64.
>
> 3)  Round off: 944.64 ≈ 945.
>
> 4)  Place that value to the right of the */ operator:
>
>     timeCounter = timeCounter */ 945

## Item-2

**Players soon figure out that the delay from red to green is 1 second. After playing it several times, they get better at predicting when to let go, and their score no longer reflects their true reaction time.**

The BASIC Stamp has a **RANDOM** command. Here is how to modify your code for a random number:

√   At the beginning of your code, add a declaration for a new variable called **value**, and set it to 23. The value 23 is called the seed because it starts the pseudo random number sequence.

```
timeCounter VAR Word
value VAR Byte                          ' <- Add this
value = 23                              ' <- Add this
```

√   Just before the pause command, use the **RANDOM** command to give **value** a new "random" value from the pseudo random sequence that started with 23.

```
RANDOM value                            ' <- Add this.
DEBUG "Delay time ", ? 1000 + value, CR ' <- Add this.
```

√ Modify the **PAUSE** command so that the random value is added to 1000 (for one second) in the **PAUSE** command's *Duration* argument.

```
PAUSE 1000 + value                              ' <- Modify this.
```

**What's an algorithm?** An algorithm is a sequence of mathematical operations.

**What's pseudo random?** Pseudo random means that it seems random, but it isn't really. Each time you start the program over again, you will get the same sequence of values.

**What's a seed?** A seed is a value that is used to start the pseudo random sequence. If you use a different value (change value from 23 to some other number), you will get a different pseudo random sequence.

### Item-3

**A player that lets go of the button before the light turns green gets an unreasonably good score (1 ms). Your microcontroller needs to figure out if a player is cheating.**

Pseudo code was introduced near the end of Activity #3 in this chapter. Here is some pseudo code to help you apply an **IF…THEN…ELSE** statement to solve the problem.

- *If the value of timeCounter equals 1*
  - o *Display a message telling the player he or she has to wait until after the light turns green to let go of the button.*
- *Else, (if the value of timeCounter is greater than 1)*
  - o *Display the value of timeCounter (just like in ReactionTimer.bs2) time in ms.*

√ Modify your program by implementing this pseudo code in PBASIC to fix the cheating player problem.

## SUMMARY

This chapter introduced the pushbutton and common pushbutton circuits. This chapter also introduced how to build and test a pushbutton circuit and how to use the BASIC Stamp to read the state of one or more pushbuttons. The BASIC Stamp was programmed to make decisions based on the state(s) of the pushbutton(s) and this information was used to control LED(s). A reaction timer game was built using these concepts. In addition to controlling LEDs, the BASIC Stamp was programmed to poll a pushbutton and take time measurements.

Reading individual pushbutton circuits using the special I/O variables built into the BASIC Stamp (IN3, IN4, etc.) was introduced. Making decisions based on these values using IF...THEN...ELSE statements, IF...ELSEIF...ELSE statements, and code blocks were also introduced. For evaluating more than one condition, the AND and OR operators were introduced. Adding a condition to a DO...LOOP using the UNTIL keyword was introduced along with nesting DO...LOOP code blocks.

### Questions

1. What is the difference between sending and receiving HIGH and LOW signals using the BASIC Stamp?
2. What does "normally open" mean in regards to a pushbutton?
3. What happens between the terminals of a normally open pushbutton when you press it?
4. What is the value of IN3 when a pushbutton connects it to Vdd? What is the value of IN3 when a pushbutton connects it to Vss?
5. What does the command DEBUG ? IN3 do?
6. What kind of code blocks can be used for making decisions based on the value of one or more pushbuttons?
7. What does the HOME formatter do in the statement DEBUG HOME?

### Exercises

1. Explain how to modify ReadPushbuttonState.bs2 on page 77 so that it reads the pushbutton every second instead of every ¼ second.
2. Explain how to modify ReadPushbuttonState.bs2 so that it reads a normally open pushbutton circuit with a pull-up resistor connected to I/O pin P6.

## Project

1. Modify ReactionTimer.bs2 so that it is a two player game. Add a second button wired to P4 for the second player.

## Solutions

Q1. Sending uses the BASIC Stamp I/O pin as an output, whereas receiving uses the I/O pin as an input.

Q2. Normally open means the pushbutton's normal state (not pressed) forms an open circuit.

Q3. When pressed, the gap between the terminals is bridged by a conductive metal. Current can then flow through the pushbutton.

Q4. **IN3** = 1 when pushbutton connects it to Vdd. **IN3** = 0 when pushbutton connects it to Vss.

Q5. **DEBUG ? IN3** sends the value of **IN3** to the Debug Terminal.

Q6. **IF...THEN...ELSE** and **IF...ELSEIF...ELSE**.

Q7. The **HOME** formatter sends the cursor to the top left position in the Debug Terminal.

E1. The **DO...LOOP** in the program repeats every ¼ second because of the command **PAUSE 250**. To repeat every second, change the **PAUSE 250** (250ms = 0.25 s = ¼ s), to **PAUSE 1000** (1000ms = 1 s).

```
DO
    DEBUG ? IN3
    PAUSE 1000
LOOP
```

E2. Replace **IN3** with **IN6**, to read I/O pin P6. The program only displays the pushbutton state, and does not use the value to make decisions, it does not matter whether the resistor is a pull-up or a pull-down. The **DEBUG** statement will display the button state either way.

```
DO
    DEBUG ? IN6
    PAUSE 250
LOOP
```

P1. First, a button was added for the second player, wired to Stamp I/O pin P4. The schematic is based on Figure 3-14 on page 90.

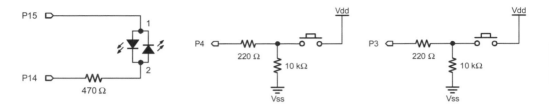

Snippets from the solution program are included below, but keep in mind solutions may be coded a variety of different ways. However, most solutions will include the following modifications:

Use two variables to keep track of two player's times.
```
timeCounterA VAR     Word       ' Time score of player A
timeCounterB VAR     Word       ' Time score of player B
```

Change instructions to reflect two pushbuttons:
```
DEBUG "Press and hold pushbuttons", CR,
DEBUG "buttons down again.", CR, CR
```

Wait for both buttons to be pressed before turning LED red, by using the **AND** operator.
```
LOOP UNTIL (IN3 = 1) AND (IN4 = 1)
```

Wait for both buttons to be released to end timing, again using the **AND** operator.
```
LOOP UNTIL (IN3 = 0) AND (IN4 = 0)
```

Add logic to decide which player's time is incremented.
```
IF (IN3 = 1) THEN
timeCounterA = timeCounterA + 1
ENDIF
IF (IN4 = 1) THEN
timeCounterB = timeCounterB + 1
ENDIF
```

Change time display to show times of both players.
```
DEBUG "Player A Time:  ", DEC timeCounterA, " ms. ", CR
     DEBUG "Player B Time:  ", DEC timeCounterB, " ms. ", CR, CR
```

Add logic to show which player had the faster reaction time.
```
IF (timeCounterA < timeCounterB) THEN
```

```
DEBUG "Player A is the winner!", CR
ELSEIF (timeCounterB < timeCounterA) THEN
DEBUG "Player B is the winner!", CR
ELSE
DEBUG "It's a tie!", CR
ENDIF
```

The complete solution is shown below.

```
' What's a Microcontroller - Ch03Prj03_TwoPlayerReactionTimer.bs2
' Test reaction time with a pushbutton and a bi-color LED.
' Add a second player with a second pushbutton. Both players
' play at once using the same LED.  Quickest to release wins.
' Pin P3: Player A Pushbutton, Active High
' Pin P4: Player B Pushbutton, Active High

' {$STAMP BS2}
' {$PBASIC 2.5}

timeCounterA VAR        Word                ' Time score of player A
timeCounterB VAR        Word                ' Time score of player B

DEBUG "Press and hold pushbuttons", CR,     ' Display reaction
                                            ' instructions.
     "to make light turn red.", CR, CR,
     "When light turns green, let", CR,
     "go as fast as you can.", CR, CR

DO                                          ' Begin main loop.

  DO                                        ' Loop until both press
  ' Nothing
  LOOP UNTIL (IN3 = 1) AND (IN4 = 1)

  LOW 14                                    ' Bi-color LED red.
  HIGH 15

  PAUSE 1000                                ' Delay 1 second.

  HIGH 14                                   ' Bi-color LED green.
  LOW 15

  timeCounterA = 0                          ' Set timeCounters to zero
  timeCounterB = 0

  DO

    PAUSE 1
    IF (IN3 = 1) THEN                       ' If button is still down,
```

```
       timeCounterA = timeCounterA + 1             ' increment counter
    ENDIF
    IF (IN4 = 1) THEN
       timeCounterB = timeCounterB + 1
    ENDIF

  LOOP UNTIL (IN3 = 0) AND (IN4 = 0)               ' Loop until both buttons
                                                   ' released.

  LOW 14                                           ' Bi-color LED off.

  DEBUG "Player A Time:  ", DEC timeCounterA, " ms. ", CR
  DEBUG "Player B Time:  ", DEC timeCounterB, " ms. ", CR, CR
  IF (timeCounterA < timeCounterB) THEN
    DEBUG "Player A is the winner!", CR
  ELSEIF (timeCounterB < timeCounterA) THEN
    DEBUG "Player B is the winner!", CR
  ELSE                                             ' A & B times are equal
    DEBUG "It's a tie!", CR
  ENDIF
  DEBUG CR

  DEBUG "To play again, hold the ", CR             ' Play again instructions.
  DEBUG "buttons down again.", CR, CR


LOOP                                               ' Back to "Begin main
```

## Further Investigation

The resources listed here are available for free download from the Parallax web site and are also included on the Parallax CD.

**"*BASIC Stamp Manual*", Users Manual, Version 2.0c, Parallax Inc., 2000**

       The *BASIC Stamp Manual* has more examples you can try and information that further explains the following: The `DEBUG HOME` and `CLS` formatters, input pin variables such `IN3`, `IN4`, and the `RANDOM` command.

**"*Basic Analog and Digital*", Student Guide, Version 2.0, Parallax Inc., 2003**

       *Basic Analog and Digital* explains binary counting using pushbuttons. It also uses pushbuttons to introduce a technique for transmitting numbers from one system to another called synchronous serial communication.

**"*BASIC Stamp Editor Help File*", PBASIC 2.5 Version 2.0 Parallax Inc., 2003**

       The PBASIC 2.5 Help File has information on the `WHILE` and `UNTIL` conditions used with `DO...LOOP`, and information on nesting and `IF...THEN...ELSE` code blocks, which is new to PBASIC 2.5. You can find this information by clicking the book icon on your BASIC Stamp Editor task bar, then selecting PBASIC Reference from the menu in the left sidebar window. This will open the PBASIC Command Reference alphabetical listing in the main window. Detailed information can be found by clicking on each command.

# Chapter #4: Controlling Motion

## MICROCONTROLLED MOTION

Microcontrollers make sure things move to the right place all around you every day. If you have an inkjet printer, the print head that goes back and forth across the page as it prints is moved by a stepper motor that is controlled by a microcontroller. The automatic grocery store doors that you walk through are controlled by microcontrollers, and the automatic eject feature in your VCR or DVD player is also controlled by a microcontroller.

## ON/OFF SIGNALS AND MOTOR MOTION

Just about all microcontrolled motors receive sequences of high and low signals similar to the ones you've been sending to LEDs. The difference is that the microcontroller has to send these signals at rates that are usually faster than the eye can detect. The timing and number of separate high/low signals differ from one motor to the next, but they can all be controlled by microcontrollers capable of delivering the high/low signals.

Some of these motors require lots of circuitry to help the microcontroller make them work. Other motors require extra mechanical parts to make them work right in machines. Of all the different types of motors to start with, the hobby servo that you will experiment with in this chapter is probably the simplest. As you will soon see, it is easy to control with the BASIC Stamp, requires little or no additional circuitry, and has a mechanical output that is easy to connect to things to make them move.

## ACTIVITY #1: CONNECTING AND TESTING THE SERVO

In this activity, you will connect a servo to a power supply and the BASIC Stamp. You will then verify that the servo is functioning properly by programming the BASIC Stamp to send signals to the servo that will control the servo's position.

### Introducing the Servo

Figure 4-1 shows a drawing of a Parallax Standard Servo. The plug (1) is used to connect the servo to a power source (Vdd and Vss) and a signal source (a BASIC Stamp I/O pin). The cable (2) conducts Vdd, Vss and the signal line from the plug into the servo. The horn (3) is the part of the servo that looks like a four-pointed star. When the servo is running, the horn is the moving part that the BASIC Stamp controls. The case (4) contains the servo's control circuits, a DC motor, and gears. These parts work together to take high/low signals from the BASIC Stamp and convert them into positions held by the servo horn.

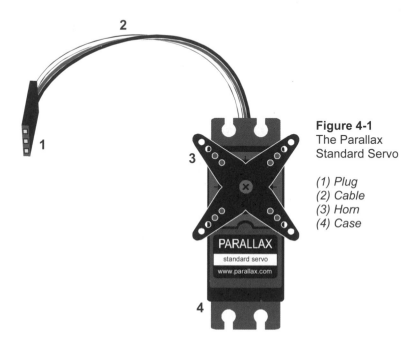

**Figure 4-1**
The Parallax
Standard Servo

*(1) Plug*
*(2) Cable*
*(3) Horn*
*(4) Case*

> **CAUTION: use only a Parallax Standard Servo for the activities in this text!**
>
> Do not substitute a Parallax Continuous Rotation Servo, as it may be quickly damaged by some of the circuits shown below. Likewise, we do not recommend using other brands or models of hobby servos, which may not be rated for use with the voltage in these circuits.

## Servo and LED Circuit Parts

An LED circuit can be used to monitor the control signal the BASIC Stamp sends to the servo. Keep in mind that the LED circuit is not required to help the servo operate. It is just there to help see what's going on with the control signals.

(1) Parallax Standard Servo

(1) Resistor – 470 Ω (yellow-violet-brown)
(1) LED – any color

## Building the Servo and LED Circuits

It's really important to be careful when connecting a servo to your BASIC Stamp. How you connect your servo depends on whether you are using the Board of Education Rev B, Rev C, or the HomeWork Board. If you are using the Board of Education, but you're not sure which Rev it is, Figure 4-2 shows an example of the Rev label on the Board of Education Rev B.

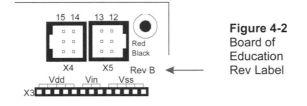

**Figure 4-2**
Board of
Education
Rev Label

√ Examine the labeling on your carrier board and figure out whether you have a HomeWork Board or a Board of Education Rev B, or Rev C.

√ Skip to instructions for connecting the servo to the BASIC Stamp on your carrier board:

- Page 105 – Board of Education Rev C
- Page 108 – BASIC Stamp HomeWork Board
- Page 111 – Board of Education Rev B

## Board of Education Rev C

Figure 4-3 shows the schematic of the circuit you will build on the Board of Education Rev C.

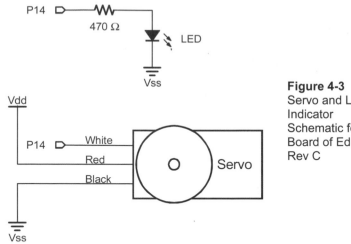

**Figure 4-3**
Servo and LED
Indicator
Schematic for
Board of Education
Rev C

√  Turn off the power as shown in Figure 4-4.

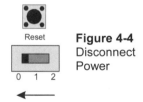

**Figure 4-4**
Disconnect
Power

Figure 4-5 shows the servo header on the Board of Education Rev C. This is where you will plug in your servo. This board features a jumper that you can use to connect the servo's power supply to either Vin or Vdd. The jumper is the removable black rectangular piece right between the two servo headers.

√  Set the jumper to Vdd as shown in Figure 4-5. This involves lifting the rectangular jumper up off of the pins it is currently on, and replacing it on the two pins closest to the Vdd label.

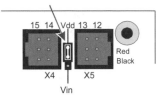

**Figure 4-5**
Servo
Header
Jumper
Set to Vdd

**4**

> **The jumper allows you to choose the power supply (Vin or Vdd) for the Parallax Standard Servo.** If you are using a 9 V battery, it is best to set it to Vdd. Either setting will work if you are using a 6 V battery pack. **Use only Vdd** if you are using a DC supply that plugs into an AC outlet. Before using a DC supply, make sure to check the specifications for acceptable DC supplies listed in Appendix D: Batteries and Power Supplies.

√ Build the circuit shown in Figure 4-6.
√ Make sure you did not plug the servo in upside-down. The white, red and black wires should line up as shown in the figure.

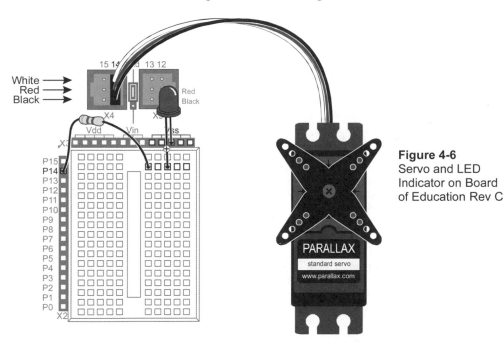

**Figure 4-6**
Servo and LED
Indicator on Board
of Education Rev C

Up until now, you have been using the 3-position switch in the 1 position. Now, you will move it to the 2 position to turn on the power to the servo header.

√ Supply power to the servo header by adjusting the 3-position switch as shown in Figure 4-7. Your servo may move a bit when you connect the power.

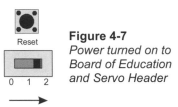

**Figure 4-7**
*Power turned on to Board of Education and Servo Header*

√ Move on to Programming Servo Control on page 113.

## BASIC Stamp HomeWork Board

If you are connecting your servo to a HomeWork Board, you will need these extra parts:

(1) 3-pin male/male header (shown in Figure 4-8).
(4) Jumper wires

**Figure 4-8**
HomeWork Board or Board of
Education – Extra Parts

*(1) 3-pin male/male header (top)*

Figure 4-9 shows the schematic of the servo and LED circuits on the HomeWork Board. The instructions that come after this figure will show you how to safely build this circuit.

---

**WARNING**

**Use only a 9 V battery when your Parallax Standard Servo is connected to the BASIC Stamp HomeWork Board. Do not use any kind of DC supply or "battery replacer" that plugs into an AC outlet. Improper use of these devices can cause the activity not to work, or even permanently damage the servo.**

For best results, make sure your battery is new. If you are using a rechargeable battery, make sure it is freshly recharged. It should also be rated for 100 mAh (milliamp hours) or more. See Appendix D: Batteries and Power Supplies for more information.

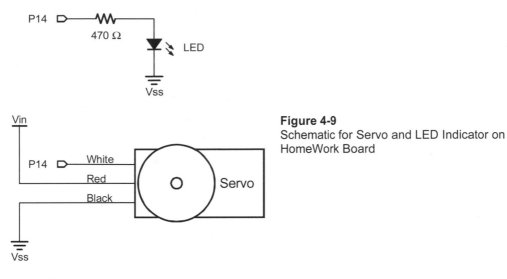

4

**Figure 4-9**
Schematic for Servo and LED Indicator on
HomeWork Board

√ Disconnect your 9 V battery from your HomeWork Board.
√ Build the LED indicator and servo header circuit shown in Figure 4-10.

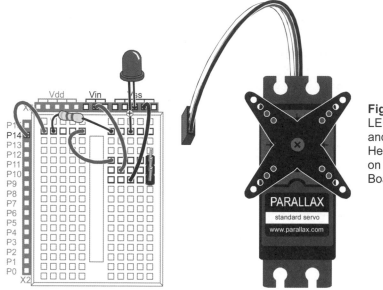

**Figure 4-10**
LED Indicator
and Servo
Header Circuits
on HomeWork
Board

√   Connect the servo to the servo header as shown in Figure 4-11.
√   Make sure that the colors on the servo's cable align properly with the colors labeled in the picture.
√   Double check your wiring.
√   Reconnect your 9 V battery to your HomeWork Board.  The servo may move a bit when you make the connection.

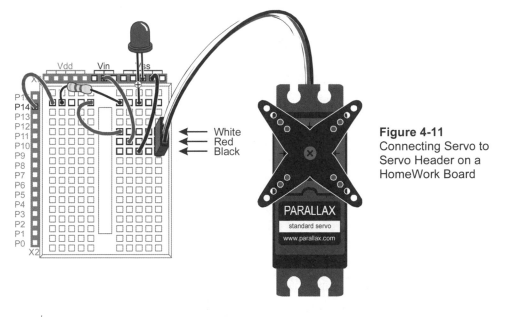

**Figure 4-11**
Connecting Servo to
Servo Header on a
HomeWork Board

White
Red
Black

4

√   Move on to **Programming Servo Control** on page 113.

## Board of Education Rev B

Figure 4-12 shows the schematic for the servo and LED circuits on the Board of
Education Rev B.  The instructions that come after this figure will show you how to
safely build this circuit on your Board of Education Rev B.

**WARNING**

**Use only a 9 V battery when your Parallax Standard Servo is connected to the Board
of Education Rev B.  Do not use any kind of DC supply or "battery replacer" that
plugs into an AC outlet.  Improper use of these devices can cause the activity not to
work, or even permanently damage the servo.**

For best results, make sure your battery is new.  If you are using a rechargeable battery,
make sure it is freshly recharged.  It should also be rated for 100 mAh (milliamp hours) or
more.  See Appendix D: Batteries and Power Supplies for more information.

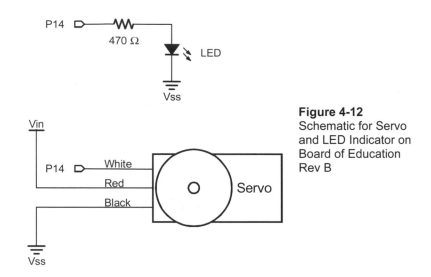

**Figure 4-12**
Schematic for Servo
and LED Indicator on
Board of Education
Rev B

√   Disconnect your battery or any other power supply from your board.
√   Build the LED circuit shown in Figure 4-12.
√   Connect the servo to the servo header as shown in Figure 4-13.

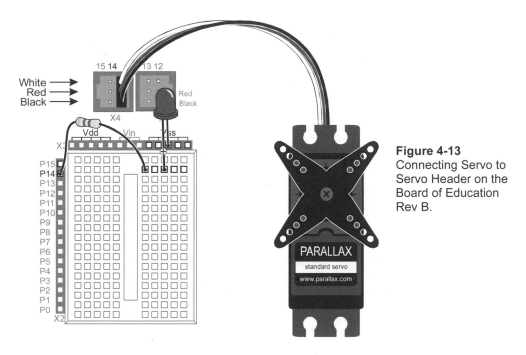

**Figure 4-13**
Connecting Servo to Servo Header on the Board of Education Rev B.

√   Make sure that the colors on the servo's cable align properly with the colors labeled in the picture.

√   Connect a 9 V battery to Board of Education Rev B. The servo may move a little bit when you make the connection.

### Programming Servo Control

A servo is controlled by very brief high signals. These high signals are sent over and over again every 20 ms. The high signals last anywhere between 1 and 2 ms. The **PULSOUT** command can be used to send a pulse (a very brief high signal) using a BASIC Stamp I/O pin. Here is the command syntax for the **PULSOUT** command:

      **PULSOUT** *Pin, Duration*

As with **HIGH** and **LOW**, the *Pin* argument is a number that tells the BASIC Stamp which I/O pin the signal is sent on. The *Duration* argument is not milliseconds, like it is in the **PAUSE** command. For the BASIC Stamp 2, the *Duration* is the number of 2-millionth-of-a-second (µs) time durations that you want the high signal to last.

> **A millionth of a second** is called a microsecond. The Greek letter μ is used in place of the word micro and the letter s is used in place of second. This is handy for writing and taking notes, because instead of writing 2 microseconds, you can write 2 μs.
>
> **Reminder: one thousandth of a second** is called a millisecond, and is abbreviated ms.
>
> **Fact: 1 ms = 1000 μs.** In other words, you can fit one thousand millionths of a second into one thousandth of a second.

The next example program will use the **PULSOUT** command to deliver pulses that instruct the servo on where to position its horn. **FOR...NEXT** loops are used to deliver a certain number of pulses, which cause the servo to hold a position for a certain amount of time.

### Example Program: ServoTest.bs2

ServoTest.bs2 will make the servo's horn start at somewhere in the neighborhood of 10 o'clock and hold that position for about three seconds. Then, the program will move the servo horn clockwise, to about the 2 o'clock position for about three seconds. After that, the servo will hold its "center position", which is about 12 o'clock, for about three seconds.

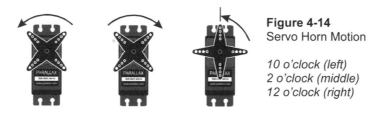

**Figure 4-14**
Servo Horn Motion

*10 o'clock (left)*
*2 o'clock (middle)*
*12 o'clock (right)*

> **What if my servo is different?** We recommend that you use a Parallax Standard Servo for these activities. There are lots of different servos, and many will respond differently to the signals that TestServo.bs2 sends. Another brand of servo might only rotate to 11 o'clock then 1 o'clock, or maybe to 9 o'clock and then 3 o'clock. It might even rotate the opposite direction and start in the clockwise direction before it goes counterclockwise. But if your servo is rated for use with a 9 V battery, and the motion is easy to observe and consistent, it will work for these activities. You can modify the example programs to get the servo to behave the way you want.

√ Enter ServoTest.bs2 into the BASIC Stamp Editor.
√ Connect power to your Board of Education or HomeWork Board.
√ Run the program.

√ Observe the servo turns at each of the three steps in the program, and record where the horn is really pointing.

√ Re-run the program and verify that the LED flickers dimly. It should be brightest when the BASIC Stamp sends the 10 o'clock signal and dimmest when the BASIC Stamp sends the 2 o'clock signal. This is because the LED circuit is only on for half as long (1 out of 21 ms instead of 2 out of 22 ms).

```
' What's a Microcontroller - ServoTest.bs2
' Test the servo at three different position signals.

' {$STAMP BS2}
' {$PBASIC 2.5}

counter          VAR     Word

DEBUG "Counterclockwise 10 o'clock", CR

FOR counter = 1 TO 150
  PULSOUT 14, 1000
  PAUSE 20
NEXT

DEBUG "Clockwise 2 o'clock", CR

FOR counter = 1 TO 150
  PULSOUT 14, 500
  PAUSE 20
NEXT

DEBUG "Center 12 o'clock", CR

FOR counter = 1 TO 150
  PULSOUT 14, 750
  PAUSE 20
NEXT

DEBUG "All done."

END
```

### How ServoTest.bs2 Works

The first **FOR…NEXT** loop delivers 150 pulses, each of which lasts 2.0 ms. These pulses instruct the servo to go to a position that is roughly 10 o'clock if you think about it in terms of a clock face.

```
        FOR counter = 1 TO 150
```

```
        PULSOUT 14, 1000
        PAUSE 20
    NEXT
```

> **ⓘ** **PULSOUT 14, 1000** sends a pulse that lasts 1000 × 2 μs.  That's 2000 μs or 2 ms.

Figure 4-15 is called a timing diagram.  It shows a picture of the high and low signals and how long they last.  The timing diagram does not show how many pulses are delivered, but it does give you information about how long the high and low signals last.  Each pulse (high signal) lasts for 2.0 ms.  Each pulse is separated by a 20 ms delay while the signal is low.

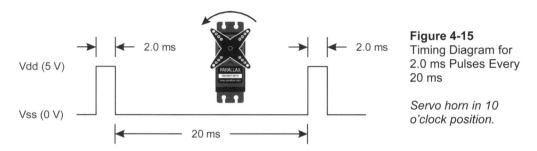

**Figure 4-15**
Timing Diagram for
2.0 ms Pulses Every
20 ms

*Servo horn in 10
o'clock position.*

The second **FOR...NEXT** loop delivers 150 pulses, but this time, each pulse only lasts 1.0 ms.  This instructs the servo to turn to the 2 o'clock position for about 3.15 seconds.

```
    FOR COUNTER = 1 TO 150
        PULSOUT 14, 500
        PAUSE 20
    NEXT
```

> **ⓘ** **PULSOUT 14, 500** sends a pulse that lasts 500 × 2 μs.  That's 1000 μs or 1 ms.

Figure 4-15 shows the timing diagram for this pulse train.  The pauses between pulses still last 20 ms.

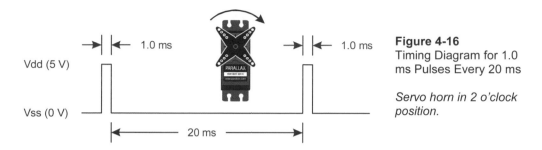

**Figure 4-16**
Timing Diagram for 1.0
ms Pulses Every 20 ms

*Servo horn in 2 o'clock
position.*

The last **FOR…NEXT** loop delivers 150 pulses, each of which lasts 1.5 ms. This instructs
the servo to go to its center position (12 o'clock) for about 3.23 seconds.

```
FOR counter = 1 TO 150
   PULSOUT 14, 750
   PAUSE 20
NEXT
```

> **i**     **PULSOUT 14, 750** sends a pulse that lasts 750 × 2 µs. That's 1500 µs or 1.5 ms.

Figure 4-17 shows the timing diagram for these pulses. While the low time is still 20
ms, the pulse now lasts for 1.5 ms.

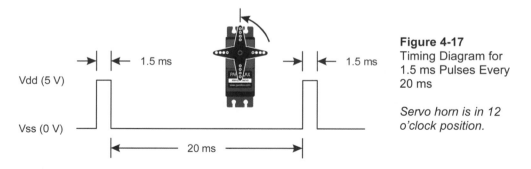

**Figure 4-17**
Timing Diagram for
1.5 ms Pulses Every
20 ms

*Servo horn is in 12
o'clock position.*

### Do the Math

If you want to convert time from milliseconds to a *Duration* you can use for **PULSOUT**,
use this equation.

$$Duration = number\ of\ ms \times 500$$

For example, if you didn't already know that the **PULSOUT** argument for 1.5 ms is 750, here is how you could calculate it.

$$Duration = 1.5 \times 500$$
$$= 750$$

You can also figure out the *Duration* of a mystery **PULSOUT** command using this equation.

$$number\ of\ ms = \frac{Duration}{500} ms$$

For example, if you see the command **PULSOUT 14, 850**, how long does that pulse really last?

$$number\ of\ ms = \frac{850}{500} ms$$
$$= 1.7\ ms$$

### Your Turn – Adjusting Position and Hold Time

The number of times each **FOR...NEXT** loop repeats is what controls how long the servo stays in a given position. The value of the **PULSOUT** command's *Duration* argument controls where the servo turns to. It's important to experiment with changing these values to be sure how they work before moving on to the next experiment.

- √ Save ServoTest.bs2 as ServoTestYourTurn.bs2.
- √ Modify all the **FOR...NEXT** loops so that they execute half as many times as the original program:

```
FOR counter = 1 to 75
```

- √ Run the modified program and verify that the servo holds each position for half as long.
- √ Modify all the **FOR...NEXT** loops so that they execute twice as many times as the original program:

```
FOR counter = 1 to 300
```

- √ Run the modified program and verify that the servo holds each position for twice as long.
- √ Modify the **PULSOUT** command in the first loop so that it reads:

```
PULSOUT 14,850
```

√ Modify the **PULSOUT** command in the second loop so that it reads:

```
PULSOUT 14,650
```

√ Run the modified program, and explain the differences in the positions the servo turns to and holds.

## ACTIVITY #2: CONTROLLING POSITION WITH YOUR COMPUTER

**4**

Factory automation often involves microcontrollers communicating with larger computers. The microcontrollers read sensors and transmit that data to the main computer. The main computer interprets and analyzes the sensor data, then sends position information back to the microcontroller. The microcontroller might then update a conveyer belt's speed, or a sorter's position, or some other mechanical, motor controlled task.

You can use the Debug Terminal to send messages from your computer to the BASIC Stamp as shown in Figure 4-18. The BASIC Stamp has to be programmed to listen for the messages you send using the Debug Terminal, and it also has to store the data you send in one or more variables.

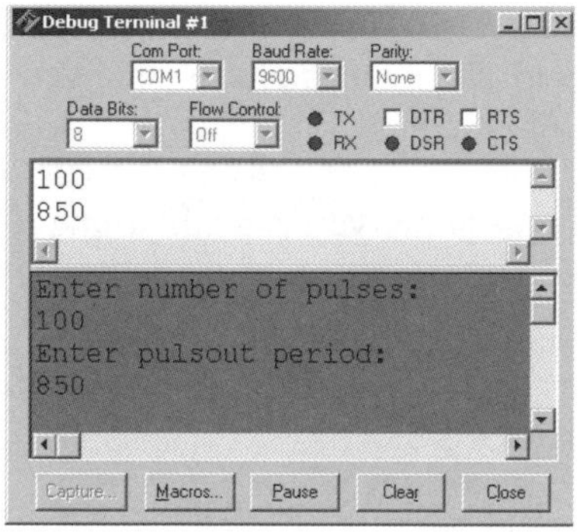

**Figure 4-18**
Sending Messages to
the BASIC Stamp

*Click the white field
above the message
display pane and type
your message. A copy
of the message you
entered appears in the
lower windowpane. This
copy is called an echo.*

In this activity, you will program the BASIC Stamp to receive two values from the Debug Terminal:

1. The number of pulses to send to the servo
2. The *Duration* value used by the **PULSOUT** command

You will also program the BASIC Stamp to use these values to control the servo.

### Parts and Circuit

Same as Activity #1

### Programming the BASIC Stamp to Receive Messages from Debug

Programming the BASIC Stamp to send messages to the Debug Terminal is done using the DEBUG command. Programming the BASIC Stamp to receive messages from the Debug Terminal is done using the DEBUGIN command. When using this command, you also have to declare one or more variables for the BASIC Stamp to store the information it receives. Here is an example of a variable you can declare for the BASIC Stamp to store a value:

```
pulses VAR Word
```

Later in the program, you can use this value to store a number received by the DEBUGIN command:

```
DEBUGIN DEC pulses
```

When the BASIC Stamp receives a numeric value from the Debug Terminal, it will store it in the **pulses** variable. The **DEC** formatter tells the **DEBUGIN** command that the characters you are sending will be digits that form a decimal number. As soon as you hit the carriage return, the BASIC Stamp will store the digits it received in the **pulses** variable as a decimal number, then move on.

Although it is not included in the example program, you can add a line to verify that the message was processed by the BASIC Stamp.

```
DEBUG CR, "You sent the value: ", DEC pulses
```

### Example Program: ServoControlWithDebug.bs2

Figure 4-19 shows a close-up view of the Transmit Windowpane in the Debug Terminal. Your Transmit Windowpane may be smaller. You can click and drag the separator between the two panes downward to make the Transmit Windowpane larger. You can type characters into the Transmit Windowpane to send them to the BASIC Stamp. In this example, somebody typed in 100, then hit the carriage return, then typed in 850. The Receive Windowpane displays the "Enter number of pulses:" message sent by the BASIC Stamp. It also displays an echo of the characters 100 that were typed into the Transmit Windowpane.

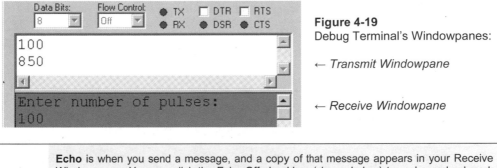

**Figure 4-19**
Debug Terminal's Windowpanes:

← *Transmit Windowpane*

← *Receive Windowpane*

**Echo** is when you send a message, and a copy of that message appears in your Receive Windowpane. You can click the Echo Off checkbox (shown below) to make a checkmark appear in it. This will make the Debug Terminal stop displaying these echoes.

√ Enter ServoControlWithDebug.bs2 into the BASIC Stamp Editor and run it.
√ If the Transmit Windowpane is too small, resize it using your mouse to click, hold, and drag the separator downward. The separator is shown just above the text message: "Enter number of pulses:" in Figure 4-19.
√ Click the upper, Transmit Windowpane to place your cursor there for typing messages.
√ When the Debug Terminal prompts you to, "Enter number of pulses:", type the number 100, then press enter.
√ When the Debug Terminal prompts you to "Enter PULSOUT duration:" type the number 850, then press enter.

**The PULSOUT *Duration* should be a number between 500 and 1000.** If you enter numbers outside that range, the servo may try to rotate to a position beyond its own mechanical limits. Although it will not break the servo, it could shorten the device's lifespan.

The BASIC Stamp will display the message "Servo is running…" while it is sending pulses to the servo. When it is done sending pulses to the servo, it will display the message "Done" for one second. Then, it will prompt you to enter the number of pulses again. Have fun with it, but make sure to follow the directive in the caution box about staying between 500 and 1000 for your PULSOUT value.

√ Experiment with entering other values between 500 and 1000 for the **PULSOUT** *Duration* and values between 1 and 65534 for the number of pulses.

> **i** **It takes between 40 and 45 pulses** to make the servo hold a position for 1 second.

```
' What's a Microcontroller - ServoControlWithDebug.bs2
' Send messages to the BASIC Stamp to control a servo using
' the Debug Terminal.

' {$STAMP BS2}
' {$PBASIC 2.5}

counter          Var     Word
pulses           Var     Word
duration         Var     Word

DO

  DEBUG CLS, "Enter number of pulses:", CR
  DEBUGIN DEC pulses

  DEBUG "Enter PULSOUT duration:", CR
  DEBUGIN DEC duration

  DEBUG "Servo is running...", CR

  FOR counter = 1 TO pulses
    PULSOUT 14, duration
    PAUSE 20
  NEXT

  DEBUG "DONE"
  PAUSE 1000

LOOP
```

## How ServoControlWithDebug.bs2 Works

Three **Word** variables are declared in this program:

```
counter          Var     WORD
pulses           Var     WORD
duration         Var     WORD
```

The `counter` variable is declared for use by a `FOR...NEXT` loop. See Chapter #2, Activity #3 for details. The `pulses` and `duration` variables are used a couple of different ways. They are both used to receive and store values sent from the Debug Terminal. The `pulses` variable is also used to set the number of repetitions in the `FOR...NEXT` loop that delivers pulses to the servo, and the `duration` variable is used to set the duration for the `PULSOUT` command.

The rest of the program is nested inside a `DO...LOOP` without a `WHILE` or `UNTIL` argument so that the commands execute over and over again.

```
DO
  ' Rest of program not shown.
LOOP
```

The `DEBUG` command is used to send you (the "user" of the software) a message to enter the number of pulses. Then, the `DEBUGIN` command waits for you to enter digits that make up the number and press the Enter key on your keyboard. The digits that you enter are converted to a value that is stored in the `pulses` variable. This process is repeated with a second `DEBUG` and `DEBUGIN` command that loads a value into the `duration` variable too.

```
DEBUG CLS, "Enter number of pulses:", CR
DEBUGIN DEC pulses

DEBUG "Enter PULSOUT duration:", CR
DEBUGIN DEC duration
```

After you enter the second value, it's useful to display a message while the servo is running so that you don't try to enter a second value:

```
DEBUG "Servo is running...", CR
```

While the servo is running, you can gently try to move the servo horn away from the position it is holding. The servo resists light pressure applied to the horn.

---

**FOR Counter = StartValue TO EndValue {STEP StepValue}...NEXT**

This is the **FOR...NEXT** loop syntax from the BASIC Stamp Manual. It shows that you need a *Counter*, *StartValue* and *EndValue* to control how many times the loop repeats itself. There is also an optional *StepValue* if you want to add a number other than 1 to the value of *Counter* each time through the loop.

As in previous examples, the `counter` variable is used as an index for the `FOR...NEXT` loop. Up until this example, all the `FOR...NEXT` loops have used constants such as 10 or 150 for `EndValue`. In this `FOR...NEXT` loop, the value of the pulses variable is used to control the `EndValue` of the `FOR...NEXT` loop. This, in turn, controls how many pulses are delivered to the servo. The end result is that the `pulses` variable controls how long the servo holds a given position. Up until now, constant values such as 500, 750, and 1000 were also used for the `PULSOUT` command's `Duration` argument. Look carefully at this `FOR...NEXT` loop to see where and how these variables are used:

```
FOR counter = 1 to pulses
   PULSOUT 14, duration
   PAUSE 20
NEXT
```

**Take some time to understand this FOR...NEXT loop.** It is one of the first examples of the amazing things you can do with variables in PBASIC command arguments, and it also highlights how useful a programmable microcontroller like the BASIC Stamp can be.

## Your Turn – Setting Limits in Software

The example program doesn't stop you or anybody else from entering a `PULSOUT` `duration` such as 1500, which is not good for the servo. This is a problem that needs to be fixed if you are designing this system into a product.

Let's imagine that this computer servo control system is one that has been developed for remote-controlling a door. Perhaps a security guard will use this to open a shipping door that he or she watches on a remote camera. Maybe a college student will use it to control doors in a maze that mice navigate in search of food. Maybe a military gunner will use it to point the cannon at a particular target. If you are designing the product for somebody else to use, the last thing you want is to give the user (security guard, college student, military gunner) the ability to enter the wrong number and damage the equipment.

To fix this problem, try this:

√   Save the example program ServoControlWithDebug.bs2 under the new name ServoControlWithDebugYourTurn.bs2.

√   Replace these two commands:

```
DEBUG "Enter pulsout duration:", CR
DEBUGIN DEC duration
```

with this code block:

```
DO
  DEBUG "Enter pulsout duration:", CR
  DEBUGIN DEC duration
  IF duration < 500 THEN
    DEBUG "Value of duration must be above 499", CR
    PAUSE 1000
  ENDIF
  IF duration > 1000 THEN
    DEBUG "Value of duration must be below 1001", CR
    PAUSE 1000
  ENDIF
LOOP UNTIL duration > 499 AND duration < 1001
```

√   Save the program.
√   Run the program and verify that it rejects values outside the appropriate range for the servo.

## ACTIVITY #3: CONVERTING POSITION TO MOTION

In this activity, you will program the servo to change position at different rates. By changing position at different rates, you will cause your servo horn to rotate at different speeds. You can use this technique to make the servo control motion instead of position.

### Programming a Rate of Change for Position

You can use a **FOR...NEXT** loop to make a servo sweep through its range of motion like this:

```
FOR counter = 500 TO 1000
  PULSOUT 14, counter
  PAUSE 20
NEXT
```

The **FOR...NEXT** loop causes the servo's horn to start at around 2 o'clock and then rotate slowly counterclockwise until it gets to 10 o'clock. Because **counter** is the index of the **FOR...NEXT** loop, it increases by one each time through. The value of counter is also used in the **PULSOUT** command's *Duration* argument, which means the *duration* of each pulse gets a little longer each time through the loop. Since the *duration* changes, so does the position of the servo's horn.

**FOR...NEXT** loops have an optional **STEP** argument. The **STEP** argument can be used to make the servo rotate faster. For example, you can use the **STEP** argument to add 8 to `counter` each time through the loop (instead of 1) by modifying the **FOR** statement like this:

```
FOR counter = 500 TO 1000 STEP 8
```

You can also make the servo turn the opposite direction by counting down instead of counting up. In PBASIC, **FOR…NEXT** loops will also count backwards if the *StartValue* argument is larger than the *EndValue* argument. Here is an example of how to make a **FOR…NEXT** loop count from 1000 to 500:

```
FOR counter = 1000 TO 500
```

You can combine counting down with a **STEP** argument to get the servo to rotate more quickly in the clockwise direction like this:

```
FOR counter = 1000 TO 500 STEP 20
```

The trick to getting the servo to turn at different rates is to use these **FOR…NEXT** loops to count up and down with different step sizes. The next example program uses these techniques to make the servo's horn rotate back and forth at different rates.

### Example Program: ServoVelocities.bs2

- √ Enter and run the program.
- √ As the program runs, watch how the value of `counter` changes in the Debug Terminal.
- √ Also, watch how the servo behaves differently through the two different **FOR…NEXT** loops. Both the servo's direction and speed change.

```
' What's a Microcontroller - ServoVelocities.bs2
' Rotate the servo counterclockwise slowly, then clockwise rapidly.

' {$STAMP BS2}
' {$PBASIC 2.5}

counter         VAR     Word

DO

DEBUG "Pulse width increment by 8", CR

  FOR counter = 500 TO 1000 STEP 8
    PULSOUT 14, counter
    PAUSE 7
    DEBUG DEC5 counter, CR, CRSRUP
  NEXT
```

```
DEBUG CR, "Pulse width decrement by 20", CR

FOR counter = 1000 TO 500 STEP 20
  PULSOUT 14, counter
  PAUSE 7
  DEBUG DEC5 counter, CR, CRSRUP
NEXT

DEBUG CR, "Repeat", CR

LOOP
```

**4**

### How ServoVelocities.bs2 Works

The first **FOR…NEXT** loop counts upwards from 500 to 1000 in steps of 8. Since the **counter** variable is used as the **PULSOUT** command's **Duration** argument, the servo horn's position rotates counterclockwise by steps that are four times the smallest possible step.

```
FOR counter = 500 TO 1000 STEP 8
  PULSOUT 14, counter
  PAUSE 7
  DEBUG DEC5 counter, CR, CRSRUP
NEXT
```

**Why PAUSE 7 instead of PAUSE 20?** The command **DEBUG DEC5 counter, CR, CRSRUP** takes about 8 ms to execute. This means that **PAUSE 12** would maintain the 20 ms delay between pulses. A few trial and error experiments showed that **PAUSE 7** gave the servo the smoothest motion. Your servo may be different.

**More DEBUG formatters and control characters** are featured in the **DEBUG** command that displays the value of the **counter** variable. This value is printed using the 5-digit decimal format (**DEC5**). After the value is printed, there is a carriage return (**CR**). After the carriage return, the formatter **CRSRUP** (cursor up) sends the cursor back up to the previous line. This causes the new value of counter to be printed over the old value each time through the loop.

The second **FOR…NEXT** loop counts downwards from 1000 back to 500 in steps of 20. The **counter** variable is also used as an argument for the **PULSOUT** command in this example, so the servo horn rotates clockwise.

```
FOR counter = 1000 TO 500 STEP 20
  PULSOUT 14, counter
```

```
      PAUSE 7
      DEBUG DEC5 counter, CR, CRSRUP
   NEXT
```

### Your Turn – Adjusting the Velocities

√   Try different **STEP** values to make the servo turn at different rates.

√   Re-run the program after each modification.

√   Observe the effect of each new **STEP** value on how fast the servo horn turns.

√   Experiment with different **PAUSE** command *Duration* values (between 3 and 12) to find the value that gives the servo the smoothest motion for each new **STEP** value.

## ACTIVITY #4: PUSHBUTTON CONTROLLED SERVO

In this chapter, you have written programs that make the servo go through a pre-recorded set of motions, and you have controlled the servo using the Debug Terminal. You can also program the BASIC Stamp to control the servo based on pushbutton inputs. In this activity you will:

- Build a circuit for a pushbutton controlled servo.
- Program the BASIC Stamp to control the servo based on the pushbutton inputs.

When you are done, you will be able to push one button to get the BASIC Stamp to rotate the servo in one direction, and another button to get the servo to rotate in the other direction. When no buttons are pressed, the servo will hold whatever position it moved to.

### Extra Parts for Pushbutton Servo Control

The same parts from the previous activities in this chapter are still used. You will need to gather the following parts for the pushbutton circuits:

(2) Pushbuttons – normally open
(2) Resistors – 10 kΩ (brown-black-orange)
(2) Resistors – 220 Ω (red-red-brown)
(3) Jumper wires

### Adding the Pushbutton Control Circuit

Figure 4-20 shows the pushbutton circuits that you will use to control the servo.

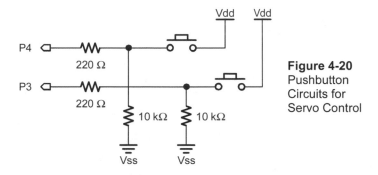

**Figure 4-20**
Pushbutton
Circuits for
Servo Control

√ Add this circuit to the servo+LED circuit that you have been using up to this point. When you are done your circuit should resemble:

- Figure 4-21 if you are using the Board of Education Rev C
- Figure 4-22 if you are using the HomeWork Board
- Figure 4-23 if you are using the Board of Education Rev B

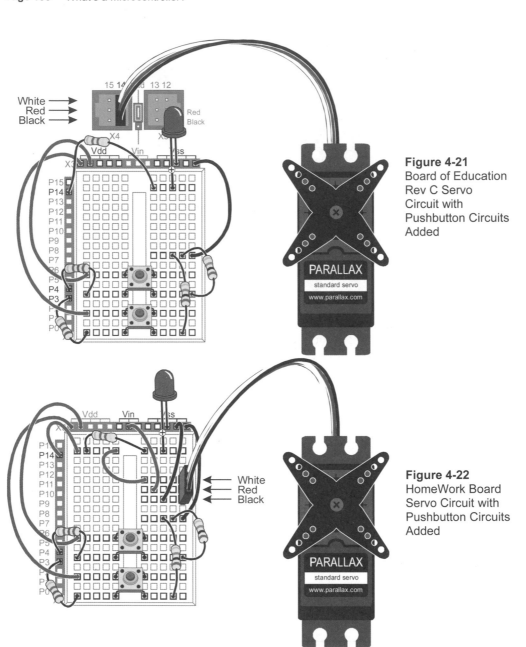

**Figure 4-21**
Board of Education
Rev C Servo
Circuit with
Pushbutton Circuits
Added

**Figure 4-22**
HomeWork Board
Servo Circuit with
Pushbutton Circuits
Added

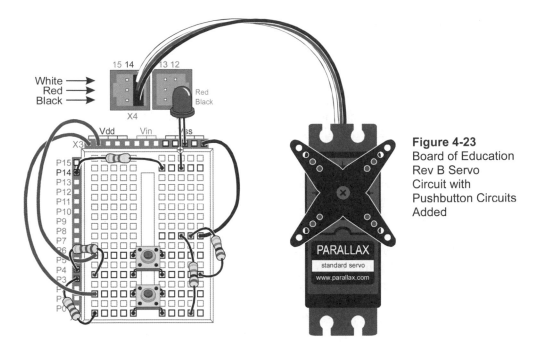

**Figure 4-23**
Board of Education
Rev B Servo
Circuit with
Pushbutton Circuits
Added

√ Test the pushbutton connected to P3 using the original version of ReadPushbuttonState.bs2. The section that has this program and the instructions on how to use it begins on page 77.
√ Modify the program so that it reads P4.
√ Run the modified program to test the pushbutton connected to P4.

## Programming Pushbutton Servo Control

Pushbutton servo control is not much different from pushbutton LED control. **IF…THEN** code blocks are used to check the pushbutton states and either add or subtract from a variable called **duration**. This variable is used in the **PULSOUT** command's *Duration* argument. If one of the pushbuttons is pressed, the value of **duration** increases. If the other pushbutton is pressed, the value of **duration** decreases. A nested **IF…THEN** statement is used to decide if the **duration** variable is too large (greater than 1000) or too small (smaller than 500).

### Example Program: ServoControlWithPushbuttons.bs2

This example program makes the servo's horn rotate counterclockwise when the pushbutton connected to P4 is pressed. The servo's horn will keep rotating so long as the pushbutton is held down and the value of **duration** is smaller than 1000. When the pushbutton connected to P3 is pressed, the servo horn rotates clockwise. The servo also is limited in its clockwise motion because the **duration** variable is not allowed to go below 500. The Debug Terminal displays the value of **duration** while the program is running.

- √ Enter the ServoControlWithPushbuttons.bs2 program into the BASIC Stamp Editor and run it.
- √ Verify that the servo turns counterclockwise when you press and hold the pushbutton connected to P4.
- √ Verify that as soon as the limit of **duration** > 1000 is reached or exceeded that the servo stops turning any further in the counterclockwise direction.
- √ Verify that the servo turns clockwise when you press and hold the pushbutton connected to P3.
- √ Verify that as soon as the limit of **duration** < 500 is reached or exceeded that the servo stops turning any further in the clockwise direction.

```
' What's a Microcontroller - ServoControlWithPushbuttons.bs2
' Press and hold P4 pushbutton to rotate the servo counterclockwise,
' or press the pushbutton connected to P3 to rotate the servo clockwise.

' {$STAMP BS2}
' {$PBASIC 2.5}

duration        VAR     Word

duration = 750

DO

  IF IN3 = 1 THEN
    IF duration > 500 THEN
      duration = duration - 25
    ENDIF
  ENDIF
```

```
  IF IN4 = 1 THEN
    IF duration < 1000 THEN
      duration = duration + 25
    ENDIF
  ENDIF

  PULSOUT 14, duration
  PAUSE 10

  DEBUG HOME, DEC4 duration, " = duration"

LOOP
```

**Your Turn – Software Stoppers**

Servos have a built in mechanical stopper that prevents them from turning too far. If you try to send a command like **PULSOUT 14, 2000**, the servo will not turn to a position that corresponds to a *Duration* argument of 2000. This is because servos have built-in mechanical stoppers that limit the range of motion. By gently turning the horn, you can feel when the servo's internal gears run into this mechanical stopper. You can modify the example program in this activity so that the BASIC Stamp limits the servo's motion to a range that is narrower than the limits imposed by the mechanical stoppers.

√   Save ServoControlWithPushbuttons.bs2 under a new name.
√   Adjust the software limits imposed on the servo's motion so that they are 650 and 850 instead of 500 and 1000.
√   Adjust the software imposed rate so that the **duration** variable is incremented or decremented by 10 instead of 25.
√   Decide what differences you expect to see in the way the servo behaves when you press the pushbutton.
√   Run the program and compare the actual results with your expected results.

## SUMMARY

This chapter introduced microcontrolled motion using a servo. A servo is a device that moves to and holds a particular position based on electronic signals it receives. These signals take the form of pulses that last anywhere between 1 and 2 ms, and they have to be delivered every 20 ms for the servo to maintain its position.

A programmer can use the **PULSOUT** command to make the BASIC Stamp send these signals. Since pulses have to be delivered every 20 ms for the servo to hold its position, the **PULSOUT** and **PAUSE** commands are usually placed in some kind of loop. Variables can be used to store the value used in the **PULSOUT** command's *Duration* argument. This causes the servo's horn to rotate in steps.

In this chapter, a variety of ways to get the values into the variables were presented. The variable can receive the value from your Debug Terminal using the **DEBUGIN** command. The value of the variable can pass through a sequence of values if the same variable is used as the index for a **FOR...NEXT** loop. This technique can be used to cause the servo to make sweeping motions. **IF...THEN** statements can be used to monitor pushbuttons and add or subtract from the variable used in the **PULSOUT** command's *Duration* argument based on whether or not a certain button is pressed. This allows both position control and sweeping motions depending on how the program is constructed and how the pushbuttons are operated.

### Questions

1.  What are the four external parts on a servo? What are they used for?
2.  Is an LED circuit required to make a servo work?
3.  What command controls the low time in the signal sent to a servo? What command controls the high time?
4.  What programming element can you use to control the amount of time that a servo holds a particular position?
5.  How do you use the Debug Terminal to send messages to the BASIC Stamp? What programming command is used to make the BASIC Stamp receive messages from the Debug Terminal?
6.  What type of code block can you write to limit the servo's range of motion?

### Exercises

1. Write a code block that sweeps the value of **PULSOUT** controlling a servo from a *Duration* of 700 to 800, then back to 700, in increments of (a) 1, (b) 4.
2. Add a nested **FOR...NEXT** loop to your answer to exercise 1b so that it delivers ten pulses before incrementing the **PULSOUT** *Duration* argument by 4.

### Project

1. Modify ServoControlWithDebug.bs2 so that it monitors a kill switch. If the kill switch (P3 pushbutton) is pressed, Debug Terminal should not accept any commands. It should display: "Press Start switch to start machinery". When the start switch (P4 pushbutton) is pressed, the program should function normally. If power is disconnected and reconnected, the program should behave as though the kill switch has been pressed.

### Solutions

Q1. 1. Plug – Connects servo to power and signal sources
2. Cable – Conducts power and signals from plug into the servo.
3. Horn – The moving part of the servo.
4. Case – Contains DC motor, gears, and control circuits.

Q2. No, the LED just helps us see what's going on with the control signals.

Q3. The low time is controlled with the **PAUSE** command. The high time is controlled with the **PULSOUT** command.

Q4. A **FOR...NEXT** loop.

Q5. Click the white field above the message display pane in the Debug Terminal and type the message you'd like to send. Use the **DEBUGIN** command to receive the typed characters in the BASIC Stamp.

Q6. A nested **IF...THEN** statement.

E1. a)
```
FOR counter = 700 TO 800
  PULSOUT 14, counter
  PAUSE 20
NEXT
FOR counter = 800 TO 700
  PULSOUT 14, counter
  PAUSE 20
NEXT
```

b) Add "**STEP 4**" to both **FOR** loops.
```
FOR counter = 700 TO 800 STEP 4
  PULSOUT 14, counter
  PAUSE 20
NEXT
FOR counter = 800 TO 700 STEP 4
  PULSOUT 14, counter
  PAUSE 20
NEXT
```

E2.
```
FOR counter = 700 TO 800 STEP 4
  FOR pulses = 1 TO 10
     PULSOUT 14, counter
     PAUSE 20
  NEXT
NEXT
FOR counter = 800 TO 700 STEP 4
  FOR pulses = 1 TO 10
     PULSOUT 14, counter
     PAUSE 20
  NEXT
NEXT
```

P1. There are many possible solutions; one is given below.

```
' What's a Microcontroller - Ch04Prj01Soln2__KillSwitch.bs2
' Send messages to the BASIC Stamp to control a servo using
' the Debug Terminal as long as kill switch is not being pressed.

' Contributed by: Professor Clark J. Radcliffe, Department
' of Mechanical Engineering, Michigan State University

' {$STAMP BS2}
' {$PBASIC 2.5}

counter VAR Word
pulses VAR Word
duration VAR Word
DO
  PAUSE 2000
  IF (IN3 = 1) AND (IN4 = 0) THEN
    DEBUG "Press Start switch to start machinery.     ", CR ,CRSRUP
  ELSEIF (IN3 = 0) AND (IN4 = 1) THEN
    DEBUG CLS, "Enter number of pulses:", CR
    DEBUGIN DEC pulses

    DEBUG "Enter PULSOUT duration:", CR
    DEBUGIN DEC duration

    DEBUG "Servo is running...", CR

    FOR counter = 1 TO pulses
      PULSOUT 14, duration
      PAUSE 20
    NEXT

    DEBUG "DONE"
    PAUSE 2000
  ENDIF
LOOP
```

## Further Investigation

The servo, and using sensors to control servos, can be investigated in detail in a variety of Stamps in Class texts.

**"*Advanced Robotics: with the Toddler*", Student Guide, Version 1.2, Parallax Inc., 2003**

> *Advanced Robotics: with the Toddler* uses servos to control the motions of the Parallax Toddler robot's legs. Although we take walking for granted, programming a machine to walk, maneuver, and keep its balance can be very challenging. This walking robot is recommended for advanced students who have already mastered the concepts in *What's a Microcontroller?* and either *Robotics with the Boe-Bot* or *SumoBot*.

**"*Robotics with the Boe-Bot*", Student Workbook, Version 2.0 Parallax Inc., 2003**

> *Robotics with the Boe-Bot* makes use of the same servo control principles you just learned with a twist; servos can also be modified and used as rolling robot motors. Using the BASIC Stamp, Board of Education, and Robotics with the Boe-Bot kit, this text starts with the basics of robot navigation, then guides you through navigation with sensors. It also introduces some more in-depth topics such as solving problems with artificial intelligence and navigation using elementary control systems.

**"*SumoBot*", Student Workbook, Version 1.1, Parallax Inc., 2002**

> Robot Sumo is a very exciting competition that is fun for observers and participants. *SumoBot* is a guided tour through building, testing, and competing with your own autonomous Mini-Sumo class SumoBot® robot. This textbook offers a condensed presentation of the *Robotics with the Boe-Bot* text material applied towards the goal of winning a robotic sumo wrestling contest.

# Chapter #5: Measuring Rotation

## ADJUSTING DIALS AND MONITORING MACHINES

Many households have dials to control the lighting in a room. Twist the dial one direction, and the light gets brighter; twist the dial in the other direction, and the light gets dimmer. Model trains use dials to control motor speed and direction. Many machines have dials or cranks used to fine tune the position of cutting blades and guiding surfaces.

Dials can also be found in audio equipment, where they are used to adjust how music and voices sound. Figure 5-1 shows a simple example of a dial with a knob that is turned to adjust the speaker's volume. By turning the knob, a circuit inside the speaker changes, and the volume of the music the speaker plays changes. Similar circuits can also be found inside joysticks, and even inside the servo used in Chapter #4: Controlling Motion.

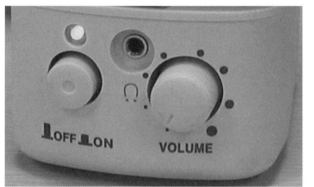

**Figure 5-1**
Volume
Adjustment
on a Speaker

## THE VARIABLE RESISTOR UNDER THE DIAL – A POTENTIOMETER

The device inside sound system dials, joysticks and servos is called a potentiometer, often abbreviated as a "pot". Figure 5-2 shows a picture of some common potentiometers. Notice that they all have three pins.

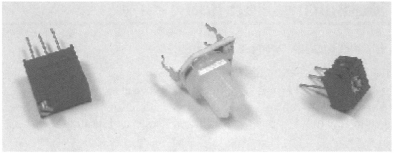

**Figure 5-2**
A Few
Potentiometer
Examples

Figure 5-3 shows the schematic symbol and part drawing of the potentiometer you will use in this chapter. Terminals A and B are connected to a 10 kΩ resistive element. Terminal W is called the wiper terminal, and it is connected to a wire that touches the resistive element somewhere between its ends.

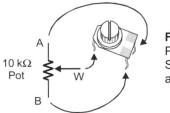

**Figure 5-3**
Potentiometer
Schematic Symbol
and Part Drawing

Figure 5-4 shows how the wiper on a potentiometer works. As you adjust the knob on top of the potentiometer, the wiper terminal contacts the resistive element at different places. As you turn the knob clockwise, the wiper gets closer to the A terminal, and as you turn the knob counterclockwise, the wiper gets closer to the B terminal.

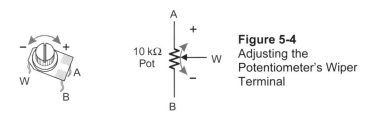

**Figure 5-4**
Adjusting the
Potentiometer's Wiper
Terminal

## ACTIVITY #1: BUILDING AND TESTING THE POTENTIOMETER CIRCUIT

Placing different size resistors in series with an LED causes different amounts of current to flow through the circuit. Large resistance in the LED circuit causes small amounts of current to flow through the circuit, and the LED glows dimly. Small resistances in the LED circuit causes more current to flow through the circuit, and the LED glows more brightly. By connecting the W and A terminals of the potentiometer, in series with an LED circuit, you can use it to adjust the resistance in the circuit. This in turn adjusts the brightness of the LED. In this activity, you will use the potentiometer as a variable resistor and use it to change the brightness of the LED.

**5**

### Dial Circuit Parts

(1) Potentiometer – 10 kΩ
(1) Resistor – 220 Ω (red-red-brown)
(1) LED – any color
(1) Jumper wire

### Building the Potentiometer Test Circuit

Figure 5-5 shows a circuit that can be used for adjusting the LED's brightness with a potentiometer.

√ Build the circuit shown in Figure 5-5.

 **Tip:** Use a needle-nose pliers to straighten the kinks out of the potentiometer's legs before plugging the device into the breadboard. When the potentiometer's legs are straight, they maintain better contact with the breadboard sockets.

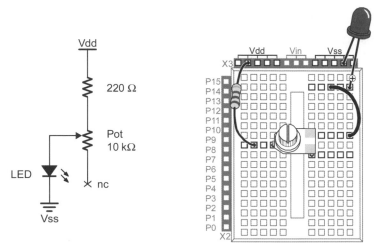

**Figure 5-5**
Potentiometer-LED
Test Circuit

## Testing the Potentiometer Circuit

√   Turn the potentiometer clockwise until it reaches its mechanical limit shown in
     Figure 5-6.

**Handle with care:** If your potentiometer will not turn this far, do not try to force it.   Just turn
it until it reaches its mechanical limit; otherwise, it might break.

√   Gradually rotate the potentiometer counterclockwise to the positions shown in
     Figure 5-6 (b), (c), (d), (e), and (f) noting the how brightly the LED glows at
     each position.

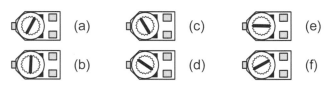

**Figure 5-6**
Potentiometer Input Shaft

*(a) through (f) show the
potentiometer's wiper
terminal set to different
positions.*

## How the Potentiometer Circuit Works

The total resistance in your test circuit is 220 Ω plus the resistance between the A and W
terminals of the potentiometer.  This value could be anywhere from 0 to 10 kΩ.  As you

turn the potentiometer's input shaft, the resistance between the A and W terminals changes. This in turn changes the current flow through the LED circuit.

## ACTIVITY #2: MEASURING RESISTANCE BY MEASURING TIME

This activity introduces a new part called a capacitor. A capacitor behaves like a rechargeable battery that only holds its charge for short durations of time. This activity also introduces RC-time, which is an abbreviation for resistor-capacitor time. RC-time is a measurement of how long it takes for a capacitor to lose a certain amount of its stored charge as it supplies current to a resistor. By measuring the time it takes for the capacitor to discharge with different size resistors and capacitors, you will become more familiar with RC-time. In this activity, you will program the BASIC Stamp to charge a capacitor and then measure the time it takes the capacitor to discharge through a resistor.

### Introducing the Capacitor

Figure 5-7 shows the schematic symbol and part drawing for the type of capacitor used in this activity. Capacitance value is measured in microfarads ($\mu$F), and the measurement is typically printed on the capacitors. The cylindrical case of the capacitor is called a canister.

> **This capacitor has a positive (+) and a negative (-) terminal.** The negative terminal is the lead that comes out of the metal canister closest to the stripe with a negative (–) sign. Always make sure to connect these terminals as shown in the circuit diagrams. Connecting one of these capacitors incorrectly can damage it. In some circuits, connecting this type of capacitor incorrectly and then connecting power can cause it to rupture or even explode.

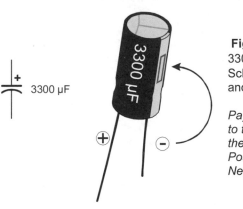

3300 $\mu$F

**Figure 5-7**
3300 $\mu$F Capacitor
Schematic Symbol
and Part Drawing

*Pay careful attention to the leads and how they connect to the Positive and Negative Terminals.*

## Resistance and Time Parts

(1) Capacitor – 3300 µF
(1) Capacitor – 1000 µF
(1) Resistors – 220 Ω (red-red-brown)
(1) Resistor – 470 Ω (yellow-violet-brown)
(1) Resistor – 1 kΩ (brown-black-red)
(1) Resistor – 2 kΩ (red-black-red)
(1) Resistor – 10 kΩ (brown-black-orange)

 **Recommended Equipment:** Safety goggles or safety glasses.

### Building and Testing the Resistance Capacitance (RC) Time Circuit

Figure 5-8 shows the circuit schematic and Figure 5-9 shows the wiring diagram for this activity. You will be taking time measurements using different resistor values in place of the resistor labeled $R_i$.

---

**SAFETY**

**Always observe polarity when connecting the 3300 µF capacitor.** Remember, the negative terminal is the lead that comes out of the metal canister closest to the stripe with a negative (–) sign. Use Figure 5-7 to identify the (+) and (-) terminals.

Your 3300 µF capacitor will work fine in this experiment so long as you make sure that the positive (+) and negative (-) terminals are connected EXACTLY as shown in Figure 5-8 and Figure 5-9.

**Never reverse the supply polarity** on the 3300 µF or any other polar capacitor. The voltage at the capacitor's (+) terminal must always be higher than the voltage at its (-) terminal. Vss is the lowest voltage (0 V) on the Board of Education and BASIC Stamp HomeWork Board. By connecting the capacitor's negative terminal to Vss, you ensure that the polarity across the capacitor's terminals will always be correct.

**Wear safety goggles or safety glasses during this activity.**

**Always disconnect power before you build or modify circuits.**

**Keep your hands and face away from this capacitor when power is connected.**

---

√ With power disconnected, build the circuit as shown starting with a 470 Ω resistor in place of the resistor labeled $R_i$.

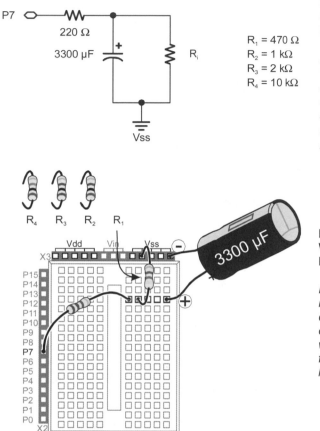

**Figure 5-8**
Schematic for Viewing
RC-time Voltage Decay

$R_1 = 470\ \Omega$
$R_2 = 1\ k\Omega$
$R_3 = 2\ k\Omega$
$R_4 = 10\ k\Omega$

*Four different resistors
will be used as $R_i$
shown in the schematic.
First, the schematic will
be built and tested with
$R_i = 470\ \Omega$, then $R_i = 1$
$k\Omega$, etc.*

**5**

**Figure 5-9**
Wiring Diagram for
Figure 5-8

*Make sure that the
negative lead of the
capacitor is connected
on your board the same
way it is shown in this
figure, with the negative
lead connected to Vss.*

## Polling the RC-Time Circuit with the BASIC Stamp

Although a stopwatch can be used to record how long it takes the capacitor's charge to
drop to a certain level, the BASIC Stamp can also be programmed to monitor the circuit
and give you a more reliable time measurement.

### Example Program: PolledRcTimer.bs2

√    Enter and run PolledRcTimer.bs2.

√   Observe how the BASIC Stamp charges the capacitor and then measures the discharge time.

√   Record the measured time (the capacitor's discharge time) in the 470 Ω row of Table 5-1.

√   Disconnect power from your Board of Education or BASIC Stamp HomeWork Board.

√   Remove the 470 Ω resistor labeled R$_i$ in Figure 5-8 and Figure 5-9 on page 145, and replace it with the 1 kΩ resistor.

√   Reconnect power to your board.

√   Record your next time measurement (for the 1 kΩ resistor).

√   Repeat these steps for each resistor value in Table 5-1.

| **Table 5-1:** Resistance and RC-time for C = 3300 µF | |
| --- | --- |
| **Resistance (Ω)** | **Measured Time (s)** |
| 470 | |
| 1 k | |
| 2 k | |
| 10 k | |

```
' What's a Microcontroller - PolledRcTimer.bs2
' Reaction timer program modified to track an RC-time voltage decay.

' {$STAMP BS2}
' {$PBASIC 2.5}

timeCounter     VAR     Word
counter         VAR     Nib

DEBUG CLS

HIGH 7
DEBUG "Capacitor Charging...", CR

FOR counter = 5 TO 0
  PAUSE 1000
  DEBUG DEC2 counter, CR, CRSRUP
NEXT

DEBUG CR, CR, "Measure decay time now!", CR, CR
INPUT 7

DO
```

```
  PAUSE 100
  timeCounter = timeCounter + 1

  DEBUG ? IN7
  DEBUG DEC5 timeCounter, CR, CRSRUP, CRSRUP

LOOP UNTIL IN7 = 0

DEBUG CR, CR, CR, "The RC decay time was ",
      DEC timeCounter, CR,
      "tenths of a second.", CR, CR

END
```

## How PolledRcTimer.bs2 Works

Two variables are declared. The **timeCounter** variable is used to track how long it takes the capacitor to discharge through $R_i$. The **counter** variable is used to count down while the capacitor is charging.

```
         timeCounter    VAR    Word
         counter        VAR    Nib
```

The command **DEBUG CLS** clears the Debug Terminal so that it doesn't get cluttered with successive measurements. **HIGH 7** sets P7 high and starts charging the capacitor, then a **"Capacitor charging…"** message is displayed. After that, a **FOR…NEXT** loop counts down while the capacitor is charging. As the capacitor charges, the voltage across its terminals increases toward anywhere between 2.5 and 4.9 V (depending on the value of $R_i$).

```
         DEBUG CLS

         HIGH 7
         DEBUG "Capacitor Charging...", CR

         FOR counter = 5 TO 0
           PAUSE 1000
           DEBUG DEC2 counter, CR, CRSRUP
         NEXT
```

A message announces when the decay starts getting polled.

```
         DEBUG CR, CR, "Measure decay time now!", CR, CR
```

In order to let the capacitor discharge itself through the $R_i$ resistor, the I/O pin is changed from **HIGH** to **INPUT**. As an input, the I/O pin, has no effect on the circuit, but it can sense high or low signals. As soon as the I/O pin releases the circuit, the capacitor discharges as it feeds current through the resistor. As the capacitor discharges, the voltage across its terminals gets lower and lower (decays).

```
INPUT 7
```

Back in the pushbutton chapter, you used the BASIC Stamp to detect a high or low signal using the variables **IN3** and **IN4**. At that time, a high signal was considered Vdd, and a low signal was considered Vss. It turns out that a high signal is any voltage above 1.4 V. Of course, it could be up to 5 V. Likewise, a low signal is anything between 1.4 V and 0 V. This **DO...LOOP** checks P7 every 100 ms until the value of **IN7** changes from 1 to 0, which indicates that the capacitor voltage decayed below 1.4 V.

```
DO

    PAUSE 100
    timeCounter = timeCounter + 1

    DEBUG ? IN7
    DEBUG DEC5 timeCounter, CR, CRSRUP, CRSRUP

LOOP UNTIL IN7 = 0
```

The result is then displayed and the program ends.

```
DEBUG CR, CR, CR, "The RC decay time was ",

    DEC timeCounter, CR,
    "tenths of a second.", CR, CR

END
```

## Your Turn – A Faster Circuit

By using a capacitor that has roughly 1/3 the capacity to hold charge, the time measurement for each resistor value that is used in the circuit will be reduced by 1/3. In Activity #3, you will use a capacitor that is 10,000 times smaller, and the BASIC Stamp will still take the time measurements for you using a command called **RCTIME**.

√ Disconnect power to your Board of Education or HomeWork Board.
√ Replace the 3300 µF capacitor with a 1000 µF capacitor.
√ **Confirm that the polarity of your capacitor is correct.** The negative terminal should be connected to Vss.

√ Reconnect power.

√ Repeat the steps in the Example Program: PolledRcTimer.bs2 section, and record your time measurements in Table 5-2.

√ Compare your time measurements to the ones you took earlier in Table 5-1. How close are they to 1/3 the value of the measurements taken with the 3300 µF capacitor?

| Table 5-2: Resistance and RC-time for C = 1000 µF | |
|---|---|
| **Resistance (Ω)** | **Measured Time (s)** |
| 470 | |
| 1 k | |
| 2 k | |
| 10 k | |

## ACTIVITY #3: READING THE DIAL WITH THE BASIC STAMP

In Activity #1, a potentiometer was used as a variable resistor. The resistance in the circuit varied depending on the position of the potentiometer's adjusting knob. In Activity #2, an RC-time circuit was used to measure different resistances. In this activity, you will build an RC-time circuit to read the potentiometer, and use the BASIC Stamp to take the time measurements. The capacitor you use will be very small, and the time measurements will only take a few milliseconds. Even though the measurements take very short durations of time, the BASIC Stamp will give you an excellent indication of the resistance between the potentiometer's A and W terminals.

### Parts for Reading RC-Time with the BASIC Stamp

(1) Potentiometer – 10 kΩ

(1) Resistor – 220 Ω (red-red-brown)

(2) Jumper wires

(1) Capacitor – 0.1 µF shown in Figure 5-10

(1) Capacitor – 0.01 µF, also shown in Figure 5-10

(2) Jumper wires

 **These capacitors do not have + and – terminals.** You can safely connect these capacitors to a circuit without worrying about positive and negative terminals.

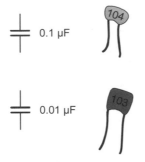

**Figure 5-10**
Ceramic Capacitors

*The 0.1 μF capacitor (above)
and the 0.01 μF capacitor
(below) are both non-polar.
You will not have to worry
about positive and negative
leads with these two parts.*

## Building an RC Time Circuit for the BASIC Stamp

Figure 5-11 shows a schematic for the fast RC-time circuit, and Figure 5-12 shows the wiring diagram. This is the circuit that you will use to monitor the position of the potentiometer's input shaft with the help of the BASIC Stamp and a PBASIC program.

√ Build the circuit shown in Figure 5-11.

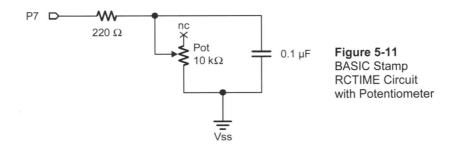

**Figure 5-11**
BASIC Stamp
RCTIME Circuit
with Potentiometer

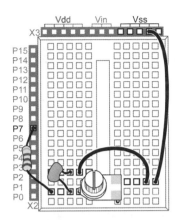

**Figure 5-12**
Wiring Diagram for
Figure 5-11

5

### Programming RC-Time Measurements

The BASIC Stamp program to measure the potentiometer's resistance will do essentially the same thing that you did by hand in Activity #2. The equivalent of pressing and holding the pushbutton is a **HIGH** command followed by a **PAUSE**. The **RCTIME** command is the BASIC Stamp module's way of letting go of the pushbutton and polling until the capacitor's voltage gets low enough to pass the threshold voltage of **IN7** (1.4 V).

### Example Program: ReadPotWithRcTime.bs2

√ Enter and run ReadPotWithRcTime.bs2
√ Try rotating the potentiometer's input shaft while monitoring the value of the **time** variable using the Debug Terminal.

```
' What's a Microcontroller - ReadPotWithRcTime.bs2
' Read potentiometer in RC-time circuit using RCTIME command.

' {$STAMP BS2}
' {$PBASIC 2.5}

time VAR Word

DO

  HIGH 7
  PAUSE 100
  RCTIME 7, 1, time
  DEBUG HOME, "time = ", DEC5 time

LOOP
```

### How ReadPotWithRcTime.bs2 Works

Here are the pseudo-code steps the program goes through to take the RC-time measurement.

- *Declare the variable* **time** *to store a time measurement.*
- *Code block within* **DO...LOOP***:*
  - o *Set I/O pin P7 to* **HIGH***.*
  - o *Wait for 100 ms (20 ms to make sure the capacitor is charged up and 80 more ms to keep the Debug Terminal display steady).*
  - o *Execute the* **RCTIME** *command.*
  - o *Store the time measurement in the* **time** *variable.*
  - o *Display the value* **time** *in the Debug Terminal.*

Before the **RCTIME** command is executed, the capacitor is fully charged. As soon as the **RCTIME** command executes, the BASIC Stamp changes the I/O pin from an output to an input. As an input, the I/O pin looks about the same to the circuit as when the pushbutton was released (open circuit) in Activity #2. The **RCTIME** command is a high speed version of the polling that was used in Activity #2, and it measures the amount of time it takes for the capacitor to lose its charge and fall below the I/O pin's 1.4 V input threshold. Instead of counting in 100 ms increments, the **RCTIME** command counts in 2 µs increments.

### Your Turn – Changing Time by Changing the Capacitor

- √   Replace the 0.1 µF capacitor with a 0.01 µF capacitor.
- √   Try the same positions on the potentiometer that you did in the main activity and compare the value displayed in the Debug Terminal with the values obtained for the 0.1 µF capacitor. Are the **RCTIME** measurements one tenth the value?
- √   Go back to the 0.1 µF capacitor.
- √   With the 0.1 µF capacitor back in the circuit and the 0.01 µF capacitor removed, make a note of the highest and lowest values for the next activity.

## ACTIVITY #4: CONTROLLING A SERVO WITH A POTENTIOMETER

Potentiometers together with servos can be used to make lots of fun things. This is the foundation for model airplanes, cars and boats. This activity shows how the BASIC Stamp can be used to monitor a potentiometer circuit and control the position of a servo.

An example of a model airplane and its radio controller are shown in Figure 5-13. The model airplane has servos to control all its flaps and the gas engine's throttle settings. These servos are controlled using the radio control (RC) unit in front of the plane. This RC unit has potentiometers under a pair of joysticks that are used to control the servos that in turn control the plane's elevator and rudder flaps.

**Figure 5-13**
Model Airplane and
Radio Controller

 **How the RC Unit Controls the Airplane:** The potentiometers under the joysticks are monitored by a circuit that converts the position of the joystick into control pulses for the servo. These control pulses are then converted to radio signals and transmitted by the handheld controller to a radio receiver in the model airplane. The radio receiver converts these signals back to control pulses which then position the servos.

## Potentiometer Controlled Servo Parts

(1) Potentiometer – 10 kΩ
(1) Resistor – 220 Ω (red-red-brown)
(1) Capacitor – 0.1 µF
(1) Parallax Standard Servo
(1) LED – any color
(2) Jumper wires

HomeWork Board users will also need:

(1) 3-pin male-male header

(4) Jumper wires

> **CAUTION: use only a Parallax Standard Servo for the activities in this text!**
>
> Do not substitute a Parallax Continuous Rotation Servo, as it may be quickly damaged by the circuits shown below. Likewise, we do not recommend using other brands of standard hobby servos, which may not be rated for use with the voltage supplied in these circuits.

## Building the Dial and Servo Circuits

This activity will use two circuits that you have already built individually: the potentiometer circuit from the activity you just finished and the servo circuit from the previous chapter.

√ Leave your potentiometer RC-time circuit from Activity #3 on your prototyping area. If you need to rebuild it, use Figure 5-11 on page 150 and Figure 5-12 on page 151. Make sure to use the 0.1 µF capacitor, not the 0.01 µF capacitor.

√ Add your servo circuit from Chapter #4, Activity #1 to the project. Remember that your servo circuit will be different depending on your carrier board. Below are the pages for the sections that you will need to jump to:

- Page 105 – Board of Education Rev C
- Page 111 – Board of Education Rev B
- Page 108 – BASIC Stamp HomeWork Board

## Programming Potentiometer Control of the Servo

You will need the smallest and largest value of the `time` variable that you recorded from your RC-time circuit while using a 0.1 µF capacitor.

√ If you have not already completed the Your Turn section of the previous activity, go back and complete it now.

For this next example, here are the `time` values that were measured by a Parallax technician; your values will probably be slightly different:

- All the way clockwise:            1
- All the way counterclockwise:   691

So how can these input values be adjusted so that they map to the values of 500 and 1000 that are needed to control the servo with the **PULSOUT** command? The answer is by using multiplication and addition. First, multiply the input values by something to make the difference between the clockwise (minimum) and counterclockwise (maximum) values 500 instead of almost 700. Then, add a constant value to the result so that its range is from 500 to 1000 instead of 1 to 500. In electronics, these operations are called scaling and offset.

Here's how the math works for the multiplication (scaling):

$$time(maximum) = 691 \times \frac{500}{691} = 691 \times 0.724 = 500$$

$$time(minimum) = 1 \times \frac{500}{691} = 0.724$$

After the values are scaled, here is the addition (offset) step.

$$time(maximum) = 500 + 500 = 1000$$

$$time(minimum) = 0.724 + 500 = 500$$

The **\*/** operator that was introduced on page 95 is built into PBASIC for scaling by fractional values, like 0.724. Here again are the steps for using **\*/** applied to 0.724:

1. Place the value or variable you want to multiply by a fractional value before the */ operator.

   ```
   time = time */
   ```

2. Take the fractional value that you want to use and multiply it by 256.

   $$new\ fractional\ value = 0.724 \times 256 = 185.344$$

3. Round off to get rid of anything to the right of the decimal point.

   $$new\ fractional\ value = 185$$

4. Place that value after the */ operator.

```
time = time */ 185
```

That takes care of the scaling, now all we need to do is add the offset of 500. This can be done with a second command that adds 500 to `time`:

```
time = time */ 185
time = time + 500
```

Now, `time` is ready to be recycled into the `PULSOUT` command's *Duration* argument.

```
time = time */ 185      ' Scale by 0.724.
time = time + 500       ' Offset by 500.
PULSOUT 14, time        ' Send pulse to servo.
```

## Example Program: ControlServoWithPot.bs2

√   Enter and run this program, then twist the potentiometer's input shaft and
    make sure that the servo's movements echo the potentiometer's movements.

```
' What's a Microcontroller - ControlServoWithPot.bs2
' Read potentiometer in RC-time circuit using RCTIME command.
' Scale time by 0.724 and offset by 500 for the servo.

' {$STAMP BS2}
' {$PBASIC 2.5}

DEBUG "Program Running!"

time            VAR     Word

DO
  HIGH 7
  PAUSE 10
  RCTIME 7, 1, time
  time = time */ 185                          ' Scale by 0.724 (X 256 for */).
  time = time + 500                           ' Offset by 500.
  PULSOUT 14, time                            ' Send pulse to servo.
LOOP
```

## Your Turn – Scaling the Servo's Relationship to the Dial

Your potentiometer and capacitor will probably give you `time` values that are somewhat different from the ones discussed in this activity. These are the values you gathered in the Your Turn section of the previous activity.

√   Repeat the math discussed in the Programming Potentiometer Control of the
    Servo section on page 154 using your maximum and minimum values.

√ Substitute your **scale** and **offset** values in ControlServoWithPot.bs2.

√ Add this line of code between the **PULSOUT** and **LOOP** commands so that you can view your results.

```
DEBUG HOME, DEC5 time    ' Display adjusted time value.
```

√ Run the modified program and check your work. Because the values were rounded off, the limits may not be exactly 500 and 1000, but they should be pretty close.

## Using Constants in Programs

In larger programs, you may end up using the **PULSOUT** command and the value of the scale factor (which was 185) and the offset (which was 500) many times in the program. You can use alias names for these values with the **CON** directive like this:

```
scaleFactor CON 185
offset CON 500
```

 **These alias names** are just about always declared near the beginning of the program so that they are easy to find.

Now, anywhere in your program that you want to use one of these values, you can use the words **offset** or **scaleFactor** instead. For example,

```
time = time */ scaleFactor                    ' Scale by 0.724.
time = time + offset                          ' Offset by 500.
```

You can also apply the same technique with the I/O pins. For example, you can declare a constant for I/O pin P7.

```
rcPin     CON 7
```

There are two places in the previous example program where the number 7 is used to refer to I/O pin P7. The first can now be written as:

```
HIGH rcPin
```

The second can be written as:

```
RCTIME rcPin, 1, time
```

If you change your circuit later, all you have to do is change the value in your constant declaration, and both the **HIGH** and **RCTIME** commands will be automatically updated.

Likewise, if you have to recalibrate your scale factor or offset, you can also just change the CON directives at the beginning of the program.

 **Assigning an alias** is what you do when you give a variable, constant or I/O pin a name using **VAR**, **CON**, or **PIN**.

### Example Program: ControlServoWithPotUsingConstants.bs2

This program makes use of aliases in place of almost all numbers.

√ Enter and run ControlServoWithPotUsingConstants.bs2.
√ Observe how the servo responds to the potentiometer and verify that it's the same as the previous example program (ControlServoWithPot.bs2).

```
' What's a Microcontroller - ControlServoWithPotUsingConstants.bs2
' Read potentiometer in RC-time circuit using RCTIME command.
' Apply scale factor and offset, then send value to servo.

' {$STAMP BS2}
' {$PBASIC 2.5}

scaleFactor     CON     185
offset          CON     500
rcPin           CON     7
delay           CON     10
servoPin        CON     14

time            VAR     Word

DO
  HIGH rcPin
  PAUSE delay
  RCTIME rcPin, 1, time
  time = time */ scaleFactor                ' Scale scaleFactor.
  time = time + offset                      ' Offset by offset.
  PULSOUT servoPin, time                    ' Send pulse to servo.
  DEBUG HOME, DEC5 time                     ' Display adjusted time value.
LOOP
```

### Your Turn – Using Constants for Calibration and Easy Updating

As mentioned earlier, if you change the I/O pin used by the **HIGH** and **RCTIME** command, you can simply change the value of the **rcPin** constant declaration.

√   Save the example program under a new name.

√   Change the `scaleFactor` and `offset` values to the unique values for your RC circuit that you determined in the previous Your Turn section.

√   Run the modified program and verify that it works correctly.

√   Modify your circuit by moving the RC-time circuit from I/O pin P7 to I/O pin P8.

√   Modify the `rcPin` declaration so that it reads:

```
rcPin    CON 8
```

√   Add this command before the `DO...LOOP` so that you can see that the `rcPin` constant really is just a way of saying the number eight:

```
DEBUG ? rcPin
```

√   Re-run the program and verify that the `HIGH` and `RCTIME` commands are still functioning properly on the different I/O pin with just one change to the `rcPin` `CON` directive.

## SUMMARY

This chapter introduced the potentiometer, a part often found under various knobs and dials. The potentiometer has a resistive element that typically connects its outer two terminals and a wiper terminal that contacts a variable point on the resistive element. The potentiometer can be used as a variable resistor if the wiper terminal and one of the two outer terminals is used in a circuit.

The capacitor was also introduced in this chapter. A capacitor can be used to store and release charge. The amount of charge a capacitor can store is related to its value, which is measured in Farads, (F). The µ is engineering notation for micro, and it means one-millionth. The capacitors used in this chapter's activities ranged from 0.01 to 3300 µF.

A resistor and a capacitor can be connected together in a circuit that takes a certain amount of time to charge and discharge. This circuit is commonly referred to as an RC-time circuit. The R and C in RC-time stand for resistor and capacitor. When one value (C in this chapter's activities) is held constant, the change in the time it takes for the circuit to discharge is related to the value of R. When the value of R changes, the value of the time it takes for the circuit to charge and discharge also changes. The overall time it takes the RC-time circuit to discharge can be scaled by using a capacitor of a different size.

Polling was used to monitor the discharge time of a capacitor in an RC circuit where the value of C was very large. Several different resistors were used to show how the discharge time changes as the value of the resistor in the circuit changes. The RCTIME command was then used to monitor a potentiometer (a variable resistor) in an RC-time circuit with smaller value capacitors. Although these capacitors cause the discharge times to range from roughly 2 to 1500 µs (millionths of a second), the BASIC Stamp has no problem tracking these time measurements with the RCTIME command. The I/O pin must be set HIGH, and then the capacitor in the RC-time circuit must be allowed to charge by using PAUSE before the RCTIME command can be used.

PBASIC programming can be used to measure a resistive sensor such as a potentiometer and scale its value so that it is useful to another device, such as a servo. This involves performing mathematical operations on the measured RC discharge time, which the RCTIME command stores in a variable. This variable can be adjusted by adding a constant value to it, which comes in handy for controlling a servo. In the Projects section, you may find yourself using multiplication and division as well. The CON directive can be used at the beginning of a program to substitute a name for a number. As with naming variables, naming constants is also called creating an alias. After an alias is created, the name can be used in place of the number throughout the program. This can come in handy, especially if you need to use the same number in 2, 3, or even 100 different places in the program. You can change the number in the CON directive, and all 2, 3, or even 100 different instances of that number are automatically updated next time you run the program.

## Questions

1. When you turn the dial or knob on a sound system, what component are you most likely adjusting?
2. In a typical potentiometer, is the resistance between the two outer terminals adjustable?
3. How is a capacitor like a rechargeable battery? How is it different?
4. What can you do with an RC-time circuit to give you an indication of the value of a variable resistor?
5. What happens to the RC discharge time as the value of R (the resistor) gets larger or smaller?
6. What does the CON directive do? Explain this in terms of a name and a number.

## Exercise

1. Let's say that you have a 0.5 µF capacitor in an RC timer circuit, and you want the measurement to take 10-times as long. Calculate the value of the new capacitor.

## Projects

1. Add a bi-color LED circuit to Activity #4. Modify the example program so that the bi-color LED is red when the servo is rotating counterclockwise, green when the servo is rotating clockwise, and off when the servo holding its position.
2. Use IF...THEN to modify the example program from Activity #4 so that the servo only rotates between PULSOUT values of 650 and 850.

## Solutions

Q1. A potentiometer.

Q2. No, it's fixed. The variable resistance is between either outer terminal and the wiper (middle) terminal.

Q3. A capacitor is like a rechargeable battery in that it can be charged up to hold voltage. The difference is that it only holds a charge for a very small amount of time.

Q4. You can measure the time it takes for the capacitor to discharge (or charge) This time is related to the resistance and capacitance. If the capacitance is known and the resistance is variable, then the discharge time gives an indication of the resistance.

Q5. As R gets larger, the RC discharge time increases in direct proportion to the increase in R. As R gets smaller, the RC discharge time decreases in direct proportion to the decrease in R.

Q6. The CON directive substitutes a name for a number.

E1. new cap = 10 x old cap value

$$= 10 \times 0.5\mu F$$
$$= 5\mu F$$

P1. Activity #4 with bi-color LED added.

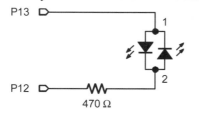

P13

1

P12

2

470 Ω

Potentiometer schematic from Figure 5-11 p. 150, servo from Figure 4-3 p. 106, bi-color LED from Figure 2-19 p. 63, with P15 and P14 changed to P13 and P12.

```
' What's a Microcontroller - Ch5Prj01_ControlServoWithPot.bs2
' Read potentiometer in RC-time circuit using RCTIME command.
' The time variable ranges from 126 to 713, and an offset of 330 is
' needed.
' Bi-color LED on P12, P13 tells direction of servo rotation:
' green for CW, red for CCW, off when servo is holding position.

' {$STAMP BS2}
' {$PBASIC 2.5}
DEBUG "Program Running!"


time             VAR     Word          ' time reading from
potentiometer
prevTime         VAR     Word          ' previous reading

DO
```

```
   prevTime = time                       ' Store previous time reading
   HIGH 7                                ' Read pot using RCTIME
   PAUSE 10
   RCTIME 7, 1, time
   time = time + 330                     ' Scale pot, match servo range

   IF ( time > prevTime + 2) THEN        ' increased, pot turned CCW
     HIGH 13                             ' Bi-color LED red
     LOW 12
   ELSEIF ( time < prevTime - 2) THEN    ' value decreased, pot turned CW
     LOW 13                              ' Bi-color LED green
     HIGH 12
   ELSE                                  ' Servo holding position
     LOW 13                              ' LED off
     LOW 12
   ENDIF

   PULSOUT 14, time
LOOP
```

P2. The key is to add **IF...THEN** blocks; an example is shown below.

```
' What's a Microcontroller - Ch5Prj02_ControlServoWithPot.bs2
' Read potentiometer in RC-time circuit using RCTIME command.
' The time variable ranges from 126 to 713, and an offset of 330 is
' needed.
' Modify so the servo only rotates from 650 to 850.
' {$STAMP BS2}
' {$PBASIC 2.5}
DEBUG "Program Running!"

time VAR Word

DO
  HIGH 7                                ' Read pot with RCTIME
  PAUSE 10
  RCTIME 7, 1, time

  time = time + 330                     ' Scale time to servo range

  IF (time < 650) THEN                  ' Constrain range from 650 to 850
    time = 650
  ENDIF
  IF (time > 850) THEN
    time = 850
  ENDIF

  PULSOUT 14, time
LOOP
```

## Further Investigation

Several different electronic components, concepts and techniques were incorporated in this chapter. Some of the more notable examples are:

- Using a potentiometer as an input device
- Measuring the resistance/capacitance of a device using `RCTIME`
- Performing math on an input value and recycling it into an output
- Controlling a motor based on a measured value

**"*Advanced Robotics: with the Toddler*", Student Workbook, Version 1.2, Parallax Inc., 2003**
**"*Robotics with the Boe-Bot*", Student Workbook, Version 2.0, Parallax Inc., 2003**
**"*SumoBot*", Student Workbook, Version 1.1, Parallax Inc., 2002**
> Every Stamps in Class robotics text uses `RCTIME` to measure resistive sensors to detect a variety of conditions. Each condition leads to math and decisions, and the end result is robot movement.

**"*Basic Analog and Digital*", Student Guide, Version 2.0, Parallax Inc., 2003**
> *Basic Analog and Digital* uses the potentiometer to create a variable voltage, called a voltage divider, which is analyzed by an analog to digital converter. A potentiometer is also used as an input device to set the frequency of a 555 timer. This text takes a closer look at the math involved in RC voltage decay.

**"*Applied Sensors*", Student Guide, Version 1.3, Parallax Inc., 2003**
> `RCTIME` is used extensively in this book to collect data from a variety of sensors.

**"*Industrial Control*", Student Guide, Version 2.0, Parallax Inc., 2002**
> This book introduces techniques used extensively in industry for controlling machines based on sensor input. The techniques fall under the general category of control systems.

# Chapter #6: Digital Display

### THE EVERY-DAY DIGITAL DISPLAY

Figure 6-1 shows a display on the front of an oven door. When the oven is not in use, it displays the time. When the oven is in use, it displays the oven's timer, cooking settings, and it flashes on and off at the same time an alarm sounds to let you know the food is done. A microcontroller inside the oven door monitors the pushbuttons and updates the display. It also monitors sensors inside the oven and switches devices that turn the heating elements on and off.

6

**Figure 6-1**
Digital Clock 7-Segment
Display on Oven Door

Each of the three digits in Figure 6-1 is called a 7-segment display. In this chapter, you will program the BASIC Stamp to display numbers and letters on a 7-segment display.

### WHAT'S A 7-SEGMENT DISPLAY?

A 7-segment display is rectangular block of 7 lines of equal length that can be lit selectively to display digits and some letters. A very common form is the 7-segment LED display, a package with a rectangular block of 7 LEDs. Figure 6-2 shows a part drawing of the 7-segment LED display you will use in this chapter's activities. It has one additional LED, a dot that can be used as a decimal point. Each of the segments (A through G) and the dot contains a separate LED, which can be controlled individually. Most of the pins have a number along with a label that corresponds with one of the LED segments. Pin 5 is labeled DP, which stands for decimal point. Pins 3 and 8 are labeled "common cathode", and they will be explained when the schematic for this part is introduced.

Common
Cathode

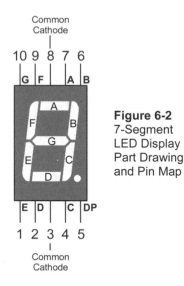

**Figure 6-2**
7-Segment
LED Display
Part Drawing
and Pin Map

Common
Cathode

 **Pin Map:** Figure 6-2 is an example of a pin map.  A pin map contains useful information that helps you connect a part to other circuits.  Pin maps usually show a number for each pin, a name for each pin, and a reference.  Take a look at Figure 6-2.  Each pin is numbered, and the name for each pin is the segment letter next to the pin.  The reference for this part is its overall appearance.  You know by looking at the top of the display that pin 1 is closest to the lower-left corner of the display.  Other parts have more subtle references, such as the flat spot on a regular LED's case.

Figure 6-3 shows a schematic of the LEDs inside the 7-segment LED display.  Each LED anode is connected to an individual pin.  All the cathodes are connected together by wire inside the part.  Because all the cathodes share a common connection, the 7-segment LED display can be called a "common cathode" display.  By connecting either pin 3 or pin 8 of the part to Vss, you will connect all the LED cathodes to Vss.

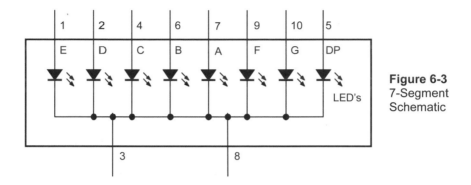

**Figure 6-3**
7-Segment
Schematic

LED's

6

## ACTIVITY #1: BUILDING AND TESTING THE 7-SEGMENT LED DISPLAY

In this activity, you will manually build circuits to test each segment in the display.

### 7-Segment LED Display Test Parts

(1) 7-segment LED display
(5) Resistors – 1 kΩ (brown-black-red)
(5) Jumper wires

### 7-Segment LED Display Test Circuits

√    With power disconnected from your Board of Education or HomeWork Board, build the circuit shown in Figure 6-4 and Figure 6-5.

√    Reconnect power and verify that the A segment emits light.

 **What's the x with the nc above it in the schematic?** The nc stands for not connected or no-connect. It indicates that a particular pin on the 7-segment LED display is not connected to anything. The x at the end of the pin also means not connected. Schematics sometimes use just the x or just the nc.

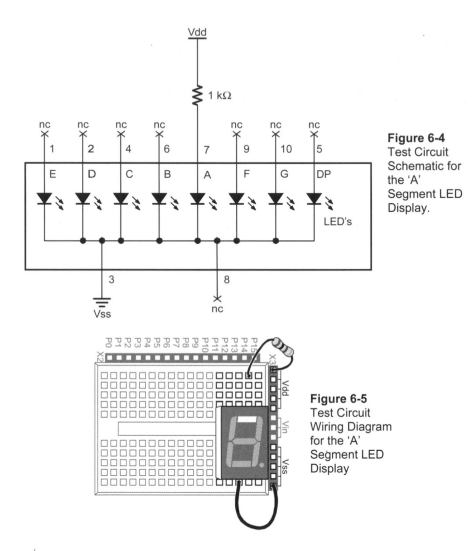

**Figure 6-4**
Test Circuit Schematic for the 'A' Segment LED Display.

**Figure 6-5**
Test Circuit Wiring Diagram for the 'A' Segment LED Display

√ Disconnect power, and modify the circuit by connecting the resistor to the B LED input as shown in Figure 6-6 and Figure 6-7.

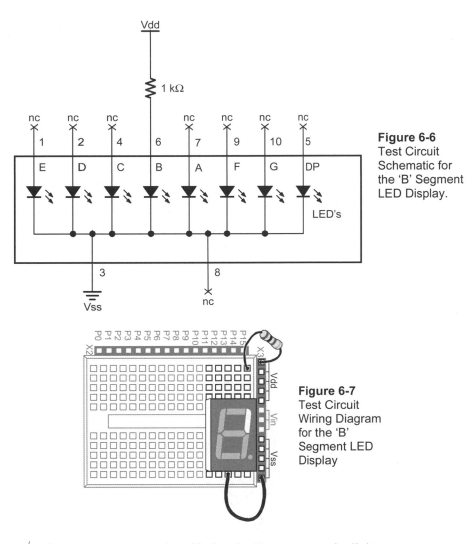

**Figure 6-6**
Test Circuit
Schematic for
the 'B' Segment
LED Display.

**Figure 6-7**
Test Circuit
Wiring Diagram
for the 'B'
Segment LED
Display

√ Reconnect power and verify that the B segment emits light.
√ Using the pin map from Figure 6-2 as a guide, repeat these steps for segments
C through G.

### Your Turn – The Letter A and the Number Two

Figure 6-8 and Figure 6-9 show the digit '3' hardwired into the 7-segment LED display.

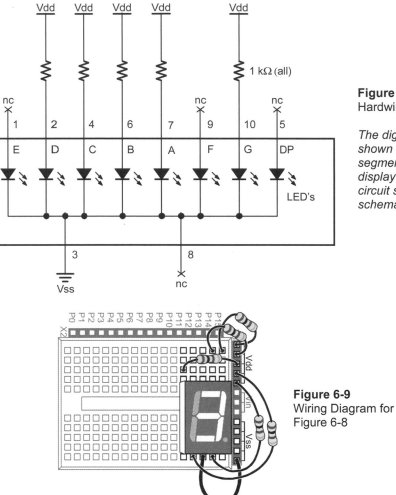

**Figure 6-8**
Hardwired Digit '3'

*The digit "3" is shown on the 7-segment LED display using the circuit shown in this schematic.*

**Figure 6-9**
Wiring Diagram for Figure 6-8

√  Build and test the circuit shown in Figure 6-8 and Figure 6-9, and verify that it displays the number three.

√  Draw a schematic that will display the number two on the 7-segment LED.

√  Build and test the circuit to make sure it works.  Trouble-shoot if necessary.

√  Repeat for the letter 'A'.

## ACTIVITY #2: CONTROLLING THE 7-SEGMENT LED DISPLAY

In this activity, you will connect the 7-segment LED display to the BASIC Stamp, and then run a simple program to test and make sure each LED is properly connected.

### 7-Segment LED Display Parts

(1) 7-segment LED display
(8) Resistors – 1 k$\Omega$ (brown-black-red)
(5) Jumper wires

### Connecting the 7-Segment LED Display to the BASIC Stamp

Figure 6-10 shows the schematic and Figure 6-11 shows the wiring diagram for this BASIC Stamp controlled 7-segment LED display example.

√ Build the circuit shown in Figure 6-10 and Figure 6-11.

 **Schematic and pin map:** If you are trying to build the circuit from the schematic in Figure 6-10 without relying on Figure 6-11, make sure to consult the 7-segment LED display's pin map (Figure 6-2, page 166).

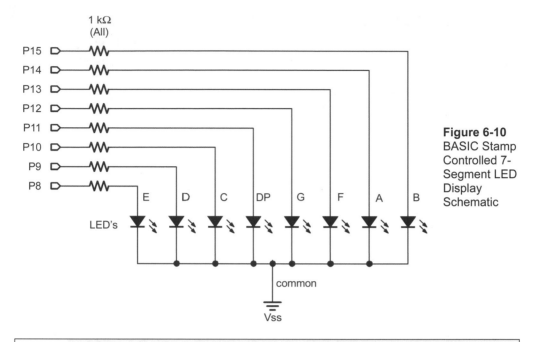

**Figure 6-10**
BASIC Stamp Controlled 7-Segment LED Display Schematic

**Be careful with the resistors connected to P13 and P14.** Look carefully at the resistors connected to P13 and P14 in Figure 6-11. There is gap between these two resistors. The gap is shown because pin 8 on the 7-segment LED display is left unconnected. A resistor connects I/O pin P13 to 7-segment LED display pin 9. Another resistor connects P14 to 7-segment LED display pin 7.

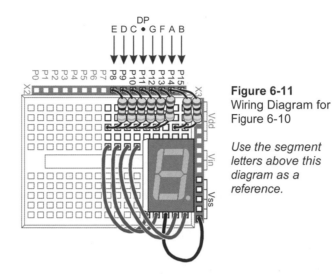

**Figure 6-11**
Wiring Diagram for
Figure 6-10

*Use the segment
letters above this
diagram as a
reference.*

6

---

**Parallel Device:** The 7-segment LED display is called a parallel device because you have to use more than one I/O line at a time to send data (high and low information) to the device. In the case of this 7-segment LED display, it takes 8 I/O pins to instruct the device what to do.

**Parallel Bus:** The wires that transmit the **HIGH/LOW** signals from the BASIC Stamp to the 7-segment LED display are called a parallel bus. Note that these wires are drawn as parallel lines in Figure 6-10. The term parallel kind of makes sense given the geometry of the schematic.

---

## Programming the 7-Segment LED Display Test

The **HIGH** and **LOW** commands will accept a variable as a pin argument.  To test each segment, one at a time, simply place the **HIGH** and **LOW** commands in a **FOR...NEXT** loop, and use the index to set the I/O pin, high, then low again.

- √ Enter and run SegmentTestWithHighLow.bs2.
- √ Verify that every segment in the 7-segement LED display lights briefly, turning on and then off again.
- √ Record a list of which segment each I/O pin controls.

## Example Program: SegmentTestWithHighLow.bs2

```
' What's a Microcontroller - SegmentTestWithHighLow.bs2
' Individually test each segment in a 7-Segment LED display.
```

```
'{$STAMP BS2}
'{$PBASIC 2.5}

pinCounter      VAR      Nib

DEBUG "I/O Pin", CR,
      "-------", CR

FOR pinCounter = 8 TO 15

  DEBUG DEC2 pinCounter, CR
  HIGH pinCounter
  PAUSE 1000
  LOW pinCounter

NEXT
```

### Your Turn – A Different Pattern

Removing the command LOW pinCounter will have an interesting effect:

√   Comment the LOW pinCounter command by adding an apostrophe to the left of it.

√   Run the modified program and observe the effect.

## ACTIVITY #3: DISPLAYING DIGITS

If you include the decimal point there are eight different BASIC Stamp I/O pins that send high/low signals to the 7-segment LED display. That's eight different HIGH or LOW commands just to display one number. If you want to count from zero to nine, that would be a huge amount of programming. Fortunately, there are special variables you can use to set the high and low values for groups of I/O pins.

In this activity, you will use 8-digit binary numbers instead of HIGH and LOW commands to control the high/low signals sent by BASIC Stamp I/O pins. By setting special variables called DIRH and OUTH equal to the binary numbers, you will be able to control the high/low signals sent by all the I/O pins connected to the 7-segment LED display circuit with a single PBASIC command.

> **8 bits:** A binary number that has 8 digits is said to have 8 bits. Each bit is a slot where you can store either a 1 or a 0.
>
> **A byte** is a variable that contains 8 bits. There are 256 different combinations of zeros and ones that you can use to count from 0 to 255 using 8 bits. This is why a byte variable can store a number between 0 and 255.

### Parts and Circuit for Displaying Digits

Same as previous activity

### Programming On/Off Patterns Using Binary Numbers

In this activity, you will experiment with the variables **DIRH** and **OUTH**. **DIRH** is a variable that controls the direction (input or output) of I/O pins P8 through P15. **OUTH** controls the high or low signals that each I/O pin sends. As you will soon see, **OUTH** is especially useful because you can use it to set the high/low signals at eight different I/O pins at once with just one command. Here is an example program that shows how these two variables can be used to count from 0 to 9 on the 7-segment LED display without using **HIGH** and **LOW** commands:

### Example Program: DisplayDigits.bs2

This example program will cycle the 7-Segment LED display through the digits 0 through 9.

  √   Enter and run DisplayDigits.bs2.
  √   Verify that the digits 0 through 9 are displayed.

```
' What's a Microcontroller - DisplayDigits.bs2
' Display the digits 0 through 9 on a 7-segment LED display.

'{$STAMP BS2}
'{$PBASIC 2.5}

DEBUG "Program Running!"

OUTH = %00000000                        ' OUTH initialized to low.
DIRH = %11111111                        ' Set P8-P15 to all output-low.
                                        ' Digit:
'        BAFG.CDE
OUTH = %11100111                        ' 0
PAUSE 1000
OUTH = %10000100                        ' 1
```

```
PAUSE 1000
OUTH = %11010011                          ' 2
PAUSE 1000
OUTH = %11010110                          ' 3
PAUSE 1000
OUTH = %10110100                          ' 4
PAUSE 1000
OUTH = %01110110                          ' 5
PAUSE 1000
OUTH = %01110111                          ' 6
PAUSE 1000
OUTH = %11000100                          ' 7
PAUSE 1000
OUTH = %11110111                          ' 8
PAUSE 1000
OUTH = %11110110                          ' 9
PAUSE 1000

DIRH = %00000000                          ' I/O pins to input,
                                          ' segments off.
END
```

### How DisplayDigits.bs2 Works

Figure 6-12 shows how you can use the DIRH and OUTH variables to control the direction and state (high/low) of I/O pins P8 through P15.

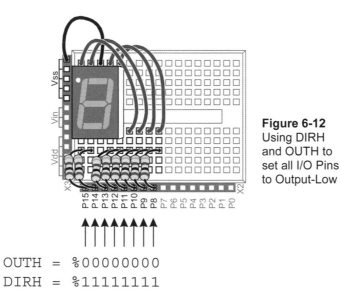

**Figure 6-12**
Using DIRH and OUTH to set all I/O Pins to Output-Low

```
OUTH = %00000000
DIRH = %11111111
```

The first command:

```
OUTH = %00000000
```

gets all the I/O pins (P8 through P15) ready to send the low signals. If they all send low signals, it will turn all the LEDs in the 7-segment LED display off. If you wanted all the I/O pins to send the high signal, you could use **OUTH = %11111111** instead.

**What does % do?** The % is used to tell the BASIC Stamp Editor that the number is a binary number. For example, the binary number %00001100 is the same as the decimal number 12. As you will see in this activity, binary numbers can make many programming tasks much easier.

The low signals will not actually be sent by the I/O pins until you use the **DIRH** variable to change all the I/O pins from input to output. The command:

```
DIRH = %11111111
```

sets all I/O pins P8 through P15 to output. As soon as this command is executed, P8 through P15 all start sending the low signal. This is because the command **OUTH = %00000000** was executed just before this **DIRH** command. As soon as the **DIRH** command set all the I/O pins to output, they started sending their low signals. You can also use **DIRH = %00000000** to change all the I/O pins back to inputs.

**Before I/O pins become outputs:** Up until the I/O pins are changed from input to output, they just listen for signals and update the **INH** variable. This is the variable that contains **IN8**, **IN9**, up through **IN15**. These variables can be used the same way that **IN3** and **IN4** were used for reading pushbuttons in Chapter #3.

**All BASIC Stamp I/O pins start out as inputs.** This is called a "default". You have to tell a BASIC Stamp I/O pin to become an output before it starts sending a high or low signal. Both the **HIGH** and **LOW** commands automatically change a BASIC Stamp I/O pin's direction to output. Placing a 1 in the **DIRH** variable also makes one of the I/O pins an output.

Figure 6-13 shows how to use the **OUTH** variable to selectively send high and low signals to P8 through P15. A binary-1 is used to send a high signal, and a binary-0 is used to send a low signal. This example displays the number three on the 7-segment LED display:

```
'        BAFG.CDE
OUTH = %11010110
```

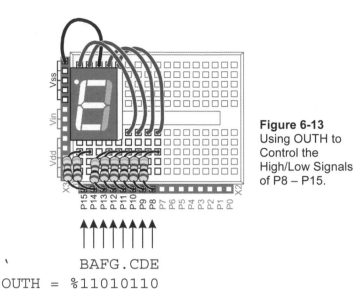

**Figure 6-13**
Using OUTH to
Control the
High/Low Signals
of P8 – P15.

```
`              BAFG.CDE
OUTH  =  %11010110
```

The display is turned so that the three on the display is upside-down because it more clearly shows how the values in **OUTH** line up with the I/O pins. The command **OUTH = %11010110** uses binary zeros to set I/O pins P8, P11, and P13 low, and it uses binary ones to set P9, P10, P12, P14 and P15 high. The line just before the command is a comment that shows the segment labels line up with the binary value that turns that segment on/off. The next example program shows how to set **OUTH** to binary numbers to make the 7-segment LED display count from zero to nine.

 **Inside the HIGH and LOW commands:** The command **HIGH 15** is really the same as **OUT15 = 1** followed by **DIR15 = 1**. Likewise, the command **LOW 15** is the same as **OUT15 = 1** followed by **DIR15 = 1**. If you want to change P15 back to an input, use **DIR15 = 0**. You can then use **IN15** to detect (instead of send) high/low signals.

### Your Turn – Displaying A through F

√   Figure out what bit patterns (combinations of zeros and ones) you will need to display the letters A, b, C, d, E, and F.

√   Modify SevenSegment0to9 so that it displays A, b, C, d, E, F.

**Decimal vs. Hexadecimal** The basic digits in the decimal (base-10) number system are: 0, 1, 2, 3, 4, 5, 6, 7, 8, and 9. In the hexadecimal (base-16) number system the basic digits are: 0, 1, 2, 3, 4, 5, 6, 7, 8, 9, A, b, C, d, E, F. Base-16 is used extensively in both computer and microcontroller programming. Once you figure out how to display the characters A through F, you can further modify your program to count in hexadecimal from 0 to F.

### Keeping Lists of On/Off Patterns

The LOOKUP command makes writing code for 7-segment LED display patterns much easier. The LOOKUP command lets you "look up" elements in a list. Here is a code example that uses the LOOKUP command:

```
LOOKUP index, [7, 85, 19, 167, 28], value
```

There are two variables used in this command, **index** and **value**. If the **index** is 0, **value** stores the **7**. If **index** is **1**, the **value** stores **85**. Since **index** is 2, in this example, the LOOKUP command places **19** into **value**, and that's what the Debug Terminal displays.

### Example Program: SimpleLookup.bs2

√ Enter and run SimpleLookup.bs2.
√ Run the program as-is, with the **index** variable set equal to 2.
√ Try setting the **index** variable equal to numbers between 0 and 4.
√ Re-run the program after each change to the **index** variable and note which value from the list gets placed in the **value** variable.
√ Optional: Modify the program by placing the LOOKUP command in a FOR...NEXT loop that counts from 0 to 4.

```
' What's a Microcontroller - SimpleLookup.bs2
' Debug a value using an index and a lookup table.

' {$STAMP BS2}
' {$PBASIC 2.5}

value           VAR     Byte
index           VAR     Nib

index = 2

DEBUG ? index

LOOKUP index, [7, 85, 19, 167, 28], value
```

```
DEBUG ? value, CR

DEBUG "Change the index variable to a ", CR,
      "different number(between 0 and 4).", CR, CR,

      "Run the modified program and ", CR,
      "check to see what number the", CR,
      "LOOKUP command places in the", CR,
      "value variable."

END
```

### Example Program: DisplayDigitsWithLookup.bs2

This example program shows how the LOOKUP command can come in really handy for storing the bit patterns used in the OUTH variable. Again, the **index** is used to choose which binary value is placed into the OUTH variable. This example program counts from 0 to 9 again. The difference between this program and DisplayDigits.bs2 is that this program is much more versatile. It is much quicker and easier to adjust for different number sequences using lookup tables.

√   Enter and run DisplayDigitsWithLookup.bs2.
√   Verify that it does the same thing as the previous program (with much less work).
√   Take a look at the Debug Terminal while the program runs. It shows how the value of **index** is used by the LOOKUP command to load the correct binary value from the list into OUTH.

```
' What's a Microcontroller - DisplayDigitsWithLookup.bs2
' Use a lookup table to store and display digits with a 7-segment LED display.

'{$STAMP BS2}
'{$PBASIC 2.5}

index           VAR     Nib

OUTH = %00000000
DIRH = %11111111

DEBUG "index  OUTH    ", CR,
      "-----  --------", CR

FOR index = 0 TO 9

  LOOKUP index, [ %11100111, %10000100, %11010011,
                  %11010110, %10110100, %01110110,
```

```
                %01110111, %11000100, %11110111, %11110110 ], OUTH

  DEBUG "   ", DEC2 index, "   ", BIN8 OUTH, CR

  PAUSE 1000

NEXT

DIRH = %00000000

END
```

### Your Turn – Displaying 0 through F Again

√ Modify DisplayDigitsWithLookup.bs2 so that it counts from 0 through F in hexadecimal. Don't forget to update the **FOR...NEXT** loop's **start** and **end** values.

## ACTIVITY #4: DISPLAYING THE POSITION OF A DIAL

In Chapter #5, Activity #4 you used the potentiometer to control the position of a servo. In this activity, you will display the position of the potentiometer using the 7-segment LED display.

### Dial and Display Parts

(1) 7-segment LED display
(8) Resistors – 1 kΩ (brown-black-red)
(1) Potentiometer – 10 kΩ
(1) Resistor – 220 Ω (red-red-brown)
(1) Capacitor – 0.1 µF
(7) Jumper wires

### Building the Dial and Display Circuits

Figure 6-14 shows a schematic of the potentiometer circuit that should be added to the project. Figure 6-15 shows a wiring diagram of the circuit from Figure 6-14 combined with the circuit from Figure 6-10 on Page 172.

√ Add the potentiometer circuit to the 7-segment LED display circuit as shown in Figure 6-15.

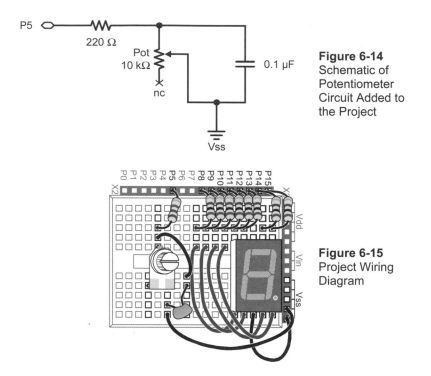

**Figure 6-14**
Schematic of
Potentiometer
Circuit Added to
the Project

**Figure 6-15**
Project Wiring
Diagram

## Programming the Dial and Display

There is a useful command called the LOOKDOWN, and yes, it is the reverse of the LOOKUP command. While the LOOKUP command gives you a number based on an index, the LOOKDOWN command gives you an index based on a number.

### Example Program: SimpleLookdown.bs2

This example program demonstrates how the LOOKDOWN command works.

√   Enter and run SimpleLookdown.bs2.
√   Run the program as-is, with the **value** variable set equal to 167, and use the Debug Terminal to observe the value of **index**.
√   Try setting the **value** variable equal to each of the other numbers listed by the LOOKDOWN command: 7, 85, 19, 28.

√ Re-run the program after each change to the **value** variable and note which value from the list gets placed in the **index** variable.

Unless you tell it to make a different kind of comparison, the LOOKDOWN command checks to see if a value is equal to an entry in the list. You can also check to see if a value is greater than, less than or equal to, etc. For example, to search for an entry that is less than or equal to the value variable, use the **<=** operator just before the first bracket that starts the list.

√ Modify SimpleLookdown.bs2 by substituting this **value** and LOOKDOWN statement:

```
value = 35
LOOKDOWN value, <= [ 7, 19, 28, 85, 167 ], index
```

√ Experiment with different values and see if the index variable displays what you would expect.

**Trick question:** What happens if your value is greater than 167? This little twist in the LOOKDOWN command can cause problems because the LOOKDOWN command doesn't make any changes to the index.

```
' What's a Microcontroller - SimpleLookdown.bs2
' Debug an index using a value and a lookup table.

' {$STAMP BS2}
' {$PBASIC 2.5}

value           VAR     Byte
index           VAR     Nib

value = 167

DEBUG ? value

LOOKDOWN value, [7, 85, 19, 167, 28], index

DEBUG ? index, CR

DEBUG "Change the value variable to a ", CR,
      "different number in this list:", CR,
      "7, 85, 19, 167, or 28.", CR, CR,

      "Run the modified program and ", CR,
```

```
        "check to see what number the ", CR,
        "LOOKDOWN command places in the ", CR,
        "index variable."

END
```

## Example Program: DialDisplay.bs2

This example program mirrors the position of the potentiometer's knob by lighting segments around the outside of the 7-segment LED display as shown in Figure 6-16.

**Figure 6-16**
Displaying the Potentiometer's Position with the 7-Segment LED Display

√    Enter and run DialDisplay.bs2.

√    Twist the potentiometer's input shaft and make sure it works.

√    When you run the example program, it may not be as precise as shown in Figure 6-16. Adjust the values in the lookdown table so that that the digital display more accurately depicts the position of the potentiometer.

```
' What's a Microcontroller - DialDisplay.bs2
' Display POT position using 7-segment LED display.

'{$STAMP BS2}
'{$PBASIC 2.5}

DEBUG "Program Running!"

index          VAR     Nib
time           VAR     Word

OUTH = %00000000
DIRH = %11111111

DO

  HIGH 5
  PAUSE 100
  RCTIME 5, 1, time
```

```
  LOOKDOWN time, <= [40, 150, 275, 400, 550, 800], index

  LOOKUP index, [ %11100101, %11100001, %01100001,
                  %00100001, %00000001, %00000000 ], OUTH

LOOP
```

### How DialDisplay.bs2 Works

This example program takes an **RCTIME** measurement of the potentiometer and stores it in a variable named **time**.

```
            HIGH 5
            PAUSE 100
            RCTIME 5, 1, time
```

The **time** variable is then used in a **LOOKDOWN** table. The **LOOKDOWN** table decides which number in the list **time** is smaller than, then loads the entry number (0 to 5 in this case) into the **index** variable.

```
            LOOKDOWN time, <= [40, 150, 275, 400, 550, 800], index
```

Then, the **index** variable is used in a **LOOKUP** table to choose the binary value to load into the **OUTH** variable.

```
            LOOKUP index, [ %11100101, %11100001, %01100001,
                            %00100001, %00000001, %00000000 ], OUTH
```

### Your Turn – Adding a Segment

DialDisplay.bs2 only makes five of the six segments turn on when you turn the dial. The sequence for turning the LEDs on in DialDisplay.bs2 is E, F, A, B, C, but not D.

√   Save DialDisplay.bs2 under the name DialDisplayYourTurn.bs2.
√   Modify DialDisplayYourTurn.bs2 so that it causes all six outer LEDs to turn on in sequence as the potentiometer is turned. The sequence should be: E, F, A, B, C, and D.

## SUMMARY

This chapter introduced the 7-segment LED display, and how to read a pin map. This chapter also introduced some techniques for devices and circuits that have parallel inputs. The **DIRH** and **OUTH** variables were introduced as a means of controlling the values of BASIC Stamp I/O pins P8 through P15. The **LOOKUP** and **LOOKDOWN** commands were introduced as a means for referencing the lists of values used to display letters and numbers.

### Questions

1. In a 7-segment LED display, what is the active ingredient that makes the display readable when a microcontroller sends a high or low signal?
2. What does common cathode mean? What do you think common anode means?
3. What is the group of wires that conduct signals to and from a parallel device called?
4. What are the names of the commands in this chapter that are used to handle lists of values?

### Exercises

1. Write an **OUTH** command to set P8, P10, P12 high and P9, P11, P13 low. Assuming all your I/O pins started as inputs, write the **DIRH** command that will cause the I/O pins to send high/low signals while leaving P14, P15 configured as inputs.
2. Write the values of **OUTH** required to make the letters: a, C, d, F, H, I, n, P, S.

### Project

1. Spell "FISH CHIPS And dIP" over and over again with your 7-segment LED display. Make each letter last for 400 ms.

### Solutions

Q1. The active ingredient is an LED.

Q2. Common cathode means that all the cathodes are connected together, i.e., they share a common connection point. Common anode would mean that all the anodes are connected together.

Q3. A parallel bus.

Q4. **LOOKUP** and **LOOKDOWN** handle list of values.

E1. The first step for configuring OUTH is set to "1" in each bit position specified as HIGH. So bits 8, 10, and 12 get set to "1". Then put a "0" for each LOW, so bits 9, 11, and 13 get a "0", as shown. To configure DIRH, the specified pins, 8, 10, 12, 9, 11, and 13 must be set as outputs by setting those bit to "1". 15 and 14 are configured as inputs by placing zeroes in bits 15 and 14. The second step is to translate this to a PBASIC statement.

```
Bit  15 14 13 12 11 10  9  8    Bit  15 14 13 12 11 10  9  8
OUTH  0  0  0  1  0  1  0  1    DIRH  0  0  1  1  1  1  1  1
```

**OUTH = %00010101**                **DIRH = %00111111**

6

E2. The key to solving this problem is to draw out each letter and note which segments must be lit. Place a 1 in every segment that is to be lit. Translate that to the binary OUTH value.

| Letter | LED Segments | B A F G . C D E | OUTL Value = | |
|--------|--------------|-----------------|--------------|---|
| a | e, f, a, b, c, g | 1 1 1 1 0 1 0 1 | %11110101 | Common Cathode |
| C | a, f, e, d | 0 1 1 0 0 0 1 1 | %01100011 | 10 9 8 7 6 |
| d | b, c, d, e, g | 1 0 0 1 0 1 1 1 | %10010111 | G F A B |
| F | a, f, e, g | 0 1 1 1 0 0 0 1 | %01110001 | |
| H | f, e, b, c, g | 1 0 1 1 0 1 0 1 | %10110101 | |
| I | f, e | 0 0 1 0 0 0 0 1 | %00100001 | |
| n | e, g, c | 0 0 0 1 0 1 0 1 | %00010101 | |
| P | all but d and e | 1 1 1 1 0 0 0 1 | %11110001 | E D C DP |
| S | a, f, g, c, d | 0 1 1 1 0 1 1 0 | %01110110 | 1 2 3 4 5 |
| | | | From Figure 6-2, p. 160 | Common Cathode |

P1. Use the Schematic from Figure 6-10 on page 172. To solve this problem, modify DisplayDigitsWithLookup.bs2, using the letter patterns worked out in Exercise 1.
In the solution, the letters have been set up as constants to make the program more intuitive. Using the binary values is fine too, but more prone to errors.

```
' What's a Microcontroller - Ch6Prj01_FishAndChips.bs2
' Use a lookup table to store and display digits with a 7-segment display.
' Spell out the message:  FISH CHIPS And dIP

'{$STAMP BS2}
'{$PBASIC 2.5}
```

```
' Patterns of 7-Segment Display to create letters
A               CON     %11110101
C               CON     %01100011
d               CON     %10010111
F               CON     %01110001
H               CON     %10110101
I               CON     %00100001
n               CON     %00010101
P               CON     %11110001
S               CON     %01110110
space           CON     %00000000

OUTH = %00000000                            ' All off to start
DIRH = %11111111                            ' All LEDs must be outputs

index           VAR     Byte                ' 19 chars in message

DO
  DEBUG "index  OUTH    ", CR,
        "-----  --------", CR

  FOR index = 0 TO 18                        ' 19 chars in message

    LOOKUP index, [ F, I, S, H, space, C, H, I, P, S, space,
                   A, n, d, space, d, I, P, space ], OUTH

    DEBUG "   ", DEC2 index, "   ", BIN8 OUTH, CR

    PAUSE 400                                ' 400 ms between letters

  NEXT
LOOP
```

## Further Investigation

As with all texts cited in this section, this one is available for free download from www.parallax.com.

### "StampWorks", Workbook, Version 1.2, Parallax Inc., 2001

*StampWorks* is written by Nuts & Volts author Jon Williams, and features a wide variety of experiments. This text is a collection of 32 experiments including several that use 7-segment LED displays and other types of displays. This text makes use of the INEX 1000 board, which has many of the components you have used in this text built into it.

# Chapter #7: Measuring Light

## DEVICES THAT CONTAIN LIGHT SENSORS

You have already worked with two different kinds of sensors. The pushbutton can be thought of as a simple pressure sensor, and the potentiometer is a position/rotation sensor. There are many kinds of sensors built into appliances and machines that are not as obvious as a button or a knob. Other common sensors measure things like temperature, smoke, vibration, tilt, and light. Although each of these different kinds of sensors can be found in one or more devices that most people use on a daily basis, light sensors are probably the most common.

One example of an every-day device that contains a light sensor is probably your television. If it can be controlled by a handheld remote, it has a built-in detector for a type of light called infrared that cannot be seen by the human eye. The handheld remote uses infrared light to transmit information about the channel, volume, and other keys that you might press to control the TV. Another common example is a digital camera. A camera's light sensors help it adjust for various lighting conditions so that the picture looks clear regardless of whether it's a sunny or cloudy day.

## INTRODUCING THE PHOTORESISTOR

Light sensors have many different functions, and they come in different shapes, sizes, and with different price tags. Some sensors are designed to sense a particular color of light, such as blue, green, red, or infrared. Some sensors don't care what color the light is because they react to how bright the light is. Other sensors look for only special kinds of light given off by certain chemical reactions. Light sensors also have a variety of ways to tell a microcontroller what they see. Some sensors send a voltage, some send a sequence of binary values, and others react to different kinds of light or light levels by changing resistance.

Of the light sensors that react to light by changing their resistance, the photoresistor shown in Figure 7-1 is probably the most common, least expensive and easiest to use. Its active ingredient is a chemical compound called cadmium sulfide (CdS). This compound changes resistance depending on how bright the light is that shines on its collecting surface. Bright light causes low resistance values between the two leads while dim light causes higher resistance values.

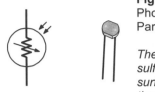

**Figure 7-1**
Photoresistor Schematic and
Part Drawing.

*The photoresistor's cadmium
sulfide coated light collecting
surface is shown at the top of
the part's drawing.*

As with a potentiometer, you can use a photoresistor in an RC-time circuit. The program to read the photoresistor is also about the same as the one used to read the potentiometer. Even though the programming is the same, light is very different from rotation or position. The activities in this chapter focus on applications that use light (instead of position) to give the microcontroller information. Along the way, some PBASIC programming techniques will be introduced that will help you with long term data storage, and with making your programs more manageable and readable.

## ACTIVITY #1: BUILDING AND TESTING THE LIGHT METER

In this activity, you will build and test an RC-time circuit that reads the value of a photoresistor. The RC-time measurement will give you an idea of the light levels sensed by the photoresistor's light collecting surface. As with the potentiometer test, the time values measured by the **RCTIME** command will be displayed in the Debug Terminal.

### Light Detector Test Parts

(1) Photoresistor
(1) Resistor – 220 Ω (red-red-brown)
(1) Capacitor – 0.01 µF
(1) Capacitor – 0.1 µF
(1) Jumper wire

 **Although there are two capacitors in the list of parts,** you will only use one capacitor in the circuit at any given time.

### Building the RC Time Circuit with a Photoresistor

Figure 7-2 shows a schematic of the RC-time circuit you will use in this chapter, and Figure 7-3 shows the wiring diagram. This circuit is different from the potentiometer circuit from Chapter #5, Activity #3 in two ways. First, the I/O pin used to measure the decay time is different (P2). Second, the variable resistor is now a photoresistor instead of a potentiometer.

√ Build the circuit shown in Figure 7-2 and Figure 7-3.

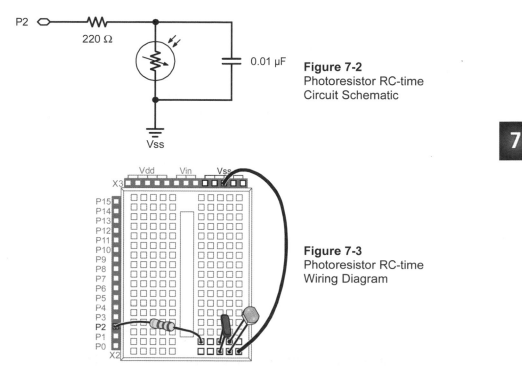

**Figure 7-2**
Photoresistor RC-time
Circuit Schematic

**Figure 7-3**
Photoresistor RC-time
Wiring Diagram

## Programming the Photoresistor Test

The first example program (TestPhotoresistor.bs2) is really just a slightly revised version of ReadPotWithRcTime.bs2 from Chapter #5, Activity #3. The potentiometer circuit from Chapter #5 was connected to I/O pin P7. The circuit in this activity is connected to P2. Because of this difference, the example program has to have two commands updated to make it work. The command that was **HIGH 7**, since the potentiometer circuit was connected to P7, is now **HIGH 2** since the photoresistor circuit is connected to P2. For the same reason, the command that was **RCTIME 7, 1, time** is now **RCTIME 2, 1, time**.

### Example Program: TestPhotoresistor.bs2

Instead of twisting the potentiometer's knob, the circuit is tested by exposing the light collecting surface of the photoresistor to different light levels. When the example program is running, the Debug Terminal should display small values for bright light conditions and large values for low light conditions.

> √ Enter and run TestPhotoresistor.bs2.
> √ While watching the value of the **time** variable on the Debug Terminal note the value under normal lighting conditions.
> √ Turn the lights in the room off or cast a shadow over the circuit with your hand and check the **time** variable again. It should be a significantly larger number.
> √ If you face the photoresistor's light collecting surface toward direct sunlight, the **time** variable should be fairly small.

```
' What's a Microcontroller - TestPhotoresistor.bs2
' Read photoresistor in RC-time circuit using RCTIME command.

' {$STAMP BS2}
' {$PBASIC 2.5}

time            VAR     Word

DO

  HIGH 2
  PAUSE 100
  RCTIME 2, 1, time
  DEBUG HOME, "time =  ", DEC5 time

LOOP
```

### Your Turn – Using a Different Capacitor for Different Light Conditions

Replacing the 0.01 µF capacitor with a 0.1 µF capacitor can be useful for more brightly lit rooms or outdoors. The time measurements with the 0.1 µF capacitor will take ten times as long, which means the value of the **time** variable displayed by the Debug Terminal should be ten times as large.

> √ Modify the circuit by replacing the 0.01 µF capacitor with a 0.1 µF capacitor.
> √ Re-run TestPhotoresistor.bs2 and verify that the RC-time measurements are roughly ten times their former values.

√ Before you move on to the next activity, return the circuit to the original one shown in Figure 7-2 by removing the 0.1 µF capacitor and replacing it with the 0.01 µF capacitor.

## ACTIVITY #2: GRAPHING LIGHT MEASUREMENTS

Factories often have to monitor many sensor inputs to make sure the products they make turn out right. From light levels in a greenhouse to fluid levels in an oil refinery to temperature levels in a nuclear reactor, the people responsible for controlling these levels often rely on graphs of the sensor measurements to get the information they need.

### Introducing Stamp Plot Lite

Figure 7-4 shows Stamp Plot Lite software graphing RC-time measurements sent by the BASIC Stamp. The line shown in Figure 7-4 is much easier to understand than the 250 RC-time measurements that were used to plot that line. Viewing the graph from left to right, the RC-time measurements gradually get larger and then suddenly drop off. Since RC-time measurements get larger when the light levels decrease and smaller when they increase, the graph tells a story. It looks like the light level being measured declined gradually, and then it suddenly increased again.

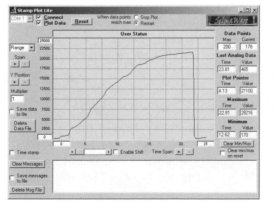

**Figure 7-4**
Stamp Plot Lite
Graphing
Measured Light
Levels

This graph could depict any number of scenarios to the technician reading it. Perhaps a microcontroller in a greenhouse switched on the artificial lights after the sunlight dropped below a certain level. Perhaps a system of motors and gears that maintains a solar panel's position for maximum sunlight exposure just readjusted the panel's position after detecting a decrease in light exposure. Regardless of the scenario, if you are familiar with the measurement being graphed, tools like Stamp Plot Lite can really help make sense out of data. It does this by converting lists of measurements into a graph.

 **Stamp Plot Lite** is free for educational use courtesy of SelmaWare Solutions and can be installed from the Parallax CD or downloaded from the Parallax web site or directly from http://www.selmaware.com/.

### Downloading and Installing Stamp Plot Lite

Before installing Stamp Plot Lite, you must have WinZip installed on your PC or laptop. WinZip can be installed from the Parallax CD or downloaded from www.winzip.com. Below are instructions for downloading and installing Stamp Plot Lite from the Parallax web site:

√    Go to the Downloads area at www.parallax.com.
√    Select BASIC Stamp Software.
√    Download the file labeled "**Stamp Plot Lite** graphing utility…"
√    Save StampPlot.zip to your disk.
√    Open StampPlot.zip by double-clicking it.
√    If you are using the WinZip wizard, follow the screen prompts, and it will run the installation program. If you are using WinZip classic, you will have to double-click Setup.exe to start the installation.
√    Follow the Stamp Plot Lite installation program's prompts to install the software.

### Programming to Send Measurements to Stamp Plot Lite

Sending values you want to graph in Stamp Plot Lite is almost the same as sending numbers to the Debug Terminal, but there are a few rules. First, values are sent using only the **DEC** formatter and the **CR** control character. We want to plot the value of the **time** variable, so all that should be sent to the Debug Terminal is the decimal value followed by a carriage return.

```
DEBUG DEC time, CR
```

You can also send display settings to Stamp Plot Lite by sending special messages in quotes. These messages are called control codes. Control codes are sent to Stamp Plot Lite at the beginning of a PBASIC program. Although you can click and adjust all the settings on the software itself, it is usually easier to program the BASIC Stamp to tell

Stamp Plot Lite those settings for you. Here is an example of some configuration settings from the next example program that will make your RC-time measurements easier to read without any adjustments to Stamp Plot Lite's display settings.

```
DEBUG "!AMAX 1250", CR,
      "!TMAX 25", CR,
      "!TMIN 0", CR,
      "!SHFT ON", CR,
      "!RSET",CR
```

 **For more information** on how to send values and control codes to Stamp Plot Lite, run Stamp Pot Lite's Help file. Click Start, select programs, select Stamp Plot, then click Stamp Plot Help.

### Example Program: PlotPhotoresistor.bs2

Follow these steps to plot the photoresistor data:

√ Use the BASIC Stamp Editor to enter and run PlotPhotoresistor.bs2.
√ Verify that there is a single column of values scrolling down the Debug Terminal. Figure 7-5 shows an example.

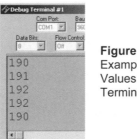

**Figure 7-5**
Example of Scrolling Values in the Debug Terminal.

√ Make a note of the COM number in the COM Port field in the upper left hand corner of the Debug Terminal.
√ Use the Windows Start Menu to run Stamp Plot Lite. Click *Start*, then select *Programs → Stamp Plot → Stamp Plot Lite*.
√ Set the COM Port field in Stamp Plot Lite to that same value. Figure 7-6 shows an example where the value is COM1 in the Debug Terminal, so Stamp Plot is also set to COM1. Your COM port value may be a different number.

Just check to see what the number is in the Debug Terminal, then set Stamp Plot Lite to that number.

√ Close the Debug Terminal (click the *X* button on the top-right or click the *Close* button near the bottom of the window).

√ In the Stamp Plot Lite window, click *Connect*, then click *Plot Data*. Checkmarks should appear in each box after you click it.

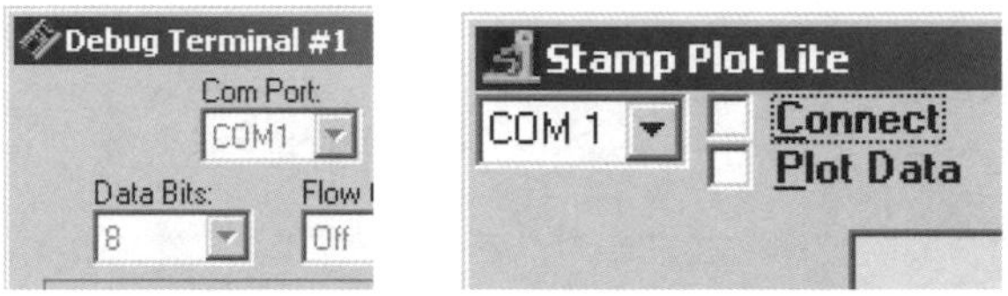

**Figure 7-6**
COM Port Settings

*Debug Terminal (left) and Stamp Plot Lite (right).*

√ Press and release the Reset button on your Board of Education or HomeWork Board. This starts the BASIC Stamp program over from the beginning, which sends the DEBUG commands that configure Stamp Plot Lite.

√ The data will start graphing as soon as you click Plot Data. Hold you hand over the photoresistor at different distances to simulate different lighting conditions. Remember, the darker the shadow you cast, the higher the value in the graph; the brighter the light, the smaller the value.

---

**IMPORTANT: Only one program can use a COM port at one time.**

Before attempting to run a different program using the BASIC Stamp Editor, you must uncheck the *Connect* and *Plot Data* checkboxes in Stamp Plot Lite.

Before reconnecting Stamp Plot Lite (by clicking the Connect and Plot Data checkboxes), you must close the Debug Terminal.

---

```
' What's a Microcontroller - PlotPhotoresistor.bs2
' Graph light levels using Stamp Plot Lite.

' {$STAMP BS2}
' {$PBASIC 2.5}

time            VAR     Word

DEBUG "!AMAX 1250", CR,
      "!TMAX 25", CR,
      "!TMIN 0", CR,
      "!SHFT ON", CR,
      "!RSET",CR
```

```
DO

  HIGH 2
  PAUSE 100
  RCTIME 2, 1, time
  DEBUG DEC time, CR

LOOP
```

### Your Turn – Adjusting the Display

Span and Time Span have + and – buttons that you can click to increase or decrease the vertical and horizontal scales. Span is to the left of the area that displays the graph, and you can use it to adjust the maximum and minimum values displayed on the graph. Time Span is below the graph, and you can use it to change how many seconds worth of values plotted in the window.

√   Experiment with increasing and decreasing these values and note their effects on the how the graph appears.

If you have difficulty finding your plot, you can always press and release the Reset button on your Board of Education or BASIC Stamp HomeWork Board to restore the default settings.

### ACTIVITY #3: TRACKING LIGHT EVENTS

One of the more useful features of the BASIC Stamp module's program memory is that you can disconnect the power, but the program is not lost. As soon as you reconnect power, the program starts running again from the beginning. Any portion of the program memory that is not used for the program can be used to store data. This memory is especially good for storing data that you do not want the BASIC Stamp to forget, even if power is disconnected and reconnected.

The chip on the BASIC Stamp that stores program memory and data is shown in Figure 7-7. This chip is called an EEPROM. EEPROM stands for electrically erasable programmable read-only memory. That's quite a mouthful, and pronouncing each of the first letters in EEPROM isn't much better. When people talk about an EEPROM, it is usually pronounced "E-E-Prom".

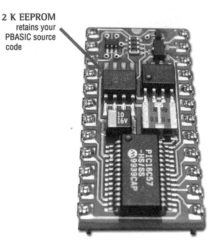

**2 K EEPROM**
retains your
PBASIC source
code

**Figure 7-7**
EEPROM Chip
on BASIC Stamp

Figure 7-8 shows a window called Memory Map. You can view this window by clicking *Run* and selecting *Memory Map*. The Memory Map uses different colors to show how both the BASIC Stamp module's RAM (variables) and EEPROM (program memory) are being used. The EEPROM Map has two graphs. The bar at the far left shows that only a small fraction of the program memory is used to store the photoresistor program from Activity #2. By scrolling to the bottom of the EEPROM Map's main window and counting the bytes highlighted in blue, you will find that only 101 bytes out of the 2048 byte EEPROM are used for the program. The remaining 1947 bytes are free to store data.

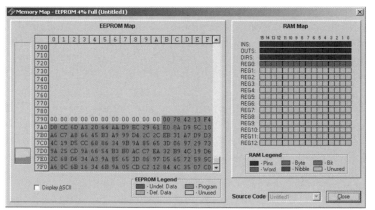

**Figure 7-8**
Memory Map

*To view this window, click Run, and select Memory Map.*

> **2048 bytes = 2 KB.** You can use 2048 bytes to store 2048 different numbers, each of which can store a value between 0 and 255.
>
> The upper-case 'B' stands for bytes. A lower-case 'b' stands for bits. This can make a big difference because 2048 Kb means that 2048 different numbers, but each number is limited to a value of either 0 or 1.
>
> Although both the upper case 'K' and the lower-case 'k' are called kilo, they are slightly different. The upper-case 'K' is used to indicate a binary kilobyte, which is $1 \times 2^{10} = 1024$. When referring to exactly 2000 bytes, you can use the lower-case k, which stands for kilo
>
> $(1 \times 10^3 = 1000)$ in the metric system.

Using the EEPROM for data storage can be very useful for remote applications. One example of a remote application would be a temperature monitor placed in a truck that hauls frozen food. A second example is a weather monitoring station. One of the pieces of data a weather station might store for later retrieval is light levels.

Since we are using a photoresistor to measure light levels, this activity introduces a technique for storing measured light levels to, and retrieving them back from the EEPROM. In this activity, you will run one PBASIC example program that stores a series of light measurements in the BASIC Stamp module's EEPROM. After that program is finished, you will run a second program that retrieves the values from EEPROM and displays them in the Debug Terminal.

### Programming Long Term Data Storage

The **WRITE** command is used to store values in the EEPROM, and the **READ** command is used to retrieve those values.

The syntax for the **WRITE** command is:

**WRITE** *Location, {WORD} Data Item*

For example, if you want to write the value 195 to address 7 in the EEPROM, you could use the command:

```
WRITE 7, 195
```

Word values can be anywhere between 0 and 65565 while byte values can only contain numbers between 0 and 255. A word value takes the space of two bytes. If you want to write a word size value to EEPROM, you have to use the optional **word** modifier. Be careful though. Since a word takes two bytes, you have to skip one of the byte size addresses in EEPROM before you can write another word. Let's say you need to save two word values to EEPROM: 659 and 50012.  You could start at address 8, but you will have to write the second value to address 10.

```
WRITE 8, Word 659
WRITE 10, Word 50012
```

**Is it possible to write over the program?** Yes, and if you do, the program is likely to either start behaving strangely or stop running altogether.  Since the PBASIC program tokens reside in the highest addresses in the EEPROM, it's best to use the lowest *Address* values for storing numbers with the **WRITE** command.

**How do I know if the *Address* I'm using is too large?** You can use the memory map to figure out the highest value not used by your PBASIC program.  The numbers on the left side of the main Memory Map graph shown in Figure 7-8 on page 198 are hexadecimal numbers, and 79A is the highest value not occupied by a program token.  Hexadecimal means base-16, so 79A is really:

$$7 \times 16^2 + 9 \times 16^1 + A \times 16^0$$

$$= 7 \times 16^2 + 9 \times 16^1 + 10 \times 16^0$$

$$= 7 \times 256 + 9 \times 16 + 10 \times 1$$

$$= 1946.$$

**Why does this add up ot 1946 instead of 1947?**  There are 1947 total addresses free, but they are numbered Address 0 through Address 1946.  You can also program the BASIC Stamp to make this conversion for you using the **DEBUG** command's **DEC** formatter and the **$** hexadecimal operator like this:

```
DEBUG DEC $79A
```

For a reminder about hexadecimal numbers, see the information box on page 179.

### Example Program: StoreLightMeasurementsInEeprom.bs2

This example program demonstrates how to use the **WRITE** command by taking light measurements every 5 seconds for 2 ½ minutes and storing them in EEPROM.

√   Enter and run StoreLightMeasurementsToEeprom.bs2 .
√   Record the measurements displayed on the Debug Terminal so that you can verify the measurements read back from the EEPROM.

**Gradually increase the shade** over the photoresistor during the 2 ½ minute test period for meaningful data.

```
' What's a Microcontroller - StoreLightMeasurementsInEeprom.bs2
' Write light measurements to EEPROM.

' {$STAMP BS2}
' {$PBASIC 2.5}

time            VAR     Word
eepromAddress   VAR     Byte

DEBUG "Starting measurements...", CR, CR,
      "Measurement    Value", CR,
      "-----------    -----", CR

PAUSE 1000

FOR eepromAddress = 0 TO 58 STEP 2
  HIGH 2
  PAUSE 5000
  RCTIME 2, 1, time
  DEBUG DEC2 eepromAddress,
        "              ", DEC time, CR
  WRITE eepromAddress, Word time
NEXT

DEBUG "All done.  Now, run:", CR,
      "ReadLightMeasurementsFromEeprom.bs2"
END
```

### How StoreLightMeasurementsInEeprom.bs2 Works

The **FOR...NEXT** loop that measures the RC-time values and stores them to EEPROM has to count in steps of 2 because word values are written into the EEPROM.

```
FOR eepromAddress = 0 to 58 STEP 2
```

The **RCTIME** command loads the time measurement into the word size **time** variable.

```
RCTIME 2, 1, time
```

The **time** variable is stored at the address given by the current value of the **eepromAddress** variable each time through the loop. Remember, the **eepromAddress** variable is incremented by two each time through the loop because a **Word** variable takes up two bytes. The address for a **WRITE** command is always in terms of bytes.

```
WRITE eepromAddress, Word time
NEXT
```

## Programming Data Retrieval

To retrieve these values from EEPROM, you can use the **READ** command. The syntax for the **READ** command is:

>  **READ** *Location, {WORD} Data Item*

While the **WRITE** command can use either a constant or a variable, the **READ** command's **DataItem** argument must be a variable, because it has to store the value fetched from the EEPROM by the **READ** command.

Let's say that the variable **eepromValueA** and **eepromValueB** are **Word** variables, and **littleEE** is a byte variable. Here are some commands to retrieve the values you stored using the write command.

```
READ 7, littleEE
READ 8, Word eepromValueA
READ 10, Word eepromValueB
```

### Example Program: ReadLightMeasurementsFromEeprom.bs2

This example program demonstrates how to use the **READ** command to retrieve the light measurements that were stored in EEPROM by StoreLightMeasurementsInEeprom.bs2.

√  After StoreLightMeasurementsToEeprom.bs2 has completed, disconnect and reconnect the power supply to the BASIC Stamp module to prove that the data is not erased from the module's EEPROM when the power is disconnected. Also, close and re-open the BASIC Stamp Editor.

√  Leave the BASIC Stamp module's power disconnected until you are ready to run ReadLightMeasurementsFromEeprom.bs2; otherwise, it will start taking measurements again.

√  Enter and run ReadLightMeasurementsFromEeprom.bs2.

Compare the table that is displayed by this program with the one displayed by StoreLightMeasurementsInEeprom.bs2, and verify that the values are the same.

```
' What's a Microcontroller - ReadLightMeasurementsFromEeprom.bs2
' Read light measurements from EEPROM.

' {$STAMP BS2}
' {$PBASIC 2.5}

time            VAR     Word
```

```
eepromAddress  VAR      Byte

DEBUG "Retrieving measurements", CR, CR,
      "Measurement    Value", CR,
      "----------    -----", CR

FOR eepromAddress = 0 TO 58 STEP 2
  READ eepromAddress, Word time
  DEBUG DEC2 eepromAddress, "              ", DEC time, CR
NEXT

END
```

### How ReadLightMeasurementsFromEeprom.bs2 Works

As with the **WRITE** command, the **READ** command uses byte-size addresses. Since words are being read from the EEPROM, the **eepromAddress** variable has to have 2 added to it each time through the **FOR...NEXT** loop.

```
        FOR eepromAddress = 0 to 58 STEP 2
```

The **READ** command gets the word size value at **eepromAddress**. This value is loaded into the **time** variable.

```
        READ eepromAddress, Word time
```

The value of the **time** and **eepromAddress** variables are displayed as columns in a table in the Debug Terminal.

```
        DEBUG DEC2 eepromAddress, "              ", DEC time, CR
      NEXT
```

### Your Turn – Plotting the Stored Data

√   Modify ReadLightMeasurementsFromEeprom.bs2 so that it displays the data to Stamp Plot Lite. Remember, the **DEBUG** statement must only display the value and a carriage return.

## ACTIVITY #4: SIMPLE LIGHT METER

Light sensor information can be communicated in a variety of ways. The light meter you will work with in this chapter changes the rate that the display flickers depending on the light intensity it detects.

## Light Meter Parts

(1) Photoresistor
(1) Resistor – 220 Ω (red-red-brown)
(1) Capacitor – 0.01 μF
(1) Capacitor – 0.1 μF
(1) 7-segment LED display
(8) Resistors – 1 kΩ (brown-black-red)
(6) Jumper wires

## Building the Light Meter Circuit

Figure 7-9 shows the 7-segment LED display and photoresistor circuit schematics that will be used to make the light meter, and Figure 7-10 shows a wiring diagram of the circuit. The photoresistor circuit is the same one you have been using in the last two activities, and the 7-segment LED display circuit is the one that was controlled by the BASIC Stamp in Chapter #6.

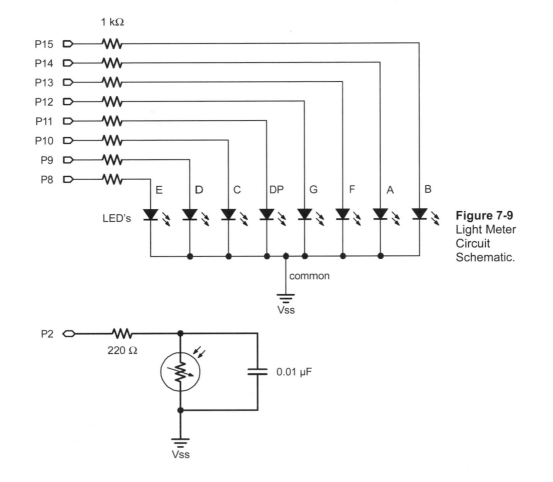

**Figure 7-9**
Light Meter
Circuit
Schematic.

7

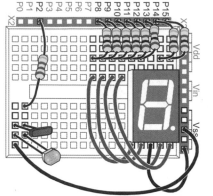

**Figure 7-10**
Wiring Diagram
for Figure 7-9

√ Build the circuit shown in Figure 7-9 and Figure 7-10.
√ Test the 7-segment LED display to make sure it is connected properly using SegmentTestWithHighLow.bs2 from Chapter #6, Activity #2.

## Using Subroutines

Most of the programs you have written so far operate inside a DO...LOOP. Since all the main activity happens inside the DO...LOOP, it is usually called the main routine. As you add more circuits and more useful functions to your program, it can get kind of difficult to keep track of all the code in the main routine. Your programs will be much easier to work with if you organize them into smaller segments of code that do certain jobs. PBASIC has some commands that you can use to make the program jump out of the main routine, do a job, and then return right back to the same spot in the main routine. This will allow you to keep each segment of code that does a particular job somewhere other than your main routine. Each time you need the program to do one of those jobs, you can write a command inside the main routine that tells the program to jump to that job, do it, and come back when the job is done. This process is called executing a subroutine.

Figure 7-11 shows an example of a subroutine and how it's used. The command GOSUB Subroutine_Name causes the program to jump to the Subroutine_Name: label. When the program gets to that label, it keeps running and executing commands until it gets to a RETURN statement. Then, the program goes back to command that comes after the GOSUB command. In the case of the example in Figure 7-11, the next command is: DEBUG "Next command".

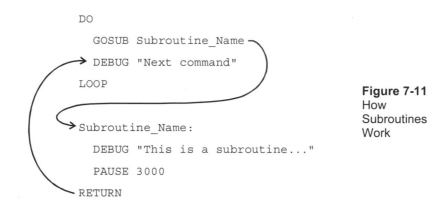

```
   DO

      GOSUB Subroutine_Name

      DEBUG "Next command"

      LOOP


   Subroutine_Name:

      DEBUG "This is a subroutine..."

      PAUSE 3000

   RETURN
```

**Figure 7-11**
How
Subroutines
Work

7

**What's a label?** A label is a name that can be used as a placeholder in your program. **GOSUB** is one of the commands you can use to jump to a label. Some others are **GOTO**, **ON GOTO**, and **ON GOSUB**. You can use these commands to jump to labels. A label must end with a colon, and for the sake of style, separate words with the underscore character. When picking a name for a label, make sure not to use a reserved word. The rest of the rules for a label name are the same as the ones for naming variables listed in the information box on page 53.

### Example Program: SimpleSubroutines.bs2

This example program shows how subroutines work by sending messages to the Debug Terminal.

√    Examine SimpleSubroutines.bs2 and try to guess the order in which the **DEBUG** commands will be executed.
√    Enter and run the program.
√    Compare the program's actual behavior with your predictions.

```
' What's a Microcontroller - SimpleSubroutines.bs2
' Demonstrate how subroutines work.

' {$STAMP BS2}
' {$PBASIC 2.5}

DO

  DEBUG CLS, "Start main routine.", CR
```

```
  PAUSE 2000
  GOSUB First_Subroutine
  DEBUG "Back in main.", CR
  PAUSE 2000
  GOSUB Second_Subroutine
  DEBUG "Repeat main...", CR
  PAUSE 2000

LOOP


First_Subroutine:

  DEBUG "  Executing first "
  DEBUG "subroutine.", CR
  PAUSE 3000

RETURN


Second_Subroutine:

  DEBUG "  Executing second "
  DEBUG "subroutine.", CR
  PAUSE 3000

RETURN
```

### How SimpleSubroutines.bs2 Works

Figure 7-12 shows how the `First_Subroutine` call in the main routine (the `DO...LOOP`) works. The command `GOSUB First_Subroutine` sends the program to the `First_Subroutine:` label. The three commands inside that subroutine are executed. When the program gets to the `RETURN` statement, it jumps back to the command that comes right after the `GOSUB` command, which is `DEBUG "Back in Main.", CR`.

 **What's a subroutine call?** When you use the `GOSUB` command to make the program jump to a subroutine, it is called a subroutine call.

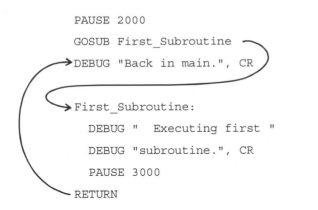

```
    PAUSE 2000
    GOSUB First_Subroutine
  → DEBUG "Back in main.", CR

  → First_Subroutine:
      DEBUG "  Executing first "
      DEBUG "subroutine.", CR
      PAUSE 3000
    RETURN
```

**Figure 7-12**
First Subroutine
Call

Figure 7-13 shows a second example of the same process with the second subroutine call
(**GOSUB Second_Subroutine**).

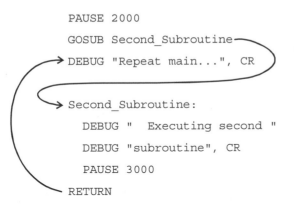

```
    PAUSE 2000
    GOSUB Second_Subroutine
  → DEBUG "Repeat main...", CR

  → Second_Subroutine:
      DEBUG "  Executing second "
      DEBUG "subroutine", CR
      PAUSE 3000
    RETURN
```

**Figure 7-13**
Second Subroutine
Call

### Your Turn – Adding and Nesting Subroutines

You can add subroutines after the two that are in the program and call them from within
the main routine.

√ Add the subroutine example in the Figure 7-11 on page 207 to
SimpleSubroutines.bs2.

√  Make any necessary adjustments to the DEBUG commands so that the display looks right with all three subroutines.

You can also call one subroutine from within another. This is called nesting subroutines.

√  Try moving the GOSUB that calls Subroutine_Name into one of the other subroutines, and see how it works.

**When nesting subroutines** the rule is no more than four deep. See the BASIC Stamp Manual for more details. Look up GOSUB and RETURN.

## Light Meter Using Subroutines

The segments on the display cycle in a circular pattern that gets faster when the light on the photoresistor gets brighter. When the light gets dimmer, the circular pattern displayed by the 7-segment LED display goes slower.

The program that runs the light meter will deal with three different operations:

1. Read the photoresistor.
2. Calculate how long to wait before updating the 7-segment LED display.
3. Update the 7-segment LED display.

Each operation is contained within its own subroutine, and the main DO...LOOP routine will cycle and call each one in sequence, over and over again.

### Example Program: LightMeter.bs2

**Controlled lighting conditions** make a big difference. For best results, conduct this test in a room lit by fluorescent lights with no direct sunlight (close the blinds). For information on how to calibrate this meter to other lighting conditions, see the Your Turn section.

√  Enter and run LightMeter.bs2.
√  Verify that the circular pattern displayed by the 7-segment LED display is controlled by the lighting conditions the photoresistor is sensing. Do this by casting a shadow over it with your hand or a piece of paper.

```
' What's a Microcontroller - LightMeter.bs2
' Indicate light level using 7-segment display.

' {$STAMP BS2}
' {$PBASIC 2.5}

DEBUG "Program Running!"

index           VAR     Nib                 ' Variable declarations.
time            VAR     Word

OUTH = %00000000                            ' Initialize 7-segment display.
DIRH = %11111111

DO                                          ' Main routine.

  GOSUB Get_Rc_Time
  GOSUB Delay
  GOSUB Update_Display

LOOP
                                            ' Subroutines

Get_Rc_Time:                                ' RC-time subroutine

  HIGH 2
  PAUSE 3
  RCTIME 2, 1, time

RETURN

Delay:                                      ' Delay subroutine.

  PAUSE time

RETURN

Update_Display:                             ' Display updating subroutine.

  IF index = 6 THEN index = 0
  '                 BAFG.CDE
  LOOKUP index, [ %01000000,
                  %10000000,
                  %00000100,
                  %00000010,
                  %00000001,
                  %00100000 ], OUTH
  index = index + 1

RETURN
```

7

### How LightMeter.bs2 Works

The first two lines of the program declare variables.  It doesn't matter whether these variables are used in subroutines or the main routine, it's always best to declare variables (and constants) at the beginning of your program.  Since this is such a common practice, this section of code has a name, variable declarations.  This name is shown in the comment to the right of the first variable declaration.

```
index VAR Nib                    ' Variable declarations.
time  VAR Word
```

Many programs also have things that need to get done once at the beginning of the program.  Setting all the 7-segment I/O pins low and then making them outputs is an example.  This section of a PBASIC program also has a name, initialization.

```
OUTH = %00000000                 ' Initialize 7-segment display.
DIRH = %11111111
```

This next segment of code is called the main routine.  The main routine calls the **Get_Rc_Time** subroutine first.  Then, it calls the **Delay** subroutine, and after that, it calls the **Update_Display** subroutine. Keep in mind that the program goes through the three subroutines as fast as it can, over and over again.

```
DO                               ' Main routine.
   GOSUB Get_Rc_Time
   GOSUB Delay
   GOSUB Update_Display
LOOP
```

All subroutines are usually placed after the main routine.  The first subroutine's name is **Get_Rc_Time:**, and it takes the RC-time measurement on the photoresistor circuit.  This subroutine has a **PAUSE** command that charges up the capacitor.  The *Duration* of this command is small because it only needs to pause long enough to make sure the capacitor is charged.  Note that the **RCTIME** command sets the value of the **time** variable.  This variable will be used by the second subroutine.

```
                                 ' Subroutines

Get_Rc_Time:                     ' RC-time subroutine
   HIGH 2
   PAUSE 3
   RCTIME 2, 1, time
```

```
    RETURN
```

The second subroutine's name is **Delay**, and all it contains is a **PAUSE** command. If you want to do some extra math on the value of the **time** variable before using it in the **PAUSE** command, it would be appropriate to do that in this subroutine.

```
    Delay:
      PAUSE time
    RETURN
```

The third subroutine is named **Update_Display**. The **LOOKUP** command in this subroutine contains a table with six bit patterns that are used to create the circular pattern around the outside of the 7-segment LED display. By adding 1 to the **index** variable each time the subroutine is called, it causes the next bit pattern in the sequence to get placed in **OUTH**. There are only entries in the **LOOKUP** command's lookup table for **index** values from 0 through 5. What happens when the value of **index** gets to 6? The lookup command doesn't automatically know to go back to the first entry, but you can use an **IF...THEN** statement to fix that problem. The command **IF index = 6 THEN index = 0** resets the value of **index** to 0 each time it gets to 6. It also causes the sequence of bit patterns placed in **OUTH** to repeat itself over and over again. This, in turn, causes the 7-segment LED display to repeat its circular pattern over and over again.

```
    Update_Display:
      IF index = 6 THEN index = 0
      '                 BAFG.CDE
      LOOKUP index, [ %01000000,
                      %10000000,
                      %00000100,
                      %00000010,
                      %00000001,
                      %00100000 ], OUTH
      index = index + 1
    RETURN
```

### Your Turn – Adjusting the Meter's Hardware and Software

There are two ways to change the sensitivity of the meter. First the software can be changed. For example, the 7-segment LED display will cycle at one-tenth the speed if you multiply the time variable by 10 in the **Delay** subroutine, and it will cycle twice as fast if you divide the time variable by 2.

√   Modify LightMeter.bs2 so that the **time** variable is multiplied by 10. The easiest way to do this is to change

```
        PAUSE time
```

to

```
        PAUSE time * 10
```

in the **Delay** subroutine.

√   Run the modified program and test to make sure the cycling of the 7-segment LED display is now one tenth of what it was before.

√   You can also try multiplying the **time** variable by other values such as 5 or 20, or dividing by 2 using **PAUSE time / 2**.

You can also make the display cycle at one tenth the speed by swapping the 0.01µF capacitor for the 0.1 µF capacitor. Remember that when you use a capacitor that is ten times as large, the RC-time measurement will become ten times as long.

√   Replace the 0.01 µF capacitor with a 0.1 µF capacitor.

√   Run the program and see if the predicted effect occurred.

**Which is better, adjusting the software or the hardware?** You should always try to use the best of both worlds. Pick a capacitor that gives you the most accurate measurements over the widest range of light levels. Once your hardware is the best it can be, use the software to automatically adjust the light meter so that it works well for the user, both indoors and outdoors. This takes a considerable amount of testing and refinement, but that's all part of the product design process.

## SUMMARY

This chapter introduced a second way to use the **RCTIME** command by using it to measure light levels with a photoresistor. Like the potentiometer, the photoresistor is a variable resistor. Unlike the potentiometer, the photoresistor's resistance changes with light levels instead of with position. Stamp Plot Lite was used to graph successive light measurements, and methods for recording and interpreting graphical data were introduced. The **WRITE** and **READ** commands were used to store and retrieve values to and from the BASIC Stamp module's EEPROM. The EEPROM was then used in an RC-time data logging application. In this chapter's last activity, a light meter application was developed. This application used subroutines to perform the three different jobs required for the light meter to function.

### Questions

1. What kind of different things can sensors detect?
2. What is the name of the chemical compound that makes a photoresistor sensitive to light?
3. How is a photoresistor similar to a potentiometer? How is it different?
4. What does EEPROM stand for?
5. How many bytes can the BASIC Stamp module's EEPROM store? How many bits can it store?
6. What command do you use to store a value in EEPROM? What command do you use to retrieve a value from EEPROM? Which one requires a variable?
7. What is a label?
8. What is a subroutine?
9. What command is used to call a subroutine? What command is used to end a subroutine?

### Exercises

1. Draw the schematic of a photoresistor RC-time circuit connected to P5.
2. Modify TestPhotoresistor.bs2 to so that it works on a circuit connected to P5 instead of P2.
3. Explain how you would modify LightMeter.bs2 so that the circular pattern displayed by the 7-segment LED display goes in the opposite direction.

## Project

1. In an earlier chapter, you used a pushbutton to make an LED blink. Instead of using a pushbutton, use a photoresistor to make the LED blink when you cast a shadow over it. Hint: You can use an **IF...THEN** statement and the greater than/less than operators to decide if your **time** measurement is above or below a certain value. The operator **>** is used for greater than, and the operator **<** is used for less than.

## Solutions

Q1. Pressure, position, rotation, temperature, smoke, vibration, tilt, light, and almost anything else you may think of: humidity, g-force, flexion, flow rate, the list goes on...

Q2. Cadmium sulfide (CdS).

Q3. Both devices have varying resistance values. The photoresistor's resistance varies according to the light level falling upon it, unlike the potentiometer, which only changes when the knob is turned.

Q4. Electrically Erasable Programmable Read-Only Memory.

Q5. 2048 bytes. 2048 x 8 = 16,384 bits.

Q6. To store a value – **WRITE**

To retrieve a value – **READ**

The **READ** command requires a variable.

Q7. A label is a name that can be used as a placeholder in a PBASIC program.

Q8. A subroutine is a small segment of code that does a certain job.

Q9. Calling: **GOSUB**; ending: **RETURN**

E1. Schematic based on Figure 7-2 on page 191, P2 changed to P5.

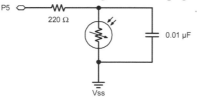

E2. The required changes are very similar to those explained on page 191.

```
DO
  HIGH 5
  PAUSE 100
  RCTIME 5, 1, time
```

```
    DEBUG HOME, "time =  ", DEC5 time
LOOP
```

E3. To go in the opposite direction, the patterns must be displayed in the reverse order. This can be done by switching the patterns around inside the **LOOKUP** statement, or by reversing the order they get looked up.

### Solution 1

```
Update_Display:
IF index = 6 THEN index = 0
'                  BAFG.CDE
LOOKUP index, [ %01000000,
                %10000000,
                %00000100,
                %00000010,
                %00000001,
                %00100000 ], OUTH
index = index + 1
RETURN
```

### Solution 2

```
Update_Display:
'                  BAFG.CDE
  LOOKUP index, [ %01000000,
                  %10000000,
                  %00000100,
                  %00000010,
                  %00000001,
                  %00100000 ], OUTH
  IF (index = 0) THEN
    index = 5
  ELSE
    index = index - 1
  ENDIF
RETURN
```

P1. Photoresistor from Figure 7-2, p.191; LED from Figure 2-11, p.48.

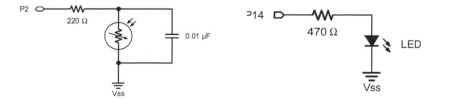

The key to solving this problem is to insert an **IF...THEN** statement that tests whether the photoresistor reading is above some threshold value. If it is, flash the LED. The threshold value can be found by running TestPhotoresistor.bs2 and observing the readings. Note the difference between an unshaded and a shaded value. Take a value somewhere in the middle and use that for your threshold. In the solution shown, the threshold value was encoded in a constant named **Dark** to make the program easier to change.

```
' What's a Microcontroller - Ch07Prj01_PhotoresistorFlasher.bs2
' Make LED on P14 flash whenever a shadow is cast over
' the photoresistor.  Change "Dark" constant for your conditions.

' {$STAMP BS2}
' {$PBASIC 2.5}

Dark    CON    25
time    VAR    Word

DO

  HIGH 2                         ' Read photoresistor with RCTIME
  PAUSE 100
  RCTIME 2, 1, time

  DEBUG HOME, "time =  ", DEC5 time ' Print value to Debug Terminal

  IF (time > Dark) THEN          ' Compare reading to known dark value
    HIGH 14                      ' Blink LED on pin P14
    PAUSE 100
    LOW 14
    PAUSE 100
  ENDIF

LOOP
```

## Further Investigation

**"*Applied Sensors*", Student Guide, Version 2.0, Parallax Inc., 2003**
    More in-depth coverage of light measurement using a photodiode, scientific units and math are featured in this text along with other sensor applications.

**"*Industrial Control*", Student Guide, Version 2.0, Parallax Inc., 2002**
    Stamp Plot Lite was developed in conjunction with this text to demonstrate the fundamentals of techniques used in industrial process control.

# Chapter #8: Frequency and Sound

## YOUR DAY AND ELECTRONIC BEEPS

Here are a few examples of beeps you might hear during a normal day: The microwave oven beeps when it's done cooking your food. The cell phone plays different tones of beeps that resemble songs to get your attention when a call is coming in. The ATM machine beeps to remind you not to forget your card. A store cash register beeps to let the teller know that the bar code of the grocery item passed over the scanner was read. Many calculators beep when the wrong keys are pressed. Let's not forget that you may have started your day with a beeping alarm clock.

## MICROCONTROLLERS, SPEAKERS, BEEPS AND ON/OFF SIGNALS

Just about all of the electronic beeps you hear during your daily routine are made by microcontrollers connected to speakers. The microcontroller creates these beeps by sending rapid high/low signals to various types of speakers. The rate of these high/low signals is called the frequency, and it determines the tone or pitch of the beep. Each time a high/low repeats itself, it is called a cycle. You will often see the number of cycles per second referred to as Hertz, and it is abbreviated Hz. For example, one of the most common frequencies for the beeps that help machines get your attention is 2 kHz. That means that the high/low signals repeat at 2000 times per second.

### Introducing the Piezoelectric Speaker

In this activity, you will experiment with sending a variety of signals to a common, small, and inexpensive speaker called a piezoelectric speaker. Its schematic symbol and part drawing are shown in Figure 8-1.

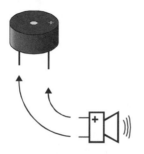

**Figure 8-1**
Piezoelectric Speaker
Schematic Symbol and
Part Drawing

**A piezoelectric speaker** is commonly referred to as a piezo speaker or piezo buzzer, and piezo is pronounced "pE-A-zO".

## ACTIVITY #1: BUILDING AND TESTING THE SPEAKER

In this activity, you will build and test the piezoelectric speaker circuit.

### Speaker Parts

(1) Piezoelectric speaker
(2) Jumper wires

### Building the Piezoelectric Speaker Circuit

The negative terminal of the piezoelectric speaker should be connected to Vss, and the positive terminal should be connected to an I/O pin. The BASIC Stamp will then be programmed to send high/low signals to the piezoelectric speaker's positive terminal.

√    Build the circuit shown in Figure 8-2.

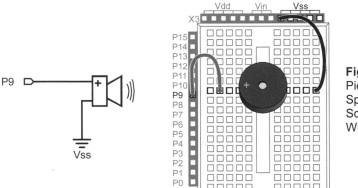

**Figure 8-2**
Piezoelectric
Speaker Circuit
Schematic and
Wiring Diagram

### How the Piezoelectric Speaker Circuit Works

When a guitar string vibrates, it causes changes in air pressure. These changes in air pressure are what your ear detects as a tone. The faster the changes in air pressure, the higher the pitch, and the slower the changes in air pressure, the lower the pitch. The element inside the piezo speaker's plastic case is called a piezoelectric element. When high/low signals are applied to the speaker's positive terminal, the piezoelectric element vibrates, and it causes changes in air pressure just as a guitar string does. As with the guitar string, your ear detects the changes in air pressure caused by the piezoelectric speaker, and it typically sounds like a beep or a tone.

## Programming Speaker Control

The **FREQOUT** command is a convenient way of sending high/low signals to a speaker to make sound. The *BASIC Stamp Manual* shows the command syntax as this:

FREQOUT *Pin, Duration, Freq1 {, Freq2}*

As with most of the other commands used in this book, **Pin** is a value you can use to choose which BASIC Stamp I/O pin to use. The **Duration** argument is a value that tells the **FREQOUT** command how long the tone should play, in milliseconds. The **Freq1** argument is used to set the frequency of the tone, in Hertz. There is an optional **Freq2** argument that can be used to mix frequencies.

Here is how to send a tone to I/O pin P9 that lasts for 1.5 seconds and has a frequency of 2 kHz:

```
FREQOUT 9, 1500, 2000
```

## Example Program: TestPiezoWithFreqout.bs2

This example program sends the 2 kHz tone to the speaker on I/O pin P9 for 1.5 seconds. You can use the Debug terminal to see when the speaker should be beeping and when it should stop.

√  Enter and run TestPiezoWithFreqout.bs2.
√  Verify that the speaker makes a clearly audible tone during the time that the Debug Terminal displays the message "Tone sending..."

```
' What's a Microcontroller - TestPiezoWithFreqout.bs2
' Send a tone to the piezo speaker using the FREQOUT command.

'{$STAMP BS2}
'{$PBASIC 2.5}

DEBUG "Tone sending...", CR

FREQOUT 9, 1500, 2000

DEBUG "Tone done."
```

### Your Turn – Adjusting Frequency and Duration

√   Save TestPiezoWithFreqout.bs2 under a different name.
√   Try some different values for the *Duration* and *Freq1* argument.
√   After each change, run the program and make a note of the effect.
√   As the *Freq1* argument gets larger, does the tone's pitch go up or down?  Try values of 1500, 2000, 2500 and 3000 to answer this question.

## ACTIVITY #2: ACTION SOUNDS

Many toys contain microcontrollers that are used to make action sounds.  Action sounds tend to involve rapidly changing the frequency played by the speaker.  You can also get some interesting effects from mixing two different tones together using the FREQOUT command's optional *Freq2* argument.  This activity introduces both techniques.

### Programming Action Sounds

Action and appliance sounds have three different components:

1.  Pause
2.  Duration
3.  Frequency

The pause is the time between tones, and you can use the PAUSE command to create that pause.  The duration is the amount of time a tone lasts, which you can set using the FREQOUT command's *Duration* argument.  The frequency determines the pitch of the tone.  The higher the frequency, the higher the pitch, the lower the frequency, the lower the pitch.  This is, of course, determined by the FREQOUT command's *Freq1* argument.

### Example Program: ActionTones.bs2

ActionTones.bs2 demonstrates a few different combinations of pause, duration, and frequency.  The first sequence of tones sounds similar to an electronic alarm clock.  The second one sounds similar to something a familiar science fiction movie robot might say.  The third is more the kind of sound effect you might hear in an old video game.

√   Enter and run ActionTones.bs2.

```
' What's a Microcontroller - ActionTones.bs2
' Demonstrate how different combinations of pause, duration, and frequency
' can be used to make sound effects.
```

```
'{$STAMP BS2}
'{$PBASIC 2.5}

duration        VAR     Word
frequency       VAR     Word

DEBUG "Alarm...", CR
   PAUSE 100
   FREQOUT 9, 500, 1500
   PAUSE 500
   FREQOUT 9, 500, 1500
   PAUSE 500
   FREQOUT 9, 500, 1500
   PAUSE 500
   FREQOUT 9, 500, 1500
   PAUSE 500

DEBUG "Robot reply...", CR
   PAUSE 100
   FREQOUT 9, 100, 2800
   FREQOUT 9, 200, 2400
   FREQOUT 9, 140, 4200
   FREQOUT 9,  30, 2000
   PAUSE 500

DEBUG "Hyperspace...", CR
  PAUSE 100
  FOR duration = 15 TO 1 STEP 1
    FOR frequency = 2000 TO 2500 STEP 20
      FREQOUT 9, duration, frequency
    NEXT
  NEXT

DEBUG "Done", CR

END
```

## How ActionTones.bs2 Works

The "Alarm" routine sounds like an alarm clock. This routine plays tones at a fixed frequency of 1.5 kHz for a duration of 0.5 s with a fixed delay between tones of 0.5 s. The "Robot reply" routine uses various frequencies for brief durations.

The "Hyperspace" routine uses no delay, but it varies both the duration and frequency. By using **FOR...NEXT** loops to rapidly change the frequency and duration, you can get some interesting sound effects. When one **FOR...NEXT** loop executes inside another one, it is called a nested loop. Here is how the nested **FOR...NEXT** loop shown below works. The duration variable starts at 15, then the frequency loop takes over and sends frequencies of 2000, then 2020, then 2040, and so on, up through 2500 to the piezo speaker. When the frequency loop is finished, the duration loop has only repeated one of its 15 passes. So it subtracts one from the value of duration and repeats the frequency loop all over again.

```
FOR duration = 15 TO 1
  FOR frequency = 2000 TO 2500 STEP 15
    FREQOUT 9, duration, frequency
  NEXT
NEXT
```

## Example Program: NestedLoops.bs2

To better understand how nested FOR...NEXT loops work, NestedLoops.bs2 uses the DEBUG command to show the value of a much less complicated version of the nested loop used in ActionTones.bs2.

√ Enter and run NestedLoops.bs2.
√ Examine the Debug Terminal output and verify how the duration and frequency arguments change each time through the loop.

```
' What's a Microcontroller - NestedLoops.bs2
' Demonstrate how the nested loop in ActionTones.bs2 works.

'{$STAMP BS2}
'{$PBASIC 2.5}

duration        VAR     Word
frequency       VAR     Word

DEBUG "Duration   Frequency", CR,
      "--------   ---------", CR

FOR duration = 4000 TO 1000 STEP 1000
  FOR frequency = 1000 TO 3000 STEP 500
    DEBUG "   "   , DEC5 duration,
          "          ", DEC5 frequency, CR
    FREQOUT 9, duration, frequency
  NEXT
  DEBUG CR
NEXT

END
```

### Your Turn – More Sound Effects

There is pretty much an endless number of ways to modify ActionTones.bs2 to get different sound combinations. Here is just one modification to the "Hyperspace" routine:

```
DEBUG "Hyperspace jump...", CR
  FOR duration = 15 TO 1 STEP 3
    FOR frequency = 2000 TO 2500 STEP 15
      FREQOUT 9, duration, frequency
    NEXT
  NEXT
  FOR duration = 1 TO 36 STEP 3
    FOR frequency = 2500 TO 2000 STEP 15
      FREQOUT 9, duration, frequency
    NEXT
  NEXT
```

√ Save your example program under the name ActionTonesYourTurn.bs2.
√ Have fun with this and other modifications of your own invention.

## Two Frequencies at Once

You can send two frequencies at the same time. In audio, this is called "mixing". Remember the **FREQOUT** command's syntax from Activity #1:

**FREQOUT** *Pin, Duration, Freq1 {, Freq2}*

You can use the optional *Freq2* argument to mix two frequencies using the **FREQOUT** command. For example, you can mix 2 and 3 kHz together like this:

```
FREQOUT 9, 1000, 2000, 3000
```

 **Each touchtone keypad tone** is also an example of two frequencies mixed together. In telecommunications, that is called DTMF (Dual Tone Multi Frequency). There is also a PBASIC command called **DTMFOUT** that is designed just for sending phone tones. For examples of projects where phone numbers are dialed, see the **DTMFOUT** command in the BASIC Stamp Manual.

### Example Program: MixingTones.bs2

This example program demonstrates the difference in tone that you get when you mix 2 and 3 kHz together. It also demonstrates an interesting phenomenon that occurs when you mix two sound waves that are very close in frequency. When you mix 2000 Hz with 2001 Hz, the tone will fade in and out once every second (at a frequency of 1 Hz). If you mix 2000 Hz with 2002 Hz, it will fade in and out twice a second (2 Hz), and so on.

**Beat** is when two tones very close in frequency are played together causing the tone you hear to fade in and out. The frequency of that fading in and out is the difference between the two frequencies. If the difference is 1 Hz, the tone will fade in and out at 1 Hz. If the difference is 2 Hz, the tone will fade in and out at 2 Hz.

The variations in air pressure made by the piezoelectric speaker are called sound waves. When the tone is loudest, the variations in air pressure caused by the two frequencies are adding to each other (called superposition). When the tone is at its quietest, the variations in air pressure are canceling each other out (called interference).

√ Enter and run MixingTones.bs2.

√ Keep an eye on the Debug Terminal as the tones play, and note the different effects that come from mixing the different tones.

```
' What's a Microcontroller - MixingTones.bs2
' Demonstrate some of the things that happen when you mix two tones.

'{$STAMP BS2}
'{$PBASIC 2.5}

DEBUG "Frequency = 2000", CR
FREQOUT 9, 4000, 2000

DEBUG "Frequency = 3000", CR
FREQOUT 9, 4000, 3000

DEBUG "Frequency = 2000 + 3000", CR
FREQOUT 9, 4000, 2000, 3000

DEBUG "Frequency = 2000 + 2001", CR
FREQOUT 9, 4000, 2000, 2001

DEBUG "Frequency = 2000 + 2002", CR
FREQOUT 9, 4000, 2000, 2002

DEBUG "Frequency = 2000 + 2003", CR
FREQOUT 9, 4000, 2000, 2003

DEBUG "Frequency = 2000 + 2005", CR
FREQOUT 9, 4000, 2000, 2005

DEBUG "Frequency = 2000 + 2010", CR
FREQOUT 9, 4000, 2000, 2010

DEBUG "Done", CR

END
```

**Your Turn – Condensing the Code**

MixingTones.bs2 was written to demonstrate some interesting things that can happen when you mix two different frequencies using the **FREQOUT** command's optional *Freq2* argument. However, it is extremely inefficient.

√ Modify MixingTones.bs2 so that it cycles through the *Freq2* arguments ranging from 2001 to 2005 using a word variable and a loop.

## ACTIVITY #3: MUSICAL NOTES AND SIMPLE SONGS

Figure 8-3 shows the rightmost 25 keys of a piano keyboard. It also shows the frequencies at which each wire inside the piano vibrates when that piano key is struck. The keys and their corresponding notes are labeled C6 through C8. These keys are separated into groups of 12. Each group spans one octave, made up of 8 white keys and 4 black keys. The sequence of notes repeats itself every 12 keys. Notes of the same letter are related by frequency, doubling with each higher octave. For example, C7 is twice the frequency of C6, and C8 is twice the frequency of C7. Likewise, if you go one octave down, the frequency will be half the value; for example, A6 is half the frequency of A7.

**Internet search for – "musical scale":** By using the words "musical scale" in a search engine like Google or Yahoo, you will find lots of fascinating information about the history, physics and psychology of the subject. The 12 note per octave scale is the main scale of western music. Other cultures use scales that contain 2 to 35 notes per octave.

If you've ever heard a singer practice his/her notes by singing the Solfege, "Do Re Mi Fa Sol La Ti Do", the singer is attempting to match the notes that you get from striking the white keys on a piano keyboard. These white keys are called natural keys. A black key on a piano can either be called sharp or flat. For example, the black key between the C and D keys is either called C-sharp ($C^\#$) or D-flat ($D^b$). Whether a key is called sharp or flat depends on the particular piece being played, and the rules for that are better left to the music classes.

**Figure 8-3**: Rightmost Piano Keys and Their Frequencies

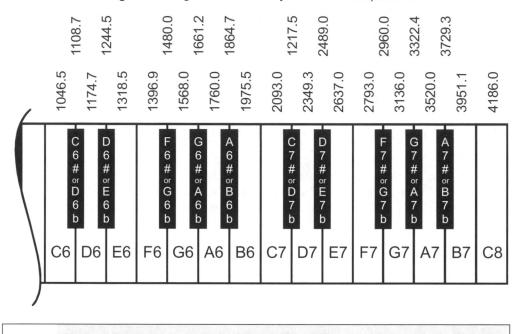

**Tuning Method:** The keyboard in Figure 8-3 uses a method of tuning called equal temperament. The frequencies are determined using a reference note, then multiplying it by $2^{(n/12)}$ for values of n = 1, 2, 3, etc. For example, you can take the frequency for A6, and multiply by $2^{(1/12)}$ to get the frequency for A6#. Multiply it by $2^{(2/12)}$ to get the frequency for B6, and so on. Here is an example of calculating the frequency for B6 using A6 as a reference frequency:

The frequency of A6 is 1760

$2^{(2/12)} = 1.1224$

1760 X 1.224 = 1975.5

1975.5 is the frequency of B6

## Programming Musical Notes

The **FREQOUT** command is also useful for musical notes. Programming the BASIC Stamp to play music using a piezospeaker involves following a variety of rules used in playing music using any other musical instrument. These rules apply to the same elements that were used to make sound effects, frequency, duration, and pause. This next example program plays some of the musical note frequencies on the piezospeaker, each with a duration of half a second.

### Example Program: DoReMiFaSolLaTiDo.bs2

√ Enter and run DoReMiFaSolLaTiDo.bs2

```
' What's a Microcontroller - DoReMiFaSolLaTiDo.bs2
' Send an octave of half second tones using a piezoelectric speaker.

'{$STAMP BS2}
'{$PBASIC 2.5}

'Solfege            Tone                  Note

DEBUG "Do...", CR:  FREQOUT 9,500,1047    ' C6

DEBUG "Re...", CR:  FREQOUT 9,500,1175    ' D6

DEBUG "Mi...", CR:  FREQOUT 9,500,1319    ' E6

DEBUG "Fa...", CR:  FREQOUT 9,500,1396    ' F6

DEBUG "Sol..", CR:  FREQOUT 9,500,1568    ' G6

DEBUG "La...", CR:  FREQOUT 9,500,1760    ' A6

DEBUG "Ti...", CR:  FREQOUT 9,500,1976    ' B6

DEBUG "Do...", CR:  FREQOUT 9,500,2093    ' C7

END
```

### Your Turn – Sharp/Flat Notes

√ Use the frequencies shown in Figure 8-3 to add the five sharp/flat notes to DoReMiFaSolLaTiDo.bs2

√ Modify your program so that it plays the next octave up. Hint: Save yourself some typing and just use the * 2 operation after each *Freq1* argument. For example, **FREQOUT 9, 500, 1175** * 2 will give you D7, the D note in the 7<sup>th</sup> octave.

## Storing and Retrieving Sequences of Musical Notes

A good way of saving musical notes is to store them using the BASIC Stamp module's EEPROM. Although you could use many **WRITE** commands to do this, a better way is to use the **DATA** directive. This is the syntax for the **DATA** directive:

    {Symbol} DATA {Word} DataItem {, {Word} DataItem, ... }

Here is an example of how to use the **DATA** directive to store the characters that correspond to musical notes.

```
Notes DATA "C","C","G","G","A","A","G"
```

You can use the **READ** command to access these characters. The letter 'C' is located at address **Notes + 0**, and a second letter 'C' is located at **Notes + 1**. Then, there's a letter 'G' at **Notes + 2**, and so on. For example, if you want to load the last letter 'G' into a byte variable called **noteLetter**, use the command:

```
READ Notes + 6, noteLetter
```

You can also store lists of numbers using the **DATA** directive. Frequency and duration values that the BASIC Stamp uses for musical notes need to be stored in word variables because they are usually greater than 255. Here is how to do that with a **DATA** directive.

```
Frequencies DATA Word 2093, Word 2093, Word 3136, Word 3136,
                 Word 3520, Word 3520, Word 3136
```

Because each of these values occupies two bytes, accessing them with the read command is different from accessing characters. The first 2093 is at **Frequencies + 0**, but the second 2093 is located at **Frequencies + 2**. The first 3136 is located at **Frequencies + 4**, and the second 3136 is located at **Frequencies + 6**.

 The values in the **Frequencies** DATA directive correspond with the musical notes in the **Notes** DATA directive.

Here is a **FOR…NEXT** loop that places the **Notes DATA** into a variable named **noteLetter**, then it places the **Frequencies DATA** into a variable named **noteFreq**.

```
FOR index = 0 to 6
  READ Notes + index, noteLetter
```

```
READ Frequencies + (index * 2), Word noteFreq
DEBUG noteLetter, "  ", DEC noteFreq, CR
NEXT
```

**What does the (index * 2) do?** Each value stored in the **Frequencies** **DATA** directive takes a word (two bytes), while each character in the **Notes** **DATA** directive only takes one byte. The value of **index** increases by one each time through the **FOR...NEXT** loop. That's fine for accessing the note characters using the command **READ** **Notes** **+** **index, noteLetter**. The problem is that for every one byte in **Notes**, the **index** variable needs to point twice as far down the **Frequencies** list. The command **READ** **Frequencies + (index * 2), Word noteFreq**, takes care of this.

The next example program stores notes and durations using **DATA**, and it uses the **FREQOUT** command to play each note frequency for a specific duration. The result is the first few notes from the children's song Twinkle Twinkle Little Star.

**The Alphabet Song** used by children to memorize their "ABCs" uses the same notes as Twinkle Twinkle Little Star.

**8**

### Example Program: TwinkleTwinkle.bs2

This example program demonstrates how to use the **DATA** directive to store lists and how to use the **READ** command to access the values in the lists.

- √   Enter and run TwinkleTwinkle.bs2
- √   Verify that the notes sound like the song Twinkle Twinkle Little Star.
- √   Use the Debug Terminal to verify that it works as expected by accessing and displaying values from the three **DATA** directives.

```
' What's a Microcontroller - TwinkleTwinkle.bs2
' Play the first seven notes from Twinkle Twinkle Little Star.

'{$STAMP BS2}
'{$PBASIC 2.5}

Notes           DATA   "C","C","G","G","A","A","G"

Frequencies     DATA   Word 2093, Word 2093, Word 3136, Word 3136,
                       Word 3520, Word 3520, Word 3136
```

```
Durations          DATA   Word 500, Word 500, Word 500, Word 500,
                          Word 500, Word 500, Word 1000

index           VAR    Nib
noteLetter      VAR    Byte
noteFreq        VAR    Word
noteDuration    VAR    Word

DEBUG    "Note  Duration  Frequency", CR,
         "----  --------  ---------", CR

FOR index = 0 TO 6

  READ Notes + index, noteLetter
  DEBUG "   ", noteLetter

  READ Durations + (index * 2), Word noteDuration
  DEBUG "        ", DEC4 noteDuration

  READ Frequencies + (index * 2), Word noteFreq
  DEBUG "          ", DEC4 noteFreq, CR

  FREQOUT 9, noteDuration, noteFreq

NEXT

END
```

### Your Turn – Adding and Playing More Notes

This program played the first seven notes from Twinkle Twinkle Little Star. The words go "Twin-kle twin-kle lit-tle star". The next phrase from the song goes "How I won-der what you are", and its notes are F, F, E, E, D, D, C. As with the first phrase the last note is held twice as long as the other notes. To add this phrase to the song from TwinkleTwinkle.bs2, you will need to expand each **DATA** directive appropriately. Don't forget to change the **FOR...NEXT** loop so that it goes from 0 to 13 instead of from 0 to 6.

√   Modify TwinkleTwinkle.bs2 so that it plays the first two phrases of the song instead of just the first phrase.

### ACTIVITY #4: MICROCONTROLLER MUSIC

Note durations are not recorded on sheet music in terms of milliseconds. Instead, they are described as whole, half, quarter, eight, sixteenth, and thirty-second notes. As the name suggests, a half note lasts half as long as a whole note. A quarter note lasts one fourth the time a whole note lasts, and so on. How long is a whole note? It depends on the piece of music being played. One piece might be played at a tempo that causes a whole note to last for four seconds, another piece might have a two second whole note, and yet another might have some other duration.

Rests are the time between notes when no tones are played. Rest durations are also measured as whole, half, quarter, eighth, sixteenth and thirty-second.

### A Better System for Storing and Retrieving Music

You can write programs that store twice as much music in your BASIC Stamp by using bytes instead of words in your DATA directives. You can also modify your program to make the musical notes easier to read by using some of the more common musical conventions for notes and duration. This activity will start by introducing how to store musical information in a way that relates to the concepts of notes, durations, and rests. Tempo is also introduced, and it will be revisited in the next activity.

Here is an example of the DATA directives that stores musical notes and durations for the next example program. When played, it should resemble the song "Frere Jacques". Only the note characters are stored in the Notes DATA directive because LOOKUP and LOOKDOWN commands will be used to match up letters to their corresponding frequencies.

```
Notes         DATA      "C","D","E","C","C","D","E","C","E","F",
                        "G","E","F","G","Q"

Durations     DATA       4,   4,   4,   4,   4,   4,   4,   4,   4,   4,
                         2,   4,   4,   2

WholeNote     CON      2000
```

The first number in the **Durations** DATA directive tells the program how long the first note in the **Notes Data** directive should last. The second duration is for the second note, and so on. The durations are no longer in terms of milliseconds. Instead, they are much smaller numbers that can be stored in bytes, so there is no Word prefix in the DATA directive. Compared to storing values in terms of milliseconds, these numbers are more closely related to sheet music. Here is a list of what each duration means.

- 1 – whole note
- 2 – half note
- 4 – quarter note
- 8 – eighth note

- 16 – sixteenth note
- 32 – thirty-second note

After each value is read from the **Durations DATA** directive, it is divided into the **WholeNote** value to get the *Duration* used in the **FREQOUT** command. The amount of time each note lasts depends on the tempo of the song. A faster tempo means each note lasts for less time, while a slower tempo means each note lasts longer. Since all the note durations are fractions of a whole note, you can use the duration of a whole note to set the tempo.

---

**What does the "Q" in Notes DATA mean?** "Q" is for quit, and a **DO WHILE…LOOP** checks for "Q" each time through the loop.

**How do I play a rest?** You can insert a rest between notes by inserting a **"P"**. The Your Turn section has the first few notes from Beethoven's 5th Symphony, which has a rest in it.

**How do I play sharp/flat notes?** NotesAndDurations.bs2 has values in its lookup tables for sharp/flat notes. When you use the lower-case version of the note, it will play the flat note. For example, if you want to play B-flat, use "b" instead of "B". Remember that this is the same frequency as A-sharp.

---

## Example Program: NotesAndDurations.bs2

√   Enter and run NotesAndDurations.bs2.
√   How does it sound?

```
' What's a Microcontroller - NotesAndDurations.bs2
' Play the first few notes from Frere Jacques.

'{$STAMP BS2}
'{$PBASIC 2.5}

DEBUG "Program Running!"

Notes           DATA    "C","D","E","C","C","D","E","C","E","F",
                        "G","E","F","G","Q"

Durations       DATA     4,   4,   4,   4,   4,   4,   4,   4,   4,   4,
                         2,   4,   4,   2

WholeNote       CON     2000

index           VAR     Byte
offset          VAR     Nib
```

```
noteLetter        VAR       Byte
noteFreq          VAR       Word
noteDuration      VAR       Word

DO UNTIL noteLetter = "Q"

  READ Notes + index, noteLetter

  LOOKDOWN noteLetter, [  "A",   "b",   "B",   "C",   "d",
                          "D",   "e",   "E",   "F",   "g",
                          "G",   "a",   "P",   "Q"    ], offset

  LOOKUP offset,      [ 1760, 1865, 1976, 2093, 2217,
                        2349, 2489, 2637, 2794, 2960,
                        3136, 3322,    0,    0    ], noteFreq

  READ Durations + index, noteDuration

  noteDuration = WholeNote / noteDuration

  FREQOUT 9, noteDuration, noteFreq

  index = index + 1

LOOP

END
```

## How NotesAndDurations.bs2 Works

The **Notes** and **Durations** DATA directives were discussed before the program. These directives combined with the **WholeNote** constant are used to store all the musical data used by the program.

The declarations for the five variables used in the program are shown below. Even though a **FOR...NEXT** loop is no longer used to access the data, there still has to be a variable (**index**) that keeps track of which DATA entry is being read in **Notes** and **Durations**. The **offset** variable is used in the **LOOKDOWN** and **LOOKUP** commands to select a particular value. The **noteLetter** variable stores a character accessed by the **READ** command. **LOOKUP** and **LOOKDOWN** commands are used to convert this character into a frequency value. This value is stored in the **noteFreq** variable and used as the **FREQOUT** command's *Freq1* argument. The **noteDuration** variable is used in a **READ** command to receive a value from the **Durations** DATA. It is also used to calculate the *Duration* used in the **FREQOUT** command.

```
index           VAR  Byte
```

```
offset          VAR   Nib

noteLetter      VAR   Byte
noteFreq        VAR   Word
noteDuration    VAR   Word
```

The main loop keeps executing until the letter 'Q' is read from the **Notes DATA**.

```
DO UNTIL noteLetter = "Q"
```

A **READ** command gets a character from the **Notes DATA**, and stores it in the **noteLetter** variable. The **noteLetter** variable is then used in a **LOOKDOWN** command to set the value of the **offset** variable. Remember that **offset** stores a 1 if "b" is detected, a 2 if "B" is detected, a 3 if "C" is detected, and so on. This **offset** value is then used in a **LOOKUP** command to figure out what the value of the **noteFreq** variable should be. If **offset** is 1, **noteFreq** will be 1865, if **offset** is 2, **noteFreq** will be 1976, if offset is 3, **noteFreq** is 2093, and so on.

```
READ Notes + index, noteLetter

LOOKDOWN noteLetter, [  "A",   "b",   "B",   "C",   "d",
                       "D",   "e",   "E",   "F",   "g",
                       "G",   "a",   "P",   "Q" ], offset

LOOKUP offset,        [ 1760, 1865, 1976, 2093, 2217,
                        2349, 2489, 2637, 2794, 2960,
                        3136, 3322,    0,    0 ], noteFreq
```

The note's frequency has been determined, but the duration still has to be figured out. The **READ** command uses the value of **index** to place a value from the **Durations DATA** into **noteDuration**.

```
READ Durations + index, noteDuration
```

Then, **noteDuration** is set equal to the **WholeNote** constant divided by the **noteDuration**. If note duration starts out as 4 from a **READ** command, it becomes 2000 ÷ 4 = 500. If **noteDuration** is 8, it becomes 1500 ÷ 8 = 250.

```
noteDuration = WholeNote / noteDuration
```

Now that **noteDuration** and **noteFreq** are determined, the **FREQOUT** command plays the note.

```
FREQOUT 9, noteDuration, noteFreq
```

Each time through the main loop, the `index` value must be increased by one. When the main loop gets back to the beginning, the first thing the program does is read the next note, using the `index` variable.

```
index = index + 1

LOOP
```

## Your Turn – Experimenting with Tempo and a Different Tune

The length of time that each note lasts is related to the tempo. You can change the tempo by adjusting the `WholeNote` constant. If you increase it to 2250, the tempo will decrease, and the song will play slower. If you increase it to 1750, the tempo will increase and the song will play more quickly.

√ Save NotesAndDurations.bs2 under the name NotesAndDurationsYourTurn.bs2.

√ Modify the tempo of NotesAndDurationsYourTurn.bs2 by adjusting the value of `WholeNote`. Try values of 1500, 1750, 2000, and 2250.

√ Re-run the program after each modification, and decide which one sounds best.

Entering musical data is much easier when all you have to do is record notes and durations. Here are the first eight notes from Beethoven's Fifth Symphony.

```
Notes      DATA "G","G","G","e","P","F","F","F","D","Q"

Durations DATA   8,  8,  8,  2,  8,  8,  8,  8,  2

WholeNote CON   2000
```

√ Save your modified program Beethoven'sFifth.bs2.

√ Replace the `Notes` and `Durations` `DATA` directives and the `WholeNote` constant declaration with the code above.

√ Run the program. Does it sound familiar?

## Adding Musical Features

The example program you just finished introduced notes, durations, and rests. It also used the duration of a whole note to determine tempo. Cell phones that play music to let you know that somebody is calling have three features that were not supported by the previous example program:

- They play "dotted" notes.
- They determine the whole note duration from a value called tempo.
- They play notes from more than one octave.

The term "dotted" refers to a dot used in sheet music to indicate that a note should be played 1 ½ times as long as its normal duration.  For example, a dotted quarter note should last for the duration of a quarter note, plus an eighth note.  A dotted half note lasts for a half plus a quarter note's duration.  You can add a data table that stores whether or not a note is dotted.  In this example, a zero means there is no dot while a 1 means there is a dot:

```
Dots               DATA      0,  0,  0,  0,  0,  0,  1,  0,  0,  0,  0,
                             0,  0,  0,  1,  0
```

Cell phones typically take the tempo for a song in beats per minute.  This is the same as saying quarter notes per minute.

```
        BeatsPerMin    CON   200
```

Figure 8-4 is a repeat of **Figure 8-3** from page 228.  It shows the 6th and 7th octaves on the piano keyboard.  These are the two octaves that sound the clearest when played by the piezospeaker.  Here is an example of a **DATA** directive you will use in the Your Turn section to play notes from more than one octave using the **Notes DATA** directive.

```
Octaves            DATA      6,  7,  6,  6,  6,  6,  6,  6,  6,  7,  6,
                             6,  6,  6
```

**Figure 8-4**
Rightmost Piano Keys and Their Frequencies

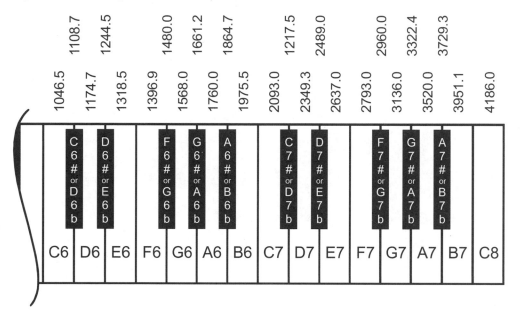

## Example Program: MusicWithMoreFeatures.bs2

This example program plays the first few notes from For He's a Jolly Good Fellow. All the notes come from the same (7th) octave, but some of the notes are dotted. In the Your turn section, you will try an example that uses notes from more than one octave, and dotted notes.

> √ Enter and run MusicWithMoreFeatures.bs2.
> √ Count notes and see if you can hear the dotted (1 ½ duration) notes.
> √ Also listen for notes in octave 7. Try changing one of those notes to octave 6. The change in the way the music sounds is pretty drastic.

```
' What's a Microcontroller - MusicWithMoreFeatures.bs2
' Play the beginning of For He's a Jolly Good Fellow.

'{$STAMP BS2}
'{$PBASIC 2.5}
```

```
DEBUG "Program Running!"

Notes           DATA    "C","E","E","E","D","E","F","E","E","D","D",
                        "D","C","D","E","C","Q"
Octaves         DATA    7,  7,  7,  7,  7,  7,  7,  7,  7,  7,  7,
                        7,  7,  7,  7,  7
Durations       DATA    4,  2,  4,  4,  4,  4,  2,  2,  4,  2,  4,
                        4,  4,  4,  2,  2
Dots            DATA    0,  0,  0,  0,  0,  0,  1,  0,  0,  0,  0,
                        0,  0,  0,  1,  0


BeatsPerMin     CON     320

index           VAR     Byte
offset          VAR     Nib

noteLetter      VAR     Byte
noteFreq        VAR     Word
noteDuration    VAR     Word
noteOctave      VAR     Nib
noteDot         VAR     Bit

wholeNote       VAR     Word
wholeNote = 60000 / BeatsPerMin * 4

DO UNTIL noteLetter = "Q"

  READ Notes + index, noteLetter

  LOOKDOWN noteLetter,  [ "C",  "d",  "D",  "e",  "E",
                          "F",  "g",  "G",  "a",  "A",
                          "b",  "B",  "P",  "Q"     ], offset

  LOOKUP offset,        [ 4186, 4435, 4699, 4978, 5274,
                          5588, 5920, 6272, 6645, 7040,
                          7459, 7902,    0,    0    ], noteFreq

  READ Octaves + index, noteOctave
  noteOctave = 8 - noteOctave
  noteFreq = noteFreq / (DCD noteOctave)

  READ Durations + index, noteDuration
  noteDuration = WholeNote / noteDuration

  READ Dots + index, noteDot
  IF noteDot = 1 THEN noteDuration = noteDuration * 3 / 2

  FREQOUT 9, noteDuration, noteFreq

  index = index + 1
```

```
LOOP

END
```

## How MusicWithMoreFeatures.bs2 Works

Below is the musical data for the entire song. For each note in the **Notes** **DATA** directive, there is a corresponding entry in the **Octaves, Durations,** and **Dots** **DATA** directives. For example, the first note is a C note in the 7th octave; it's a quarter note and it's not dotted. Here is another example: the second from the last note (not including "Q") is an E note, in the 7th octave. It's a half note, and it is dotted. There is also a **BeatsPerMin** constant that sets the tempo for the song.

```
Notes          DATA      "C","E","E","E","D","E","F","E","E","D","D",
                         "D","C","D","E","C","Q"
Octaves        DATA       7,   7,   7,   7,   7,   7,   7,   7,   7,   7,   7,
                          7,   7,   7,   7,   7
Durations      DATA       4,   2,   4,   4,   4,   4,   2,   2,   4,   2,   4,
                          4,   4,   4,   2,   2
Dots           DATA       0,   0,   0,   0,   0,   0,   1,   0,   0,   0,   0,
                          0,   0,   0,   1,   0

BeatsPerMin    CON       320
```

In the previous example program, **WholeNote** was a constant. This time, it's a variable that will hold the duration of a whole note in ms. After this value is calculated, **WholeNote** will be used to determine all the other note durations, just like in the previous program. The **index, offset, noteLetter,** and **noteDuration** variables are also used in the same manner they were in the previous program. The **noteFreq** variable is handled a little differently since now it has to be adjusted depending on the octave the note is played in. The **noteOctave** and **noteDot** variables have been added to handle the octave and dot features.

```
        wholeNote      VAR  Word

        index          VAR  Byte
        offset         VAR  Nib

        noteLetter     VAR  Byte
        noteFreq       VAR  Word
        noteDuration   VAR  Word
        noteOctave     VAR  Nib
        noteDot        VAR  Bit
```

The `wholeNote` variable is calculated using the `BeatsPerMin`. The tempo of the song is defined in beats per minute, and the program has to divide `BeatsPerMin` into 60000 ms, then multiply by 4. The result is the correct value for a whole note.

```
wholeNote = 60000 / BeatsPerMin * 4
```

> **Math executes from left to right.** In the calculation `wholeNote = 60000 / beatsPerMin * 4`, the BASIC Stamp first calculates `60000 / beatsPerMin`. Then, it multiplies that result by 4.
>
> **Parentheses can be used to group operations.** If you want to divide 4 into beatsPerMin first, you can do this: `wholeNote = 60000 / (beatsPerMin * 4)`.

This is all the same as the previous program:

```
DO UNTIL noteLetter = "Q"

  READ Notes + index, noteLetter

  LOOKDOWN noteLetter,  [ "C",  "d",  "D",  "e",  "E",
                          "F",  "g",  "G",  "a",  "A",
                          "b",  "B",  "P",  "Q"     ], offset
```

Now that octaves are in the mix, the part of the code that figures out the note frequency has changed. The `LOOKUP` command's table of values contains note frequencies from the $8^{th}$ octave. These values can be divided by 1 if you want to play notes in the $8^{th}$ octave, by 2 if you want to play notes in the $7^{th}$ octave, by 4 if you want to play notes in the $6^{th}$ octave and by 8 if you want to play notes in the $5^{th}$ octave. The division happens next. All this `LOOKUP` command does is place a note from the $8^{th}$ octave into the `noteFreq` variable.

```
  LOOKUP offset,         [ 4186, 4435, 4699, 4978, 5274,
                           5588, 5920, 6272, 6645, 7040,
                           7459, 7902,    0,    0     ], noteFreq
```

Here is how the `noteFreq` variable is adjusted for the correct octave. First, the `READ` command grabs the octave value stored in the `Octaves DATA`. This could be a value between 5 and 8.

```
  READ Octaves + index, noteOctave
```

Depending on the octave, we want to divide `noteFreq` by either 1, 2, 4, or 8. That means that the goal is really to divide by $2^0 = 1$, $2^1 = 2$, $2^2 = 4$, or $2^3 = 8$. The statement below takes the value of `noteOctave`, which could be a value between 5 and 8, and subtracts that value from 8. If `noteOctave` was 8, now it's 0. If `noteOctave` was 7, now it's 1. If `noteOctave` was 6, now it's 2, and if `noteOctave` was 5, now it's 3.

```
noteOctave = 8 - noteOctave
```

Now, `noteOctave` is a value that can be used as an exponent of 2, but how do you raise 2 to a power in PBASIC? One answer is to use the `DCD` operator. `DCD 0` is 1, `DCD 1` is 2, `DCD 2` is 4, and `DCD 3` is 8. Dividing `noteFreq` by `DCD noteOctave` means you are dividing by 1, 2, 4, or 8, which divides `noteFreq` down by the correct value. The end result is that `noteFreq` is set to the correct octave. You will use the Debug Terminal in the Your Turn section to take a closer look at how this works.

```
noteFreq = noteFreq / (DCD noteOctave)
```

**How am I supposed to know to use the DCD operator?** Keep learning and practicing. Every time you see a new command, operator, or any other keyword used in an example, look it up in the BASIC Stamp manual. Read about it, and try using it in a program of your own design. Get in the habit of periodically reading the BASIC Stamp Manual and trying the short example programs. That's the best way to get familiar with the various commands and operators and how they work. By doing these things, you will develop a habit of always adding to the list of programming tools you can use to solve problems.

The first two lines of code for determining the note duration are about the same as the code from the previous example program. Now, however, any note could be dotted, which means the duration might have to be multiplied by 1.5. A `READ` command is used to access values stored in `EEPROM` by the `Dots DATA` directive. An `IF...THEN` statement is used to multiply by 3 and divide by 2 whenever the value of the `noteDot` variable is 1.

```
READ Durations + index, noteDuration
noteDuration = WholeNote / noteDuration

READ Dots + index, noteDot
IF noteDot = 1 THEN noteDuration = noteDuration * 3 / 2
```

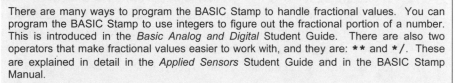

**Integer math** The BASIC Stamp does not automatically process a number like 1.5. When performing math, it only works with integers: ..., -5, -4, -3, -2, -1, 0, 1, 2, 3, ... The best solution for multiplying by 1.5 is to multiply by 3/2. First, multiply by 3, and then divide by 2.

There are many ways to program the BASIC Stamp to handle fractional values. You can program the BASIC Stamp to use integers to figure out the fractional portion of a number. This is introduced in the *Basic Analog and Digital* Student Guide. There are also two operators that make fractional values easier to work with, and they are: `**` and `*/`. These are explained in detail in the *Applied Sensors* Student Guide and in the BASIC Stamp Manual.

The remainder of this example program works the same way that it did in the previous example program:

```
        FREQOUT 9, noteDuration, noteFreq
        index = index + 1
   LOOP
   END
```

### Your Turn – Playing a Tune with More than One Octave

MusicWithMoreFeatures.bs2 made use of rests, but it stayed in one octave. The tune "Take Me Out to the Ball Game" shown below plays most of its notes in the 6th octave. There are two notes in the 7th octave, and they make a big difference to the way it sounds.

   √   Save the example program under the name
       MusicWithMoreFeaturesYourTurn.bs2.
   √   Modify the program by replacing the four data directives and one constant declaration with these:

```
Notes           DATA      "C","C","A","G","E","G","D","P","C","C","A",
                          "G","E","G","Q"
Octaves         DATA       6,  7,  6,  6,  6,  6,  6,  6,  6,  7,  6,
                           6,  6,  6
Durations       DATA       2,  4,  4,  4,  4,  2,  2,  4,  2,  4,  4,
                           4,  4,  2
Dots            DATA       0,  0,  0,  0,  0,  1,  0,  0,  0,  0,  0,
                           0,  0,  1

BeatsPerMin     CON       240
```

   √   Run the program and verify that it sounds right.

Those two notes in the 7th octave are essential for making the tune sound right. It's interesting to hear what happens if those 7 values are changed to 6.

   √   Try changing the two 7 values in the **Octaves DATA** directive so that they are 6. Keep in mind, this will make "Take Me out to the Ball Game" sound weird.
   √   Run the program, and listen to the effect of the wrong octaves on the song.
   √   Change the **Octaves DATA** back to its original state.
   √   Run the program again and listen to see if it sounds correct again.

## ACTIVITY #5: CELL PHONE RINGTONES

Many cell phones play music that can be downloaded from web pages. The computer sends the data about the notes to the microcontroller in the phone, then plays the notes whenever a call comes in. These are called ringing tones or often just ringtones.

One of the most widely used way of composing, recording and posting notes is one that features strings of text that describe each note in the song. Here is an example of how the first few notes from Beethoven's 5th look in RTTTL format:

Beethoven5:d=8,o=7,b=125:g,g,g,2d#,p,f,f,f,2d

This format for storing musical data is called RTTTL, which stand for Ringing Tone Text Transfer Language. The great thing about RTTTL files is that they are widely shared via the World Wide Web. Many sites have RTTTL files available for free download. There are also free software programs that can be used to compose and emulate these files as well as download them to your cell phone. The RTTTL specification is also published on the World Wide Web. Appendix G summarizes how an RTTTL file stores notes, durations, pauses, tempo, and dotted notes.

This activity introduces some PBASIC programming techniques that can be used to recognize different elements of text. The ability to recognize different characters or groups of characters and take action based on what those characters contain is extremely useful. In fact, it's the key to converting RTTTL format ringtone (like Beethoven5 above) into music. At the end of this activity, there is an application program that you can use to play RTTTL format ringtones.

### Selecting which Code Block to Execute on a Case by Case Basis

The **SELECT...CASE** statement is probably the best programming tool for recognizing characters or values. Keep in mind that this is one of the tools used to convert an RTTTL ringtone into musical notes. In general, **SELECT...CASE** is used to:

- Select a variable or expression.
- Evaluate that variable or expression on a case by case basis.
- Execute different blocks of code depending on which case that variable's value fits into.

Here is the syntax for **SELECT...CASE**:

```
SELECT expression
  CASE condition(s)
    statement(s)
ENDSELECT
```

You can try the next two example programs to see how **SELECT...CASE** works. SelectCaseWithValues.bs2 takes numeric values you enter into the Debug Terminal and it tells you the minimum variable size you will need to hold that value. SelectCaseWithCharacters.bs2 tells you whether the character you entered into the Debug Terminal is upper or lower case, a digit, or punctuation.

Remember to use the upper Windowpane in the Debug Terminal to transmit the characters you type to the BASIC Stamp. The Transmit and Receive Windowpanes are shown in Figure 8-5.

**Windowpanes**

Transmit →

Receive →

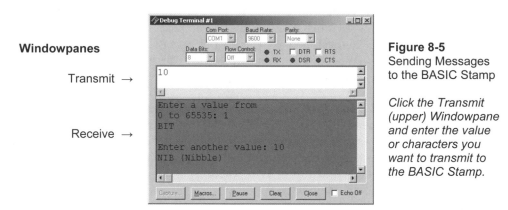

**Figure 8-5**
Sending Messages
to the BASIC Stamp

*Click the Transmit
(upper) Windowpane
and enter the value
or characters you
want to transmit to
the BASIC Stamp.*

### Example Program: SelectCaseWithValues.bs2

√   Enter and run SelectCaseWithValues.bs2.
√   Click the Debug Terminal's Transmit Windowpane.
√   Enter a value between 0 and 65535, and press the *Enter* key.

**What happens if you enter a number larger than 65535?**  If you enter the number 65536, the BASIC Stamp will store the number 0.  If you enter the number 65537, the BASIC Stamp will store the number 1, and so on.  When a number is too large for the variable it fits into, it is called overflow.

√ Use Table 2-2 to verify that the example program makes the right decisions about the size of the numbers you enter into the Debug Terminal.

| Table 2-2: Variable Types and Values They Can Store | |
|---|---|
| **Variable type** | **Range of Values** |
| Bit | 0 to 1 |
| Nib | 0 to 15 |
| Byte | 0 to 255 |
| Word | 0 to 65535 |

```
' What's a Microcontroller - SelectCaseWithValues.bs2
' Enter a value and see the minimum variable size required to hold it.

'{$STAMP BS2}
'{$PBASIC 2.5}

value          VAR     Word

DEBUG "Enter a value from", CR,
      "0 to 65535: "

DO

  DEBUGIN DEC value

  SELECT value

    CASE 0, 1
      DEBUG "Bit", CR
      PAUSE 100

    CASE 2 TO 15
      DEBUG "Nib (Nibble)", CR
      PAUSE 200

    CASE 16 TO 255
      DEBUG "Byte", CR
      PAUSE 300

    CASE 256 TO 65535
      DEBUG "Word", CR
      PAUSE 400

  ENDSELECT

  DEBUG CR, "Enter another value: "

LOOP
```

8

### How SelectCaseWithValues.bs2 Works

A word variable is declared to hold the values entered into the Debug Terminal.

```
value VAR Word
```

The **DEBUGIN** command takes the number you enter and places it into the **value** variable.

```
DEBUGIN DEC value
```

The **SELECT** statement chooses the **value** variable as the one to evaluate cases for.

```
SELECT value
```

The first case is if the **value** variable equals either 0 or 1. If **value** equals either of those numbers, the **DEBUG** and **PAUSE** commands that follow it are executed.

```
CASE 0, 1
  DEBUG "BIT", CR
  PAUSE 100
```

The second case is if **value** equals any number from 2 to 15. If it does equal any of those numbers, the **DEBUG** and **PAUSE** commands below it are executed.

```
CASE 2 to 15
  DEBUG "NIB (Nibble)", CR
  PAUSE 200
```

When all the cases are done, the **ENDSELECT** keyword is used to complete the **SELECT..CASE** statement.

```
ENDSELECT
```

### Example Program: SelectCaseWithCharacters.bs2

This example program evaluates each character you enter into the Debug Terminal's Transmit Windowpane. It can recognize upper and lower case characters, digits, and some punctuation. If you enter a character the program does not recognize, it will tell you to try again (entering a different character).

- √   Enter and run SelectCaseWithCharacters.bs2.
- √   Click Debug Terminal's Transmit Windowpane, enter characters and observe the results.

```
' What's a Microcontroller - SelectCaseWithCharacters.bs2
' Program that can identify some characters: case, digit, punctuation.
```

```
'{$STAMP BS2}
'{$PBASIC 2.5}

character          VAR      Byte

DEBUG "Enter a character: ", CR

DO

  DEBUGIN character

  SELECT character

    CASE "A" TO "Z"
      DEBUG CR, "Upper case", CR

    CASE "a" TO "z"
      DEBUG CR, "Lower case", CR

    CASE "0" TO "9"
      DEBUG CR, "Digit", CR

    CASE "!", "?", ".", ","
      DEBUG CR, "Punctuation", CR

    CASE ELSE
      DEBUG CR, "Character not known.", CR,
                "Try a different one."

  ENDSELECT

  DEBUG CR, "Enter another character", CR

LOOP
```

### How SelectCaseWithCharacters.bs2 Works

When compared to SelectCaseWithValues.bs2, this example program has a few differences. First, the name of the **value** variable was changed to **character**, and its size was changed from word to byte. This is because all characters in PBASIC are byte size. The **SELECT** statement chooses the **character** variable for case by case evaluation.

```
        SELECT character
```

The quotation marks are used to tell the BASIC Stamp Editor that you are referring to characters.

```
        SELECT character
```

```
CASE "A" to "Z"
  DEBUG CR, "Upper case", CR

CASE "a" to "z"
  DEBUG CR, "Lower case", CR

CASE "0" to "9"
  DEBUG CR, "Digit", CR

CASE "!", "?", ".", ","
  DEBUG CR, "Punctuation", CR
```

There is also one different **CASE** statement that was not used in the previous example:

```
CASE ELSE
  DEBUG CR, "Character not known.", CR,
            "Try a different one."
```

This **CASE** statement tells the **SELECT** code block what to do if none of the other cases are true. You can get this case to work by entering a character such as % or $.

### Your Turn – Selecting Based on Ranges

√   Modify the **SELECT…CASE** statement in SelectCaseWithCharacters.bs2 so that it displays "Special character" when you enter one of these characters: @, #, $, %, '^' , &, *, (, ), _, or +.

### RTTTL Ringtone Player Application Program

Below is the RTTTL file that contains the musical information used in the next example program. There are five more **RTTTL_File DATA** directives that you can try in the Your Turn section. This program plays a tune called Reveille, which is the bugle call played at military camps first thing in the morning. You may have heard it in any number of movies or television shows.

```
RTTTL_File    DATA    "Reveille:d=4,o=7,b=140:8g6,8c,16e,16c,8g6,8e,",
                      "8c,16e,16c,8g6,8e,8c,16e,16c,8a6,8c,e,8c,8g6,",
                      "8c,16e,16c,8g6,8e,8c,16e,16c,8g6,8e,8c,16e,",
                      "16c,8g6,8e,c,p,8e,8e,8e,8e,g,8e,8c,8e,8c,8e,8c,",
                      "e,8c,8e,8e,8e,8e,8e,g,8e,8c,8e,8c,8g6,8g6,c."
```

### Example Program: MicroMusicWithRtttl.bs2

This application program is pretty long, and it's a good idea to download the latest version from the www.parallax.com → Downloads → Educational Curriculum page.

Look for a link named *Selected Example Programs* near the What's a Microcontroller PDF downloads. Downloading the program and opening it with the BASIC Stamp Editor should save you a significant amount of time. The alternative, of course, is to hand enter and debug four pages of code.

√ Use the BASIC Stamp Editor to open your downloaded MicroMusicWithRtttl.bs2 file, or hand enter the example below very carefully.

√ Run the program, and verify that the piece is recognizable as the Reveille bugle call.

√ Go to the Your Turn section and try some more tunes (RTTTL_File DATA directives).

```
' What's a Microcontroller - MicroMusicWithRtttl.bs2
' Play Nokia RTTTL format ringtones using DATA.

'{$STAMP BS2}
'{$PBASIC 2.5}
DEBUG "Program Running!"

' -----[ I/O Definitions ]-------------------------------------------

  SpeakerPin      CON     9                  ' Piezospeaker connected to P9.

' -----[ Variables ]-------------------------------------------------

  counter         VAR     Word               ' General purpose counter.
  char            VAR     Byte               ' Variable stores characters.
  index           VAR     Word               ' Index for pointing at data.

  noteLetter      VAR     Byte               ' Stores note character.
  noteFreq        VAR     Word               ' Stores note frequency.
  noteOctave      VAR     Word               ' Stores note octave.

  duration        VAR     Word               ' Stores note duration.
  tempo           VAR     Word               ' Stores tempo.

  default_d       VAR     Byte               ' Stores default duration.
  default_o       VAR     Byte               ' Stores default octave.
  default_b       VAR     Word               ' Stores default beats/min.

' -----[ EEPROM Data ]-----------------------------------------------

  RTTTL_File      DATA    "Reveille:d=4,o=7,b=140:8g6,8c,16e,16c,8g6,8e,",
                          "8c,16e,16c,8g6,8e,8c,16e,16c,8a6,8c,e,8c,8g6,",
                          "8c,16e,16c,8g6,8e,8c,16e,16c,8g6,8e,8c,16e,",
                          "16c,8g6,8e,c,p,8e,8e,8e,8e,g,8e,8c,8e,8c,8e,8c,",
                          "e,8c,8e,8e,8e,8e,8e,g,8e,8c,8e,8c,8g6,8g6,c."
```

8

```
Done            DATA      ",q,"

Notes           DATA      "p",        "a",        "#",        "b",
                          "c",        "#",        "d",        "#",
                          "e",        "f",        "#",        "g",
                          "#"
Octave8         DATA      Word 0,     Word 3520, Word 3729, Word 3951,
                          Word 4186, Word 4435, Word 4699, Word 4978,
                          Word 5274, Word 5588, Word 5920, Word 6272,
                          Word 6645


' -----[ Initialization ]-------------------------------------------------

counter = 0                               ' Initialize counter.

GOSUB FindEquals                          ' Find first '=' in file.
GOSUB ProcessDuration                     ' Get default duration.
GOSUB FindEquals                          ' Find next '='.
GOSUB ProcessOctave                       ' Get default octave.
GOSUB FindEquals                          ' Find last '='.
GOSUB GetTempo                            ' Get default tempo.

' -----[ Program Code ]---------------------------------------------------

DO UNTIL char = "q"                       ' Loop until 'q' in DATA.
  GOSUB ProcessDuration                   ' Get note duration.
  GOSUB ProcessNote                       ' Get index value of note.
  GOSUB CheckForDot                       ' If dot, 3/2 duration.
  GOSUB ProcessOctave                     ' Get octave.
  GOSUB PlayNote                          ' Get freq, play note, next.
LOOP                                      ' End of main loop.

END                                       ' End of program.

' -----[ Subroutine - Find Equals Character ]-----------------------------

FindEquals:                               ' Go through characters in
                                          ' RTTTL file looking for
  DO                                      ' '='.  Increment counter
    READ RTTTL_File + counter, char       ' until '=' is found, then
    counter = counter + 1                 ' return.
  LOOP UNTIL char = "="

  RETURN

' -----[ Subroutine - Read Tempo from RTTTL Header ]----------------------
' Each keyboard character has a unique number called an ASCII value.
' The characters 0, 1, 2,...9 have ASCII values of 48, 49, 50,...57.
' You can always convert from the character representing a digit to
' to its value by subtracting 48 from the variable storing the digit.
```

```
' You can examine this by comparing DEBUG DEC 49 and DEBUG 49.

  GetTempo:                              ' Parse RTTTL file for Tempo.
                                         ' Convert characters to
    default_b = 0                        ' digits by subtracting 48
    DO                                   ' from each character's ASCII
      READ RTTTL_File + counter, char    ' value.  Iteratively multiply
      IF char = ":" THEN                 ' each digit by 10 if there
        default_b = default_b / 10       ' is another digit, then add
        counter = counter + 1            ' the most recent digit to
        EXIT                             ' one's column.
      ENDIF                              ' For example, the string
        default_b = default_b + char - 48  ' "120" is (1 X 10 X 10)
        counter = counter + 1            ' + (2 X 10) + 0.  The '1'
        default_b = default_b * 10       ' is converted first, then
    LOOP UNTIL char = ":"                ' multiplied by 10.  The '2'
                                         ' is then converted/added.
    RETURN                               ' 0 is converted/added, done.

' -----[ Subroutine - Look up Octave ]----------------------------------

  ProcessOctave:                         ' Octave may or may not be
                                         ' included in a given note
    READ RTTTL_File + counter, char      ' because any note that is
    SELECT char                          ' played in the default
      CASE "5" TO "8"                    ' octave does not specify
        noteOctave = char - "0"          ' the octave.  If a char
        counter = counter + 1            ' from '5' to '8' then use
      CASE ELSE                          ' it, else use default_o.
        noteOctave = default_o           ' Characters are converted
    ENDSELECT                            ' to digits by subtracting
    IF default_o = 0 THEN                ' '0', which is the same as
      default_o = noteOctave             ' subtracting 48. The first
    ENDIF                                ' time this subroutine is
                                         ' called, default_o is 0.
    RETURN                               ' If 0, then set default_o.

' -----[ Subroutine - Find Index of Note ]------------------------------

  ProcessNote:                           ' Set index value for lookup
                                         ' of note frequency based on
    READ RTTTL_File + counter, char      ' note character. If 'p',
    SELECT char                          ' index is 0.  If 'a' to 'g',
      CASE "p"                           ' read character values in
        index = 0                        ' DATA table and find match.
        counter = counter + 1            ' Record index value when
      CASE "a" TO "g"                    ' match is found.  If next
        FOR index = 1 TO 12              ' char is a sharp (#), add
          READ Notes + index, noteLetter ' 1 to the index value to
          IF noteLetter = char THEN EXIT ' increase the index (and
        NEXT                             ' frequency) by 1 notch.
```

```
         counter = counter + 1           ' As with other subroutines,
         READ RTTTL_File + counter, char ' increment counter for each
         SELECT char                     ' character that is processed.
           CASE "#"
             index = index + 1
             counter = counter + 1
         ENDSELECT
     ENDSELECT

     RETURN

' -----[ Subroutine - Determine Note Duration ]--------------------------

   ProcessDuration:                       ' Check to see if characters
                                          ' form 1, 2, 4, 8, 16 or 32.
     READ RTTTL_File + counter, char      ' If yes, then convert from
                                          ' ASCII character to a value
     SELECT char                          ' by subtracting 48. In the
       CASE "1", "2", "3", "4", "8"       ' case of 16 or 32, multiply
         duration = char - 48             ' by 10 and add the next
         counter = counter + 1            ' digit to the ones column.
         READ RTTTL_File + counter, char
         SELECT char
           CASE "6", "2"
             duration = duration * 10 + char - 48
             counter = counter + 1
         ENDSELECT
       CASE ELSE                          ' If no duration, use
         duration = default_d             ' use default.
     ENDSELECT

     IF default_d <> 0 THEN               ' If default_d not defined
       duration = 60000/default_b/duration*3 ' (if default_d = 0), then
     ELSE                                 ' set default_d = to the
       default_d = duration               ' duration from the d=#.
     ENDIF

     RETURN

' -----[ Subroutine - Check For '.' Indicating 1.5 Duration ]-------------

   CheckForDot:                           ' Check for dot indicating
                                          ' multiply duration by 3/2.
     READ RTTTL_File + counter, char      ' If dot found, multiply by
     SELECT char                          ' 3/2 and increment counter,
       CASE "."                           ' else, do nothing and
         duration = duration * 3 / 2      ' return.
         counter = counter + 1
     ENDSELECT

     RETURN
```

```
' -----[ Subroutine - Find Comma and Play Note/Duration ]-----------------

  PlayNote:                                  ' Find last comma in the
                                             ' current note entry.  Then,
    READ RTTTL_File + counter, char          ' fetch the note frequency
    SELECT char                              ' from data, and play it, or
      CASE ","                               ' pause if frequency = 0.
        counter = counter + 1
        READ Octave8 + (index * 2), Word noteFreq
        noteOctave = 8 - noteOctave
        noteFreq = noteFreq / (DCD noteOctave)
        IF noteFreq = 0 THEN
           PAUSE duration
        ELSE
           FREQOUT SpeakerPin, duration, noteFreq
        ENDIF
    ENDSELECT

  RETURN
```

### How MicroMusicWithRtttl.bs2 Works

This example program is fun to use, and it shows the kind of code you will be able to write with some practice. However, it was included in this text more for fun than for the coding concepts it employs.

If you examine the code briefly, you might notice that you have already used all of the commands and operators in the program. Here is a list of the elements in this application example that should, by now, be familiar:

- Comments to help explain your code
- Constant and variable declarations
- **DATA** declarations
- **READ** commands
- **IF...ELSE...ENDIF** blocks
- **DO...LOOP** both with and without **WHILE** and **UNTIL**
- Subroutines with **GOSUB**, labels, and **RETURN**
- **FOR...NEXT** loops
- **LOOKUP** and **LOOKDOWN** commands
- The **FREQOUT** and **PAUSE** commands
- **SELECT...CASE**

## Your Turn – Different Tunes

√  Try replacing the **RTTTL_File DATA** directive in MicroMusicWithRTTTL.bs2
   with each of the five different music files below.

 **Only one RTTTL_File DATA directive at a time!** Make sure to replace, not add, your
new **RTTTL_File DATA** directive.

√  Run MicroMusicWithRTTTL.bs2 to test each RTTTL file.

```
RTTTL_File      DATA      "TwinkleTwinkle:d=4,o=7,b=120:c,c,g,g,a,a,2g,f,",
                         "f,e,e,d,d,2c,g,g,f,f,e,e,2d,g,g,f,f,e,e,2d,c,c,",
                         "g,g,a,a,2g,f,f,e,e,d,d,1c"

RTTTL_File      DATA      "FrereJacques:d=4,o=7,b=125:c,d,e,c,c,d,e,c,e,f,",
                         ",2g,e,f,2g,8g,8a,8g,8f,e,c,8g,8a,8g,8f,e,c,c,g6",
                         ",2c,c,g6,2c"

RTTTL_File      DATA      "Beethoven5:d=8,o=7,b=125:g,g,g,2d#,p,f,f,f,2d"

RTTTL_File      DATA      "ForHe'sAJollyGoodFellow:d=4,o=7,b=320:c,2e,e,e,",
                         "d,e,2f.,2e,e,2d,d,d,c,d,2e.,2c,d,2e,e,e,d,e,2f,",
                         "g,2a,a,g,g,g,2f,d,2c"

RTTTL_File      DATA      "TakeMeOutToTheBallgame:d=4,o=7,b=225:2c6,c,a6,",
                         "g6,e6,2g.6,2d6,p,2c6,c,a6,g6,e6,2g.6,g6,p,p,a6",
                         ",g#6,a6,e6,f6,g6,a6,p,f6,2d6,p,2a6,a6,a6,b6,c,",
                         "d,b6,a6,g6"
```

 **Downloading RTTTL Files:** There are lots of RTTTL files available for download from
various sites on the World Wide Web. These files are contributed by ring-tone enthusiasts,
many of whom are not music experts. Some phone tones are pretty good, others are barely
recognizable. If you want to download and play some more RTTTL files, make sure to
remove any spaces from between characters, then insert the text file between quotes.

## SUMMARY

This chapter introduced techniques for making sounds and musical tones using the BASIC Stamp and a piezoelectric speaker. The **FREQOUT** command can be used to send a piezoelectric speaker high/low signals that cause it to make sound effects and/or musical notes. The **FREQOUT** command has arguments that control the I/O Pin the signal is sent to, the *Duration* of the tone, the frequency of the tone (*Freq1*). The optional *Freq2* argument can be used to mix tones.

Sound effects can be made by adjusting the frequency and duration of tones and the pauses between. The value of the frequency can also be swept across a range of values or mixed to create a variety of effects.

Making musical notes also depends on frequency, duration, and pauses. The value of the **FREQOUT** command's *Duration* argument is determined by the tempo of the song and the duration of the note (whole, half, quarter, etc.). The *Freq1* value of the note is determined by the note's letter and octave. Rests between notes are used to set the duration of the **PAUSE** command.

Playing simple songs using the BASIC Stamp can be done with a sequence of **FREQOUT** commands, but there are better ways to store and retrieve musical data. **DATA** directives along with their optional *Symbol* labels were used to store byte values using no prefix and word values using the **Word** prefix. The **READ** command was used to retrieve values stored by **DATA** directives. The **READ** command's *Address* argument always used the **DATA** directive's optional *Symbol* label to differentiate between different types of data. Some the symbol labels that were used were **Notes**, **Durations**, **Dots**, and **Octaves**.

Musical data can be stored in formats that lend themselves to translation from sheet music. The sheet music style data can then be converted into **Frequency** using the **LOOKUP** and **LOOKDOWN** commands. Mathematic operations can also be performed on variable values to change the octave of a note by dividing its frequency by a power of two. Mathematic operations are also useful for note durations given either the tempo or the duration of a whole note.

**SELECT...CASE** was introduced as a way of evaluating a variable on a case by case basis. **SELECT...CASE** is particularly useful for examining characters or numbers when there are many choices as to what the variable could be and many different sets of actions that

8

need to be taken based on the variable's value. A program that converts strings of characters that describe musical tones for cell phones (called RTTTL files) was used to introduce a larger program that makes use of all the programming techniques introduced in this text. **SELECT...CASE** played a prominent role in this program because it is used to examine characters selected in an RTTTL file on a case-by-case basis.

## Questions

1. What causes a tone to sound high-pitched? What causes a tone to sound low-pitched?
2. What does **FREQOUT 15, 1000, 3000** do? What effect does each of the numbers have?
3. How can you modify the **FREQOUT** command from Question 2 so that it sends two frequencies at once?
4. If you strike a piano's B6 key, what frequency does it send?
5. How do you modify a **DATA** directive or **READ** command if you want to store and retrieve word values?
6. Can you have more than one **DATA** directive? If so, how would you tell a **READ** command to get data from one or the other **DATA** directive?
7. What's an octave? If you know the frequency of a note in one octave, what do you have to do to that frequency to play it in the next higher octave?
8. What does **SELECT...CASE** do?

## Exercises

1. Modify the "Alarm..." tone from ActionTones.bs2 so that the frequency of the tone it plays increases by 500 each time the tone repeats.
2. Explain how to modify MusicWithMoreFeatures.bs2 so that it displays an alert message in the Debug Terminal each time a dotted note is played.

## Project

1. Build pushbutton controlled tone generator. If one pushbutton is pressed, the speaker should make a 2 kHz beep for 1/5 of a second. If the other pushbutton is pressed the speaker should make a 3 kHz beep for 1/10 of a second.

## Solutions

Q1. Our ears detect changes in air pressure as tones. A high pitched tone is from faster changes in air pressure, a low pitched tone from slower changes in air pressure.

Q2. **FREQOUT 15, 1000, 3000** sends a 3000 Hz signal out pin 15 for one second (1000 ms).

The effect of each number:

15 – pin number 15.

1000 – duration of tone equals 1000 ms or one second.

3000 – the frequency of the tone, in Hertz, so this sends a 3000 Hz tone.

Q3. Use the optional *Freq2* argument. To mix 3000 Hz and say, 2000 Hz, we simply add the second frequency to the command, after a comma:

**FREQOUT 15, 1000, 3000, 2000**

Q4. 1975.5 Hz, see Figure 8-3 on page 228.

Q5. Use the optional **Word** modifier before each data item.

Q6. Yes. Each **DATA** directive has a different symbol parameter. To specify which **DATA** directive to get the data from, include the symbol parameter after the **READ** keyword. For example: **READ Notes, noteLetter**. In this example, **Notes** is the symbol parameter.

Q7. An octave is a group of 8 whole and 4 chromatic notes. To get a given note in the next higher octave, multiply the frequency by two.

Q8. **SELECT...CASE** selects a variable or expression, evaluates it on a case by case basis, and executes different blocks of code depending on which case the variable's value fits into.

E1. This problem can be solved either by manually increasing each tone by 500, or by utilizing a **FOR...NEXT** loop with a **STEP** value of 500.

Utilizing **FOR...NEXT** loop:

```
DEBUG "Increasing alarm...", CR
    PAUSE 100
    FOR frequency = 1500 TO 3000 STEP 500
      FREQOUT 9, 500, frequency
      PAUSE 500
    NEXT
```

Manually increasing tone:

```
DEBUG "Increasing Alarm...",CR
    PAUSE 100
    FREQOUT 9, 500, 1500
    PAUSE 500
    FREQOUT 9, 500, 2000
    PAUSE 500
    FREQOUT 9, 500, 2500
    PAUSE 500
    FREQOUT 9, 500, 3000
    PAUSE 500
```

E2. Modify the lines that check for the dotted note:

```
READ Dots + index, noteDot
```

8

```
      IF noteDot = 1 THEN noteDuration = noteDuration * 3 / 2
```
Add a **DEBUG** command to the **IF...THEN**. Don't forget the **ENDIF**.
```
      READ Dots + index, noteDot
      IF noteDot = 1 THEN
        noteDuration = noteDuration * 3 / 2
        DEBUG "Dotted Note!", CR
      ENDIF
```

P1. Use the piezospeaker circuit from Figure 8-2, p. 220; pushbutton circuits from Figure 4-20, p. 129.

```
' What's a Microcontroller - Ch8Prj01_PushButtonToneGenerator.bs2
' P4 Pressed:  2 kHz beep for 1/5 second. 2 kHz = 2000 Hz.
'              1/5 s = 1000 / 5 ms = 200 ms
' P3 Pressed:  3 kHz beep for 1/10 second. 3 kHz = 3000 Hz.
'              1/10 s =  1000 / 10 ms = 100 ms
'{$STAMP BS2}
'{$PBASIC 2.5}
DEBUG "Program Running!"


DO
  IF (IN4 = 1) THEN
    FREQOUT 9, 200, 2000                    ' 2000 Hz for 200 ms
  ELSEIF (IN3 = 1) THEN
    FREQOUT 9, 100, 3000                    ' 3000 Hz for 100 ms
  ENDIF
LOOP
```

## Further Investigation

**"*Applied Sensors*", Student Guide, Version 2.0, Parallax Inc., 2003**

More sound effects, clicks, crickets are introduced using the piezoelectric speaker. The pentatonic and equal temperament scale are the basis for discussion of math fractions. The speaker is also used as feedback for a variety of sensor measurements.

**"*Basic Analog and Digital*", Student Guide, Version 2.0, Parallax Inc., 2003**

The speaker is used to make a frequency generated by a 555 timer audible. The BASIC Stamp measures the frequency of the tone with a **COUNT** command.

**"*Understanding Signals*", Student Guide, Version 1.0, Parallax Inc., 2003**

You can use this book to view the output of the **FREQOUT** command, both as digital pulses, and as sine waves.

# Chapter #9: Electronic Building Blocks

## THOSE LITTLE BLACK CHIPS

You need look no further than your BASIC Stamp (see Figure 9-1) to find examples of "those little black chips". Each of these chips has a special function. The upper-right chip is the voltage regulator. This chip takes the battery voltage and converts it to almost exactly 5.0 V, which is what the rest of the components on the BASIC Stamp need to run properly. The upper-left chip is the BASIC Stamp module's EEPROM. PBASIC programs are condensed to numbers called tokens that are downloaded to the BASIC Stamp. These tokens are stored in the EEPROM, and you can view them by clicking *Run* and then *Memory Map* in the BASIC Stamp Editor. The largest chip is called the Interpreter chip. It fetches the tokens from the EEPROM and then interprets the PBASIC command that the token represents. Then, it executes the command, fetches the next token, and so on. This process is called "fetch and execute".

**9**

2 K EEPROM
retains your
PBASIC source
code even with
power loss

5 V regulator
accepts an
input voltage
of 5-15 VDC

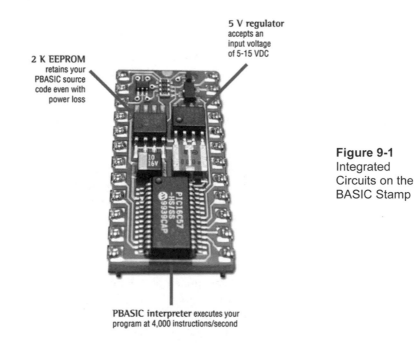

**Figure 9-1**
Integrated
Circuits on the
BASIC Stamp

PBASIC **interpreter** executes your
program at 4,000 instructions/second

People use the term "integrated circuit" (IC) to talk about little black chips. The integrated circuit is actually a tiny silicon chip that's contained inside the black plastic or ceramic case. Depending on the chip, it may have anywhere between hundreds and millions of transistors. A transistor is the basic building block for integrated circuits, and you will have the opportunity to experiment with a transistor in this chapter. Other familiar components that are designed into silicon chips include diodes, resistors and capacitors.

Take a moment to think about the activities you've tried in this book so far. The list includes switching LEDs on and off, reading pushbuttons, controlling servos, reading potentiometers, measuring light, controlling displays, and making sounds. Even though that's just the beginning, it's still pretty impressive, especially considering that you can combine these activities to make more complex gizmos and gadgets. The core of the system that made all those activities possible is comprised of just the three integrated circuits shown in Figure 9-1 and a few other parts. It just goes to show how powerful integrated circuits can be when they are designed to work together.

## EXPAND YOUR PROJECTS WITH PERIPHERAL INTEGRATED CIRCUITS

There are thousands of integrated circuits designed to be used with microcontrollers. Sometimes different integrated circuit manufacturers make chips that perform the same function. Sometimes each chip's features differ slightly, and other times, the chips are identical, but one might cost a little less than the other. Each one of the thousands of different integrated circuits can be used as a building block for a variety of designs. Companies publish information on how each of their integrated circuits work in documents called datasheets that are published on the World Wide Web. These manufacturers also publish application notes, which show how to use their integrated circuit in unique or useful ways that make it easier to design products. The integrated circuit manufacturers give away this information in hopes that engineers will use it to build their chip onto the latest must-have toy or appliance. If thousands of toys are sold, it means the company sells thousands of their integrated circuits.

In this chapter, you will experiment with a transistor, and a special-purpose integrated circuit called a digital potentiometer. As mentioned earlier, the transistor is the basic building block for integrated circuits. It's also a basic building block for lots of other circuits as well. The digital potentiometer also has a variety of uses. Keep in mind that for each activity you have done, there are probably hundreds of different ways that you could use each of these integrated circuits.

## ACTIVITY #1: CONTROL CURRENT FLOW WITH A TRANSISTOR

In this activity, you will use a transistor as a way to control the current passing through an LED. You can use the LED to monitor the current since it glows more brightly when more current passes through it and less brightly when less current passes through it.

### Introducing the Transistor

Figure 9-2 shows the schematic symbol and part drawing of the 2N3904 transistor. There are many different types of transistors. This one is called NPN, which refers to the type of materials used to manufacture the transistor and the way those materials are layered on the silicon. The best way to get started thinking about a transistor is to imagine it as a valve that is used to control current. Different transistors control how much current passes through by different means. This transistor controls how much current passes into C (collector) and back out of E (emitter). It uses the amount of current allowed into the B (base) terminal to control the current passing from C through E. With a very small amount of current allowed into B, a current flow of about 416 times that amount flows through the transistor into C and out of E.

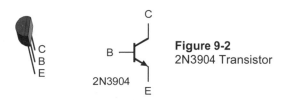

**Figure 9-2**
2N3904 Transistor

---

**The 2N3904 Part Datasheet:** As mentioned earlier, semiconductor manufacturers publish documents called datasheets for the parts they make. These datasheets contain information engineers use to design the part into a product. To see an example of a part datasheet for the 2N3904: Go to www.fairchildsemi.com. Enter 2N3904 into the Search field on Fairchild Semiconductor's home page, and click Go. One of the search results should be a link to the 2N3904 Product Folder. Follow the link to the product folder, then click Download this Datasheet link. Most web browsers display the datasheet by opening it with Adobe Acrobat Reader.

---

### Transistor Example Parts

(1) Transistor – 2N3904
(2) Resistors – 100 kΩ (brown-black-yellow)
(1) LED – any color

(1) Potentiometer – 10 kΩ
(3) Jumper wires

### Building and Testing the Transistor Circuit

Figure 9-3 shows a circuit that you can use to manually control how much current the transistor allows through the LED. By twisting the knob on the potentiometer, the circuit will deliver different amounts of current to the transistor's base. This will cause a change in the amount of current the transistor allows to pass from its collector to its emitter. The LED will give you a clear indication of the change by glowing more or less brightly.

√  Build the circuit shown in Figure 9-3.
√  Turn the knob on the potentiometer and verify that the LED changes brightness in response to a change in the position of the potentiometer's wiper terminal.

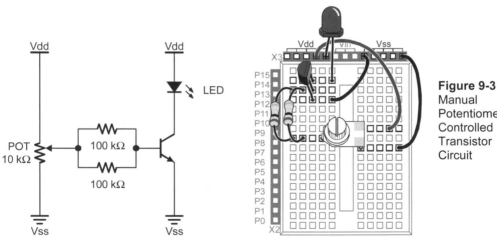

**Figure 9-3**
Manual
Potentiometer
Controlled
Transistor
Circuit

### Your Turn – Switching the Transistor On/Off

If all you want to do is switch a transistor on and off, you can use the circuit shown in Figure 9-4. When the BASIC Stamp sends a high signal to this circuit, it will make it so that the transistor conducts as much current as if you adjusted the potentiometer for maximum brightness. When the BASIC Stamp sends a low signal to this circuit, it will cause the transistor to stop conducting current, and the LED should emit no light.

> **What's the difference between this and connecting an LED circuit to an I/O pin?**
> BASIC Stamp I/O pins have limitations on how much current they can deliver. Transistors have limitations too, but they are much higher. In the *Industrial Control Student Guide*, a transistor is used to drive a small DC fan. It is also used to supply large amounts of current to a small resistor that is used as a heating element. Either of these two applications would draw so much current that they would quickly damage the BASIC Stamp, but the transistor takes it in stride.

√  Build the circuit shown in Figure 9-4.

√  Write a program that sends high and low signals to P8 twice every second. HINT: LedOnOff.bs2 from Chapter #2 needs only to be modified to send high/low signals to P8 instead of P3. Remember to save it under a new name before making the modifications.

√  Run the program and verify that it gives you on/off control of the LED.

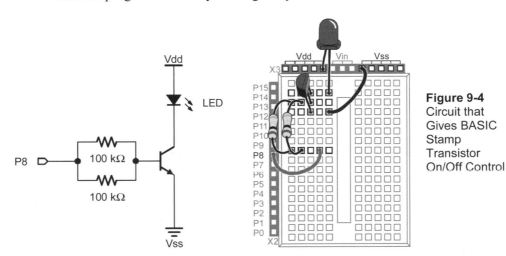

**Figure 9-4**
Circuit that Gives BASIC Stamp Transistor On/Off Control

## ACTIVITY #2: INTRODUCING THE DIGITAL POTENTIOMETER

In this activity, you will replace the manually adjusted potentiometer with an integrated circuit potentiometer that is digitally adjusted. You will then program the BASIC Stamp to adjust the digital potentiometer, which will in turn adjust the LED's brightness in the same way the manual potentiometer did in the previous activity.

## Introducing the Digital Potentiometer

Figure 9-5 shows a pin map of the digital potentiometer you will use in this activity. This chip has 8 pins, four on each side that are spaced to make it easy to plug into a breadboard (1/10 inch apart). The manufacturer places a reference notch on the plastic case so that you can tell the difference between pin 1 and pin 5. The reference notch is a small half-circle in the chip's case. You can use this notch as a reference for the pin numbers on the chip. The pin numbers on the chip count upwards, counterclockwise from the reference notch.

 **Part Substitutions:** It is sometimes necessary for Parallax to make a part substitution. The part will function the same, but the label on it may be different. If you find that the digital potentiometer included in your What's a Microcontroller Parts Kit is not labeled AD5220, rest assured that it will still work the same way and perform correctly in this activity.

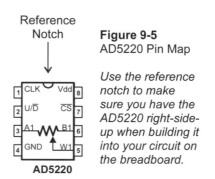

Reference Notch

**Figure 9-5**
AD5220 Pin Map

*Use the reference notch to make sure you have the AD5220 right-side-up when building it into your circuit on the breadboard.*

Here is a summary of each of the AD5220's pins and functions:

1. CLK – The pin that receives clock pulses (low-high-low signals) to move the wiper terminal.
2. U/D – The pin that receives a high signal to make the wiper (W1) terminal move towards A1, and a low signal to make it move towards B1. This pin just sets the direction, the wiper terminal doesn't actually move until a pulse (a low – high – low signal) is sent to the CLK pin.
3. A1 – The potentiometer's A terminal.
4. GND – The ground connection. The ground on the Board of Education and BASIC Stamp HomeWork Board is the Vss terminal.
5. W1 – The potentiometer's wiper (W) terminal.

6. B1 – The potentiometer's B terminal.
7. CS – The chip select pin. Apply a high signal to this pin, and the chip ignores all control signals sent to CLK and U/D. Apply a low signal to this pin, and it acts on any control signals it receives.
8. Vdd – Connect to +5 V, which is Vdd on the Board of Education and BASIC Stamp HomeWork Board.

---

**(i)** **The AD5220 Part Datasheet:** To see the part datasheet for the AD5220: Go to www.analog.com. Enter AD5220 into the Search field on Analog Devices' home page, and click the Search button. Click the Data Sheets link. Click the link that reads "AD5220: Increment/Decrement Digital Potentiometer Datasheet".

---

## Digital Pot Controlled Transistor Parts

(1) Transistor – 2N3904
(2) Resistors – 100 kΩ (brown-black-yellow)
(1) LED – any color
(1) Digital potentiometer – AD5220

## Building the Digital Potentiometer Circuit

Figure 9-6 shows a circuit schematic with the digital potentiometer used in place of a manual potentiometer, and Figure 9-7 shows a wiring diagram for the circuit. The BASIC Stamp can control the digital potentiometer by issuing control signals to P5 and P6.

√ Build the circuit shown in Figure 9-6 and Figure 9-7.

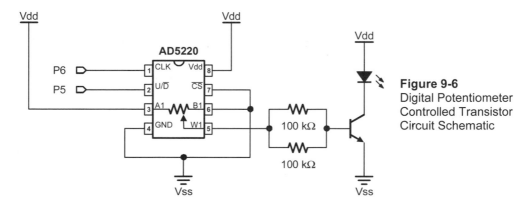

**Figure 9-6**
Digital Potentiometer
Controlled Transistor
Circuit Schematic

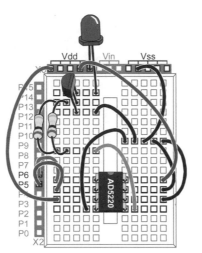

**Figure 9-7**
Digital
Potentiometer
Controlled
Transistor
Wiring Diagram

## Programming Digital Potentiometer Control

Imagine that the knob on the manual potentiometer from the previous exercise has 128 positions. Imagine also that the potentiometer is in the middle of its range of motion. That means you could rotate the knob one direction by 63 steps and the other direction by 64 steps.

Let's say you turn the potentiometer's knob one step clockwise. The LED will get only slightly brighter. This would be the same as sending a high signal to the AD5220's U/D pin and sending one pulse (high-low-high) to the CLK pin.

```
HIGH 5
PULSOUT 6, 1
```

Imagine next that you turn your manual potentiometer 3 steps counterclockwise. The LED will get a little bit dimmer. This would be the same as sending a low signal to the U/D pin on the AD5220 and sending three pulses to the CLK pin.

```
LOW 5
FOR counter = 1 TO 3
  PULSOUT 6, 1
  PAUSE 1
NEXT
```

Imagine next that you turn the potentiometer all the way clockwise. That's the same as sending a high signal to the AD5220's U/D pin and sending 65 pulses to the CLK pin. Now the LED should be shining brightly.

```
HIGH 5
FOR counter = 1 TO 65
   PULSOUT 6, 1
   PAUSE 1
NEXT
```

Finally, imagine that you turn your manual potentiometer all the way counterclockwise. The LED should emit no light. That's the same as sending a low signal to the U/D pin, and applying 128 pulses to the CLK pin

```
LOW 5
FOR counter = 0 TO 127
   PULSOUT 6, 1
   PAUSE 1
NEXT
```

### Example Program: DigitalPotUpDown.bs2

This example program adjusts the potentiometer up and down, from one end of its range to the other, causing the LED to get gradually brighter, then gradually dimmer.

√   Enter and run DigitalPotUpDown.bs2.

```
' What's a Microcontroller - DigitalPotUpDown.bs2
' Sweep digital pot through values.

' {$STAMP BS2}
' {$PBASIC 2.5}

DEBUG "Program Running!"

counter         VAR     Byte

DO

  LOW 5

  FOR counter = 0 TO 127
    PULSOUT 6, 1
    PAUSE 10
  NEXT

  HIGH 5
```

```
   FOR counter = 0 TO 127
     PULSOUT 6, 1
     PAUSE 10
   NEXT

LOOP
```

## Your Turn – Changing the Rate and Condensing the Code

You can increase or decrease the rate at which the LED gets brighter and dimmer by changing the **PAUSE** command's *Duration* argument.

√   Modify and re-run the program using **PAUSE 20** and note the difference in the rate that the LED gets brighter and dimmer.
√   Repeat for **PAUSE 5**.

You can also use a command called **TOGGLE** to make this program simpler. **TOGGLE** changes the state of a BASIC Stamp I/O pin. If the I/O pin was sending a high signal, **TOGGLE** makes it send a low signal. If the I/O pin was sending a low signal, **TOGGLE** makes it send a high signal.

√   Save DigitalPotUpDown.bs2 as DigitalPotUpDownWithToggle.bs2.
√   Modify the program so that it looks like the one below.
√   Run the program and verify that it functions the same as the DigitalPotUpDown.bs2.
√   Compare the number of lines of code it took to do the same job.

**Running out of program memory** is a problem many people encounter when their BASIC Stamp projects get large and complicated. Using **TOGGLE** instead of two **FOR...NEXT** loops is just one example of many techniques that can be used to do the same job with half the code.

```
' What's a Microcontroller - DigitalPotUpDownWithToggle.bs2
' Sweep digital pot through values.

' {$STAMP BS2}
' {$PBASIC 2.5}
DEBUG "Program Running!"

counter          VAR      Byte
```

```
LOW 5

DO
  FOR counter = 0 TO 127
    PULSOUT 6,5
    PAUSE 10
  NEXT
  TOGGLE 5
LOOP
```

### Looking Inside the Digital Potentiometer

Figure 9-8 shows a diagram of the potentiometer inside the AD5220. The AD5220 has 128 resistive elements, each of which is 78.125 Ω (nominal value). All 128 of these add up to 10,000 Ω or 10 kΩ.

 **A nominal value** means a named value. Parts like resistors and capacitors typically have a nominal value and a tolerance. Each of the AD5220's resistive elements has a nominal value of 78.125 Ω, with a tolerance of 30% (23.438 Ω) above or below the nominal value.

Between each of these resistive elements is a switch, called a tap. Each switch is actually a group of transistors that are switched on or off to let current pass or not pass. Only one of these switches can be closed at one time. If one of the upper switches is closed (like pos. 125, 126, or 127), it's like having the manual potentiometer knob turned most or all the way clockwise. If pos. 0 or 1 is closed, it's like having a manual potentiometer turned most or all the way counterclockwise.

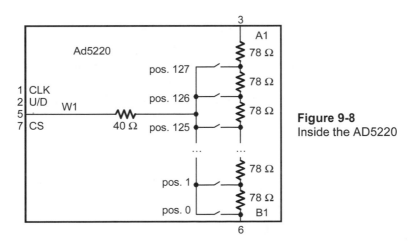

**Figure 9-8**
Inside the AD5220

Imagine that Pos. 126 is closed. If you want to set the tap to 125, (open pos. 126 and close pos. 125), set U/D low, then apply a pulse to CLK. If you want to set the tap to Pos 127, set U/D high, and apply 2 pulses. If you want to bring the tap down to 1, set U/D low, and apply 126 pulses.

This next example program uses the Debug Terminal to ask you which tap setting you want. Then it decides whether to set the U/D pin high or low, and applies the correct number of pulses to move the tap from its old setting to the new setting.

With the exception of EEPROM Data, the next example program also has all the sections you could normally expect to find in an application program:

- Title – comments that include the filename of a program, its description, and the Stamp and PBASIC directives.
- EEPROM Data – The **DATA** declarations used by the program.
- I/O Definitions – constant declarations that define I/O pin numbers.
- Constants – constant declarations that define other values used in the program.
- Variables – variable declarations.
- Initialization – a routine that gets the program started on the right foot. In this next program, the potentiometer's tap needs to be brought down to zero.
- Main – the routine that handles the primary jobs the program has to do.
- Subroutines – the segments of code that do specific jobs, either for each other, or in this case, for the main routine.

### Example Program: TerminalControlledDigtialPot.bs2

You can use this example program and the Debug Terminal to set the digital pot's tap. By changing the tap setting on the digital pot, you change the brightness of the LED connected to the transistor that the digital pot controls. Figure 9-9 shows an example of entering the value 120 into the Debug Terminal's Transmit Windowpane while the program is running. Since the old tap setting was 65, the LED becomes nearly twice as bright when it is adjusted to 120.

**Windowpanes**

Transmit →

Receive →

**Figure 9-9**
Sending Messages
to the BASIC Stamp

*Click the Transmit
(upper) Windowpane
and enter the
numbers for the new
tap setting.*

√     Enter and run TerminalControlledDigtialPot.bs2.
√     Enter values between 0 and 127 into the Debug Terminal. Make sure to press
       the enter key after you type in the digits.

```
' -----[ Title ]-------------------------------------------------------------
' What's a Microcontroller - TerminalControlledDigitalPot.bs2
' Update digital pot's tap based on Debug Terminal user input.

' {$STAMP BS2}
' {$PBASIC 2.5}

' -----[ EEPROM Data ]-------------------------------------------------------


' -----[ I/O Definitions ]---------------------------------------------------

UdPin           CON     5                       ' Set values of I/O pins
ClkPin          CON     6                       ' connected to CLK and U/D.

' -----[ Constants ]---------------------------------------------------------

DelayPulses     CON     10                      ' Delay to observe LED fade.
DelayReader     CON     2000

' -----[ Variables ]---------------------------------------------------------

counter         VAR     Byte                    ' Counter for FOR...NEXT.
oldTapSetting   VAR     Byte                    ' Previous tap setting.
newTapSetting   VAR     Byte                    ' New tap setting.

' -----[ Initialization ]----------------------------------------------------

oldTapSetting = 0                               ' Initialize new and old
newTapSetting = 0                               ' tap settings to zero.
```

9

```
LOW UdPin                                      ' Set U/D pin for Down.
FOR counter = 0 TO 127                         ' Set tap to lowest position.
  PULSOUT 6,5
  PAUSE 1
NEXT

' -----[ Main Routine ]----------------------------------------------------

DO

  GOSUB Get_New_Tap_Setting                    ' User display and get input.
  GOSUB Set_Ud_Pin                             ' Set U/D pin for up/down.
  GOSUB Pulse_Clk_pin                          ' Deliver pulses.

LOOP

' -----[ Subroutines ]------------------------------------------------------

Get_New_Tap_Setting:                           ' Display instructions and
                                               ' get user input for new
  DEBUG CLS, "Tap setting is: ",               ' tap setting value.
        DEC newTapSetting, CR, CR
  DEBUG "Enter new tap", CR, "setting (0 TO 127): "
  DEBUGIN DEC newTapSetting

  RETURN

Set_Ud_Pin:                                    ' Examine new and old tap values
                                               ' to decide value of U/D pin.
  IF newTapSetting > oldTapSetting THEN        ' Notify user if values are
    HIGH UdPin                                 ' equal.
    oldTapSetting = oldTapSetting + 1          ' Increment for Pulse_Clk_pin.
  ELSEIF newTapSetting < oldTapSetting THEN
    LOW UdPin
    oldTapSetting = oldTapSetting - 1          ' Decrement for Pulse_Clk_pin.

  ELSE
    DEBUG CR, "New and old settings", CR,
             "are the same, try ", CR,
             "again...", CR
    PAUSE DelayReader                          ' Give reader time to view
  ENDIF                                        ' Message.

  RETURN

Pulse_Clk_pin:

  ' Deliver pulses from old to new values.  Keep in mind that Set_Ud_Pin
  ' adjusted the value of oldTapSetting toward newTapSetting by one.
  ' This keeps the FOR...NEXT loop from executing one too many times.
```

```
FOR counter = oldTapSetting TO newTapSetting
  PULSOUT ClkPin, 1
  PAUSE DelayPulses
NEXT

oldTapSetting = newTapSetting                    ' Keep track of new and old
                                                 ' tapSetting values.
RETURN
```

9

## SUMMARY

This chapter introduced integrated circuits and how they can be used with the BASIC Stamp. A transistor was used as a current valve, and a digital potentiometer was used to control the amount of current passing through the transistor. Examining the digital potentiometer introduced the reference notch and pin map as important elements of electronic chips. The function of each of the digital potentiometer pins was discussed, as well as the device's internal structure. The PBASIC command TOGGLE was introduced as a means to save program memory.

## Questions

1. What are the names of the terminals on the transistor you used in this chapter?
2. Which terminal controls the current passing through the transistor?
3. What can you do to increase or decrease the current passing through the transistor?

## Exercise

1. Write a program that adjusts the tap in the digital pot to position 0 regardless of its current setting.

## Project

1. Add a photoresistor to your project and cause the brightness of the LED to adjust with the brightness seen by the photoresistor.

## Solutions

Q1. Emitter, base, and collector.
Q2. The base controls the current passing through the transistor.
Q3. Increase or decrease the current allowed into the transistor's base.
E1. To solve this exercise, look at TerminalControlledDigitalPot.bs2. The first thing it does, in the Initialization section, is to set the tap to the lowest position. This exact code is used in the solution below.

```
' What's a Microcontroller - Ch9Ex01_SetTapToZero.bs2
' Turn tap on digital pot all the way down to zero
' {$STAMP BS2}
' {$PBASIC 2.5}
DEBUG "Program Running!"
```

```
UdPin          CON    5            ' Set values of I/O pins
ClkPin         CON    6            ' connected to CLK and U/D.
counter        VAR    Byte            ' Counter for FOR...NEXT.

LOW UdPin                          ' Set U/D pin for Down.
FOR counter = 0 TO 128             ' Set tap to lowest position.
  PULSOUT ClkPin,5
  PAUSE 1
NEXT
```

P1. Use the digital potentiometer circuit from Figure 9-6, p. 267 and the photoresistor circuit from Figure 7-2, p. 191.

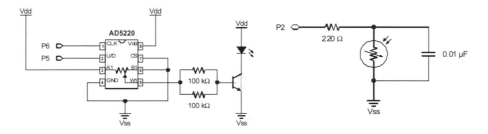

This solution is based on TerminalControlledDigitalPot.bs2, except instead of being controlled by typing in the Debug Terminal, it is controlled by reading the photoresistor. A subroutine, **Read_Photoresistor**, reads the photoresistor using **RCTIME** as shown in Chapter 5. The reading from the photoresistor becomes the new tap setting, and the original program does the work to set the tap. The parts of the original program that ask for input from the Debug Terminal were deleted, including the **Get_New_Tap_Setting** subroutine.

```
' What's a Microcontroller - Ch9Prj01_PhotoControlledDigitalPot.bs2
' Update digital pot's tap based on photoresistor reading
' {$STAMP BS2}
' {$PBASIC 2.5}
DEBUG "Program Running!"

' -----[ Declarations and Initialization]-----------------------------
UdPin          CON    5            ' Set values of I/O pins
ClkPin         CON    6            ' connected to CLK and U/D.
PhotoPin       CON    2            ' Photoresistor on pin P2
DelayPulses    CON    10           ' Delay to observe LED fade.
DelayReader    CON    2000
```

9

```
counter         VAR     Byte            ' Counter for FOR...NEXT.
oldTapSetting   VAR     Byte            ' Previous tap setting.
newTapSetting   VAR     Byte            ' New tap setting.
lightReading    VAR     Word            ' reading from photoresistor

oldTapSetting = 0                       ' Initialize new and old
newTapSetting = 0                       ' tap settings to zero.

LOW UdPin                               ' Set U/D pin for Down.
FOR counter = 0 TO 128                  ' Set tap to lowest position.
  PULSOUT 6,5
  PAUSE 1
NEXT

' -----[ Main Routine ]-------------------------------------------
DO
  GOSUB Read_Photoresistor
  newTapSetting = lightReading
  GOSUB Set_Ud_Pin                      ' Set U/D pin for up/down.
  GOSUB Pulse_Clk_pin                   ' Deliver pulses.
LOOP

' -----[ Subroutines ]--------------------------------------------
Set_Ud_Pin:                             ' Examine old and new
  IF newTapSetting > oldTapSetting THEN ' tap values to decide
  ELSEIF newTapSetting < oldTapSetting THEN ' value of UdPin. Notify
    LOW UdPin                           ' user if values are
  ENDIF                                 ' equal.
  RETURN

Pulse_Clk_pin:                          ' Deliver pulses
  FOR counter = oldTapSetting TO newTapSetting ' from old to new
    PULSOUT ClkPin, 1                   ' values.
    PAUSE DelayPulses
  NEXT
  oldTapSetting = newTapSetting         ' Keep track of new and old
  RETURN                                ' tapSetting values.

Read_Photoresistor:
  HIGH PhotoPin
  PAUSE 100
  RCTIME PhotoPin, 1, lightReading
  RETURN
```

## Further Investigation

### "*Industrial Control*", Student Guide, Version 2.0, Parallax Inc., 2002

*Industrial Control* uses the transistor as an on/off switch for a resistor heating element. It also uses a phototransistor to detect the passage of stripes on a spinning wheel.

# Chapter #10: Running the Whole Show

## SUBSYSTEM INTEGRATION

Most of the activities in this text introduce how to program the BASIC Stamp to interact with one or two circuits at a time. Many microcontrollers have to handle tens or even hundreds of circuits. This chapter will demonstrate a few of the techniques used to manage a variety of circuits with a single microcontroller. Programming the microcontroller to orchestrate the activities of different circuits performing unique functions is called subsystem integration.

The example in this chapter uses a sensor array consisting of two pushbutton circuits, a potentiometer circuit and a photoresistor circuit. The activities in this chapter will guide you through building and testing each subsystem individually. After each subsystem is built and tested, you will then write a program that combines each subsystem into a working unit. Figure 10-1 shows the circuit schematic for the system you will build, and the master parts list is below.

Always remember: whenever possible, test each subsystem individually before trying to make them work together. If you follow this rule, your projects will go much more smoothly, and your chances of success will be greatly improved. The activities in this chapter will guide you through the process.

**10**

### Sensor Array Parts List

(4) Resistors – 220 Ω (red-red-brown)
(2) Resistors – 10 kΩ (brown-black-orange)
(2) Pushbuttons – normally open
(2) Capacitors – 0.1 μF
(1) Potentiometer – 10 kΩ
(1) Photoresistor
(5) Jumper wires

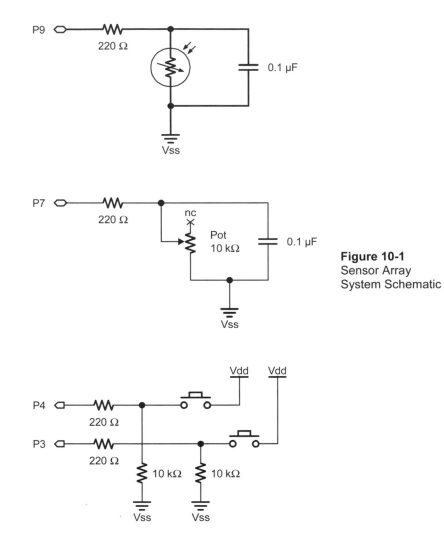

**Figure 10-1**
Sensor Array
System Schematic

## ACTIVITY #1: BUILDING AND TESTING EACH PUSHBUTTON CIRCUIT

This activity begins with building and testing a single pushbutton circuit. Once you have confirmed that the first pushbutton circuit is operating properly, you can then move on to building and testing the second pushbutton circuit.

### Pushbutton Circuit Parts

(2) Pushbuttons – normally open
(2) Resistors – 10 kΩ (brown-black-orange)
(2) Resistors – 220 Ω (red-red-brown)
(2) Jumper wires

### Building the First Pushbutton Circuit

Build the pushbutton circuit shown in Figure 10-2.

**Figure 10-2**
First Pushbutton Circuit

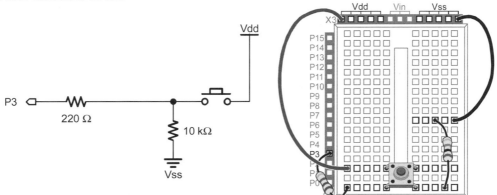

### Testing the First Pushbutton Circuit

Writing a program to test this circuit should be very simple by now, especially since you've already done it before.

### Example Program: ReadPushbuttonState.bs2

This is a repeat of the program for testing pushbuttons from Chapter #3:

- √ Enter and run the ReadPushbuttonState.bs2.
- √ Verify that the BASIC Stamp is able to read the pushbutton.
- √ Correct any problems you catch before moving on to the next circuit.

```
' What's a Microcontroller - ReadPushbuttonState.bs2
' Check and send pushbutton state to Debug Terminal every 1/4 second.

' {$STAMP BS2}
' {$PBASIC 2.5}

DO

  DEBUG ? IN3
  PAUSE 250

LOOP
```

### Your Turn – Building and Testing the Second Pushbutton Circuit

Once the first pushbutton circuit has been built and tested, the process can be repeated for the second pushbutton.

- √ Add the pushbutton circuit shown in Figure 10-3.
- √ Test the second pushbutton circuit by modifying ReadPushbuttonState.bs2 so that it reads the circuit connected to P4. Run the program and verify that the second pushbutton works.
- √ Correct any problems you catch before moving on to the next activity.

**Figure 10-3**
Adding a Second Pushbutton Circuit to the Project

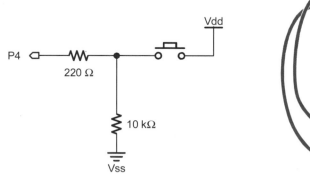
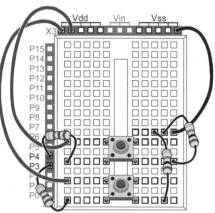

## ACTIVITY #2: BUILDING AND TESTING EACH RC-TIME CIRCUIT

Now that the two pushbutton circuits are built and tested, you can move on to the RC-time circuits.

### Extra Parts for Potentiometer and Photoresistor Circuits

(2) Resistors – 220 Ω (red-red-brown)
(2) Capacitors – 0.1 µF
(4) Jumper wires
(1) Photoresistor
(1) Potentiometer – 10 kΩ

### Building the Potentiometer Circuit

√   Add the potentiometer circuit shown in Figure 10-4 to the project.

**Figure 10-4**
Adding a Potentiometer Circuit

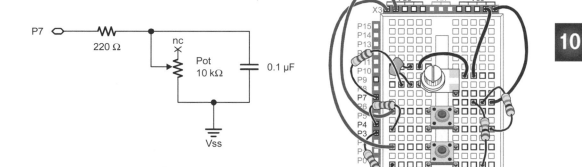

### Testing the Potentiometer Circuit

You can test this circuit using ReadPotWithRcTime.bs2. This program was first used in Chapter #5 to read the potentiometer circuit.

### Example Program: ReadPotWithRcTime.bs2

√   Enter and run the ReadPotWithRcTime.bs2.

√ Verify that the BASIC Stamp gets reliable measurements from the potentiometer.

√ Correct any problems you catch before moving on to the next circuit.

```
' What's a Microcontroller - ReadPotWithRcTime.bs2
' Read potentiometer in RC-time circuit using RCTIME command.

' {$STAMP BS2}
' {$PBASIC 2.5}

time            VAR     Word

DO

  HIGH 7
  PAUSE 100
  RCTIME 7, 1, time
  DEBUG HOME, " time =  ", DEC5 time

LOOP
```

### Your Turn – Building and Testing the Photoresistor Circuit

Once the first RC-time circuit has been built and tested, the process can be repeated for the second RC-time circuit.

√ Add the photoresistor circuit shown in Figure 10-5 to your project on the breadboard.

√ Modify ReadPotWithRcTime.bs2 so the photoresistor is connected to P9.

√ Correct any problems you catch before moving on to the next activity.

**Figure 10-5**
Adding the Photoresistor Circuit

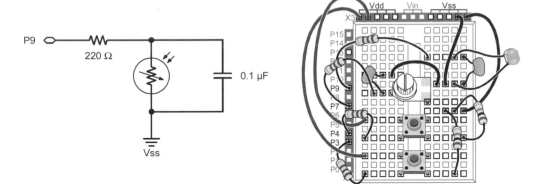

## ACTIVITY #3: SUBSYSTEM INTEGRATION EXAMPLE

Now that all the elements in the sensor array are built and tested, you can now write a program that makes use of all four sensor circuits. This example will demonstrate how to program the BASIC Stamp to display a terminal with a menu that a technician might use to monitor the sensors.

### Programming a Menu System and Using the Input/Output PIN Directive

The ON...GOSUB command can be very useful for menus.

> ON *offset* , GOSUB *Target1, {Target2, Target3,...}*

In the next example program, the ON...GOSUB command uses the value of a variable named **request** to direct it to one of four subroutines. If the value of **request** is 0, the program executes a GOSUB **Read_Pushbutton_1**. If the Value of **request** is 1, the program executes a GOSUB **Read_Pushbutton_2**, and so on.

```
ON request GOSUB Read_Pushbutton_1, Read_Pushbutton_2,
               Read_Pot, Read_Photoresistor
```

You can use the **PIN** directive to give a name to each I/O pin you are going to use in a PBASIC program. The BASIC Stamp Editor will then figure out whether you are using the I/O pin as an input or an output (or both). The **PIN** directive's syntax is:

> *PinName* **PIN** *PinNumber*

10

The next example program demonstrates how you can declare and then use a *PinName*. For example, the BASIC Stamp Editor assumes that you want to display the input value of an I/O pin (IN3) if you are using the Pb1Pin *PinName* in a DEBUG command. This DEBUG command will display a 1 or 0 depending on whether the pushbutton connected to P3 is pressed or not pressed. Why? Because the BASIC Stamp Editor knows to substitute IN3 for Pb1Pin.

```
Pb1Pin          PIN     3
DEBUG CLS, ? Pb1Pin
```

Here is another example where the BASIC Stamp Editor knows to substitute the value of 9 because the PhotoPin *PinName* is used in a HIGH command and an RCTIME command.

```
PhotoPin        PIN     9
HIGH PhotoPin
RCTIME PhotoPin, 1, time
```

### Example Program: TerminalOperatedSensorArray.bs2

Figure 10-6 shows the Debug Terminal displayed by TerminalOperatedSensorArray.bs2. The main menu is shown on the left, and an example of the display when '4' is selected is shown on the right. Remember to use the upper Windowpane to send your menu selections to the BASIC Stamp.

√   Enter and run TerminalOperatedSensorArray.bs2.
√   Click the Debug Terminal's upper Windowpane, and type digits to make your menu selections.
√   The measurement displayed is the one taken at the instant the menu selection is made, and it is displayed for 1.5 seconds. Keep this in mind when you press and hold the pushbuttons, adjust the potentiometer and cast shade onto the photoresistor.

**Figure 10-6**
Using the Debug Terminal to Select from a Menu

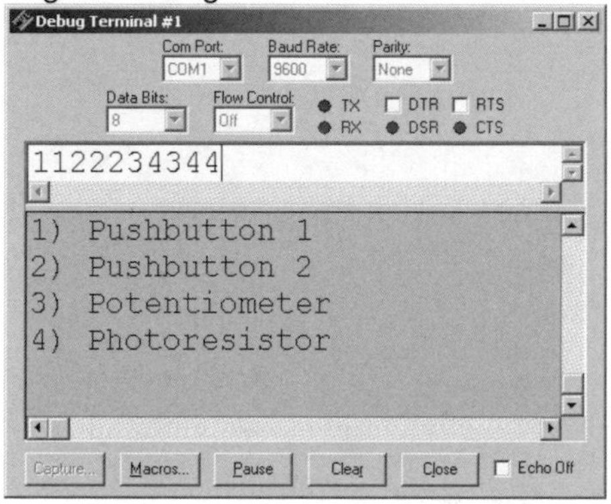

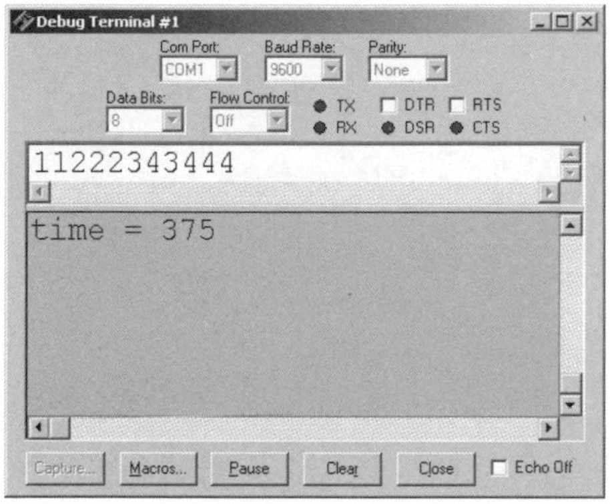

```
' -----[ Title ]-------------------------------------------------------------
' What's a Microcontroller - TerminalOperatedSensorArray.bs2
' Use Debug Terminal to choose to read one of four sensors.

' {$STAMP BS2}
' {$PBASIC 2.5}

' -----[ I/O Definitions ]---------------------------------------------------

Pb1Pin          PIN      3
Pb2Pin          PIN      4
PotPin          PIN      7
PhotoPin        PIN      9

' -----[ Constants ]---------------------------------------------------------

DelayRc         CON      100
DelayReader     CON      1500

' -----[ Variables ]---------------------------------------------------------

request         VAR      Nib
time            VAR      Word

' -----[ Main Routine ]------------------------------------------------------

DO

  GOSUB Display_Menu
  GOSUB Get_Request
  ON request GOSUB Read_Pushbutton_1, Read_Pushbutton_2,
                   Read_Pot, Read_Photoresistor
```

```
LOOP

' -----[ Subroutine - Display_Menu ]------------------------------------

Display_Menu:

  DEBUG CLS, "MENU: ", CR, CR,
            "1) Pushbutton 1", CR,
            "2) Pushbutton 2", CR,
            "3) Potentiometer", CR,
            "4) Photoresistor", CR, CR
  RETURN

' -----[ Subroutine - Get_Request ]-------------------------------------

Get_Request:

  DEBUGIN DEC1 request
  request = request - 1

  RETURN

' -----[ Subroutine - Read_Pushbutton_1 ]-------------------------------

Read_Pushbutton_1:

  DEBUG CLS, ? Pb1Pin
  PAUSE DelayReader

  RETURN


' -----[ Subroutine - Read_Pushbutton_2 ]-------------------------------

Read_Pushbutton_2:

  DEBUG CLS, ? Pb2Pin
  PAUSE DelayReader

  RETURN

' -----[ Subroutine - Read_Pot ]----------------------------------------

Read_Pot:

  HIGH PotPin
  PAUSE DelayRc
  RCTIME PotPin, 1, time
  DEBUG CLS, ? time, "       "
  PAUSE DelayReader
```

```
   RETURN

' -----[ Subroutine - Read_Photoresistor ]-----------------------------------

Read_Photoresistor:

  HIGH PhotoPin
  PAUSE DelayRc
  RCTIME PhotoPin, 1, time
  DEBUG CLS, ? time, "        "
  PAUSE DelayReader

  RETURN
```

### Your Turn – Modifying Subroutines

Terminals are not the only application for **ON…GOSUB**. For example, if you want to call the four different subroutines one after another, here is a way to do it:

```
DO

  ' GOSUB Display_Menu
  ' GOSUB Get_Request
  FOR request = 0 TO 3
    ON request GOSUB Read_Pushbutton_1, Read_Pushbutton_2,
                     Read_Pot, Read_Photoresistor
  NEXT

LOOP
```

Notice that the two subroutines that do the terminal work were commented and the **ON…GOSUB** command was placed in a **FOR…NEXT** loop.

√  Save your example program under the new name: TerminalOperatedSensorArrayYourTurn.bs2.
√  Modify the main routine by making the changes just discussed.
√  Run the program and verify that it cycles through the measurements.

## ACTIVITY #4: DEVELOPING AND ADDING A SOFTWARE SUBSYSTEM

Let's say that your sensor array is getting placed in a device that only certain employees are allowed to use, and they have to supply a password. This means you will have to expand your program so that it saves and verifies a password. It's better to write a password program that functions on its own first, and then add it to your larger program.

### Programming a Password Checker

You can save a password in a PBASIC program by using a **DATA** directive. For example:

```
Password        DATA      "pass!"
```

 **The same as:** This **DATA** directive is the same as **Password DATA "p", "a", "s", "s", "!"**.

You will need a few variables for storing other values in the program:

```
index           VAR       Nib
temp            VAR       Byte
```

If you are using a five character password, there is a special kind of variable declaration (called an array declaration) that you use to declare five variables with the same name.

```
userEntry       VAR       Byte(5)
```

Now you have five byte variables named userEntry: **userEntry(0)**, **userEntry(1)**, **userEntry(2)**, **userEntry(3)**, and **userEntry(4)**.

The **DEBUGIN** command has a formatter called **STR** that automatically loads characters into an array. For example, you can use:

```
DEBUGIN STR userEntry \5
```

If you type five characters in the Debug Terminal's Transmit Windowpane, the first will get placed in **userEntry(0)**, the second will get placed in **userEntry(1)**, etc.

There is a PBASIC keyword called **EXIT** that you can use to break out of a loop. To check a password, you can use an **IF...THEN** statement with an **EXIT** command to cause the loop to end early if not all the characters are identical. When the loop ends early, it means that **index** has not counted all the way up to five, which in turn means the password was not correct:

```
FOR index = 0 TO 4
  READ Password + index, temp
  IF temp <> userEntry(index) THEN EXIT
NEXT

IF index <> 5 THEN
  DEBUG CR,"Password not correct.", CR
ENDIF
```

This next example program places the DEBUGIN command, the FOR...NEXT loop, and the IF...THEN statement inside a DO...LOOP UNTIL statement that keeps executing until the value of index gets to 5 (indicating the correct password was entered).

### Example Program: PasswordChecker.bs2

Figure 10-7 shows the Debug Terminal displayed by PasswordChecker.bs2. When run, this program will wait for you to type the letters "pass!" in response to the prompt.

√ Enter and run PasswordChecker.bs2.
√ Try entering some letter combinations that are not the password, then enter the letter combination that is the password: "pass!".

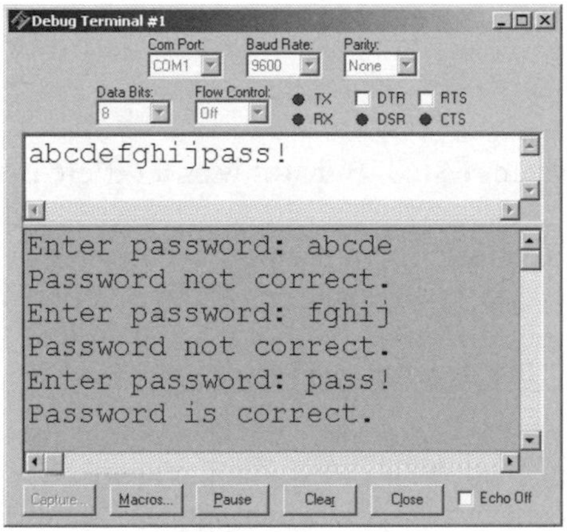

**Figure 10-7**
Entering Password into the Transmit Windowpane

*Click the Transmit (upper) Windowpane and enter the password.*

10

```
' What's a Microcontroller - PasswordChecker.bs2
' Check password entered in Debug Terminal's Transmit Windowpane.

' {$STAMP BS2}
' {$PBASIC 2.5}

Password      DATA     "pass!"                 ' Store "secret" password here.

index         VAR      Nib                     ' Index variable.
temp          VAR      Byte                    ' Stores single char.
userEntry     VAR      Byte(5)                 ' Store user entered password.

DO

  DEBUG "Enter password: "                     ' User instructions.
```

```
   DEBUGIN STR userEntry \5                  ' Get user input password.

   FOR index = 0 TO 4                        ' Check array against DATA
     READ Password + index, temp            ' Get next password char
     IF temp <> userEntry(index) THEN EXIT  ' Compare to user input,
   NEXT                                      ' exit if not equal.

   IF index <> 5 THEN                        ' If exit, then index not equal
     DEBUG CR,"Password not correct.", CR   ' to 5 and pass is not correct.
   ENDIF

LOOP UNTIL index = 5                         ' Only get out of loop when
                                             ' index = 5.

DEBUG CR, "Password is correct;", CR,        ' Program can move on when
         "program can continue..."           ' password is correct.
END
```

## Your Turn – Modifying Passwords

- √ Modify the **Password DATA** directive so that it uses a different five character password.
- √ By changing five different values in the program, you can also modify it so that it accepts a four character password instead of a five character password.

## Modifying Password Checker for Use in a Larger Program

The goal is to make it easy to fit the PasswordChecker.bs2 program into the example program from Activity #3. Two things will help. First, the password checking program should be modified so that it does most of its work in a subroutine. The different parts of the program should also be labeled with commented headings to help make it clear how to combine the two programs.

## Example Program: ReusablePasswordChecker.bs2

ReusablePasswordChecker.bs2 works the same as PasswordChecker.bs2, but it now uses a subroutine to do the work, and it has been reorganized into labeled sections.

- √ Verify that the program still works the same as PasswordChecker.bs2.
- √ Examine how the **DO...LOOP UNTIL** code block was placed into a subroutine.

```
' -----[ Title ]-----------------------------------------------------
' What's a Microcontroller - ReusablePasswordChecker.bs2
' Check password entered in Debug Terminal's Transmit Windowpane.

' {$STAMP BS2}
' {$PBASIC 2.5}

' -----[ DATA Directives ]-------------------------------------------

Password        DATA      "pass!"              ' Store "secret" password here.

' -----[ Variable Declarations ]-------------------------------------

index           VAR       Nib                  ' Index variable.
temp            VAR       Byte                 ' Stores single char.
userEntry       VAR       Byte(5)              ' Store user entered password.

' -----[ Initialization Routine ]------------------------------------

GOSUB Check_Password

' -----[ Main Routine ]----------------------------------------------

' There is no main routine in this program.

DEBUG CR, "All Done"

END

' -----[ Subroutine - Check for Correct Password ]-------------------

Check_Password:

  DO

    DEBUG "Enter password: "                    ' User instructions.

    DEBUGIN STR userEntry \5                     ' Get user input password.

    FOR index = 0 TO 4                           ' Check array against DATA
      READ Password + index, temp                ' Get next password char
      IF temp <> userEntry(index) THEN EXIT      ' Compare to user input,
    NEXT                                         ' exit if not equal.

    IF index <> 5 THEN                           ' If exit, then index not equal
      DEBUG CR,"Password not correct.", CR       ' to 5 and pass is not correct.
    ENDIF

  LOOP UNTIL index = 5                           ' Only get out of loop when
                                                 ' index = 5.
```

10

```
    DEBUG CR, "Password is correct."          ' Program can move on when
                                              ' password is correct.

RETURN                                        ' Return when pass is correct.
```

### Advanced Topic: Your Turn – Combining the two Programs

Now that both TerminalOperatedSensorArray.bs2 and ReusablePasswordChecker.bs2 have both been tested, the task is to combine the two. The final program should check your password before allowing you to choose which sensor to read using the Debug Terminal.

> √   You can open both programs (ReusablePasswordChecker.bs2 and TerminalOperatedSensorArray.bs2) in the BASIC Stamp Editor.
> √   Save TerminalOperatedSensorArray.bs2 as PasswordedSensorTerminal.bs2

You will need to tab between each program while copying sections from ReusablePasswordChecker.bs2 and pasting them into PasswordedSensorTerminal.bs2.

> √   Copy the **Password DATA** directive (including the commented heading with the dashed line) from ReusablePasswordChecker.bs2 into PasswordedSensorTerminal.bs2 just before the **I/O Definitions** section.
> √   Copy and paste the variable declarations from ReusablePasswordChecker.bs2 into PasswordedSensorTerminal.bs2. These variable declarations are added to the ones in PasswordedSensorTerminal.bs2, so don't worry about copying and pasting the commented **Variables** heading.
> √   Copy the **Initialization** section (including the commented heading) from ReusablePasswordChecker.bs2, and paste it between the **Variables** section and the **Main Routine** in PasswordedSensorTerminal.bs2.
> √   Copy the entire **Subroutine** section from ReusablePasswordChecker.bs2 and paste it after the end of the last subroutine in PasswordedSensorTerminal.bs2.
> √   Test PasswordedSensorTerminal.bs2, and see if it works, debug as needed.

## SUMMARY

This chapter introduced the technique of individually testing each circuit-subsystem before integrating it into a larger system. This chapter also introduced the ON...GOSUB command, which is particularly useful for menu systems. The useful PIN directive was demonstrated as a way to name your I/O pins and then let the BASIC Stamp Editor figure out whether to read an input or write to an output. A password program was used to introduce variable arrays, the EXIT command, and the DEBUGIN command's STR formatter. The password program was then integrated into a larger sensor terminal program to give it more functionality.

### Questions

1. When should you test subsystems individually before trying to make them work together? Why?
2. How many programs did you use in this chapter that were from other chapters?
3. How does the PIN directive differ from the CON and VAR directives?
4. What's the difference between EXIT and END?

### Exercises

1. Describe the general 3-step process you would use to add a piezospeaker circuit to your project.
2. Modify PasswordChecker.bs2 from page 291 so that the message "you entered: " appears in the Debug Terminal along with the text of the password.

### Projects

1. Add a piezospeaker circuit to the sensor array you developed in this chapter, and write a program to test it.
2. Modify TerminalOperatedSensorArray.bs2 so that it has a 5th menu item that makes the piezospeaker beep at 2 kHz for 1.5 seconds.
3. While working on one of the activities and projects in this book you may have thought to yourself, "hey, I could use this to build a >> insert your project here: _____ <<!" Use the material you have learned in this book to invent a gadget or gizmo of your own design.

10

## Solutions

Q1. Whenever possible! It is much easier to find, isolate and prevent problems.

Q2. Two. ReadPushbuttonState.bs2 from Chapter #3 and ReadPotWithRcTime.bs2 from Chapter #5.

Q3. While the **CON** directive assigns a name to a number, and while the **VAR** directive assigns a name to RAM, the **PIN** directive assigns a name to a BASIC Stamp I/O pin. This name can then be used in place of the I/O pin number throughout the program. PBASIC figures out whether you are using it as an output to send a high/low signal or as an input variable to store the state sensed by the I/O pin (1 or 0).

Q4. **END** ends the program, it doesn't run anymore. By contrast **EXIT** just breaks out of the loop, and then the program keeps on running.

E1. a. Build the piezospeaker circuit on the breadboard.

b. Run TestPiezoWithFreqout.bs2 from Chapter 8 to test the speaker.

c. Integrate the piezospeaker into the program.

E2. The key to solving this problem is to use the **STR** formatter with **DEBUG**. The text introduced the **STR** formatter with **DEBUGIN**, so it makes sense to guess that the **STR** formatter will also work with **DEBUG**. This can be done by adding this line of code below the **DEBUGIN** statement.

```
DEBUG CR, CR, "You entered: ", STR userEntry, CR
```

P1. Project 1 uses the same schematic as Figure 10-1. p. 280 with the addition of a piezo speaker connected to P11.

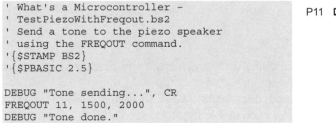
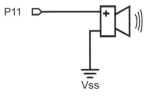

```
' What's a Microcontroller -
' TestPiezoWithFreqout.bs2
' Send a tone to the piezo speaker
' using the FREQOUT command.
'{$STAMP BS2}
'{$PBASIC 2.5}

DEBUG "Tone sending...", CR
FREQOUT 11, 1500, 2000
DEBUG "Tone done."
```

P2. Project 2 uses the same schematic as Project 1.

```
' What's a Microcontroller - Ch10Prj02_AddSpeakerToSensorArray.bs2
' Use Debug Terminal to choose to read one of five sensors.
' Project 2 - Add a 5th menu item that makes a piezo speaker beep
' for 1.5 seconds at a frequency of 2kHz.
' {$STAMP BS2}
' {$PBASIC 2.5}
```

```
' -----[ I/O Definitions ]-----------------------------------------------

Pb1Pin          CON     3
Pb2Pin          CON     4
PotPin          CON     7
PhotoPin        CON     9
SpkrPin         CON     11

' -----[ Constants ]-----------------------------------------------------

DelayRc         CON     100
DelayReader     CON     1500

' -----[ Variables ]-----------------------------------------------------

request         VAR     Nib
time            VAR     Word

' -----[ Main Routine ]--------------------------------------------------

DO
  GOSUB Display_Menu
  GOSUB Get_Request
  ON request GOSUB Read_Pushbutton_1, Read_Pushbutton_2,
                   Read_Pot, Read_Photoresistor, Beep_Speaker
LOOP

' -----[ Subroutines]----------------------------------------------------

Display_Menu:

  DEBUG CLS, "MENU: ", CR,CR,
             "1) Pushbutton 1", CR,
             "2) Pushbutton 2", CR,
             "3) Potentiometer", CR,
             "4) Photoresistor", CR,
             "5) Piezo Speaker", CR, CR
  RETURN

Get_Request:
  DEBUGIN DEC1 request
  request = request - 1
  RETURN

Read_Pushbutton_1:
  DEBUG CLS, ? IN3
  PAUSE DelayReader
  RETURN

Read_Pushbutton_2:
```

10

```
   DEBUG CLS, ? IN4
   PAUSE DelayReader
   RETURN

Read_Pot:
  HIGH 7
  PAUSE DelayRc
  RCTIME 7, 1, time
  DEBUG CLS, DEC time, "        "
  PAUSE DelayReader
  RETURN

Read_Photoresistor:
  HIGH 9
  PAUSE DelayRc
  RCTIME 9, 1, time
  DEBUG CLS, DEC time, "        "
  PAUSE DelayReader
  RETURN

Beep_Speaker:
  DEBUG CLS, "2000 Hz beep for 1.5 seconds", CR
  FREQOUT SpkrPin, 1500, 2000                     ' 2000 Hz beep for 1.5 s
  RETURN
```

P3. If you have created an interesting application with your What's a Microcontroller? Kit and you want to share it with other students and teachers, consider joining our Stamps In Class Yahoo Group. See the Web Site and Discussion Lists section right after the title page at the front of this book for details.

## Further Investigation

Please go back to the Preface and read the section titles The Stamps in Class Curriculum. All of the books listed there are available for free download from www.parallax.com and are also on the Parallax CD. They contain a wealth of knowledge and instructions for continuing your explorations into electronics, programming, robotics, and engineering. In addition, we highly recommend that you visit www.parallax.com and check out our many free downloads and applications for industry professionals, educators, students, hobbyists, and the naturally curious.

**A**

# Appendix A: USB to Serial Adapter

At the time of this writing, the US232B/LC USB to Serial Adapter made by Future Technology Devices International is the recommended adapter for use with Parallax products. The US232B/LC comes with the hardware shown in Figure A-1 and a mini-CD ROM with drivers for use with various operating systems including Microsoft Windows®.

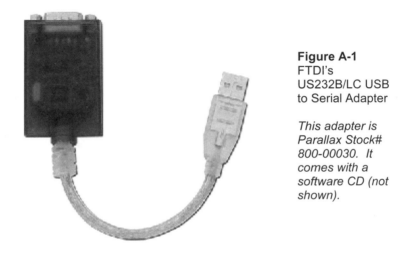

**Figure A-1**
FTDI's
US232B/LC USB
to Serial Adapter

*This adapter is
Parallax Stock#
800-00030. It
comes with a
software CD (not
shown).*

 **US232B/LC Driver Software Downloads:** The software drivers and other information about this product can be downloaded from: http://www.ftdichip.com/FT232.htm.

# Appendix B: Equipment and Parts Lists

To complete the exercises in this book, you need to have one of the following Parallax hardware options:

**Option 1**:
- **Board of Education® Full Kit (#28102)** - *AND-*
- **What's a Microcontroller Parts Kit (#28152 with text, #28122 without text)**

These two kits are also sold separately. The Board of Education Full Kit (contents listed below) is the core equipment of the Stamps in Class curriculum, and it can be used with any of the Stamps in Class texts and kits.

| Board of Education® Full Kit (#28102) | | |
|---|---|---|
| Parts and quantities subject to change without notice | | |
| **Parallax Part #** | **Description** | **Quantity** |
| 550-00022 | Board of Education | 1 |
| 800-00016 | Pluggable wires | 10 |
| BS2-IC | BASIC Stamp® 2 module | 1 |
| 800-00003 | Serial cable | 1 |
| 750-00008 | DC power supply – 9 V, 300 mA | 1 |
| 27000 | Parallax CD – includes software | 1 |
| 700-00037 | Rubber feet – set of 4 | 1 |

You may purchase the What's a Microcontroller Parts Kit alone (#28122), or with the parts and the *What's a Microcontroller?* printed text together (#28152). These parts kits are assembled to support the activities and projects in the current printed version of the text. The What's a Microcontroller Parts Kit contents are listed in the table on the following page.

| What's a Microcontroller Parts Kit #28122<br>What's a Microcontroller Parts & Text #28152<br>Parts and quantities subject to change without notice | | |
|---|---|---|
| **Parallax Part #** | **Description** | **Quantity** |
| 150-01020 | Resistor, 5%, 1/4W, 1 kΩ | 10 |
| 150-01030 | Resistor, 5%, 1/4W, 10 kΩ | 4 |
| 150-01040 | Resistor, 5%, 1/4W, 100 kΩ | 2 |
| 150-02020 | Resistor, 5%, 1/4W, 2 kΩ | 2 |
| 150-02210 | Resistor, 5%, 1/4W, 220 Ω | 6 |
| 150-04710 | Resistor, 5%, 1/4W, 470 Ω | 6 |
| 152-01031 | Potentiometer - 10 kΩ | 1 |
| 200-01031 | Capacitor, 0.01 µF, 50 V | 1 |
| 200-01040 | Capacitor, 0.1 µF, 100 V | 2 |
| 201-01080 | Capacitor, 1000 µF, 10 V | 1 |
| 201-03080 | Capacitor 3300 µF, 16 V | 1 |
| 28123 | *What's a Microcontroller?* text<br>(Included in #28152 only.) | 1 |
| 350-00001 | LED - Green - T1 3/4 | 2 |
| 350-00005 | LED - Bi-Color - T1 3/4 | 1 |
| 350-00006 | LED - Red - T1 3/4 | 2 |
| 350-00007 | LED - Yellow - T1 3/4 | 2 |
| 350-00009 | Photoresistor | 1 |
| 350-00027 | 7-segment LED Display | 1 |
| 400-00002 | Pushbutton – Normally Open | 2 |
| 451-00303 | 3 Pin Header – Male/Male | 1 |
| 500-00001 | Transistor – 2N3904 | 1 |
| 604-00010 | 10 kΩ digital potentiometer | 1 |
| 800-00016 | 3" Jumper Wires – Bag of 10 | 2 |
| 900-00001 | Piezo Speaker | 1 |
| 900-00005 | Parallax Standard Servo | 1 |

**B**

## Option 2:

- **BASIC Stamp What's a Microcontroller Kit (#90005)**

This kit features the What's a Microcontroller Parts & Text, with a HomeWork Board and accessories that are otherwise sold separately. The BASIC Stamp HomeWork Board can be used with the *What's a Microcontroller?* text in place of the Board of Education and BASIC Stamp 2 module. The HomeWork Board can also be used in the majority of the activities in the Stamps in Class curriculum, though occasional circuit modifications are necessary for certain activities. The BASIC Stamp What's a Microcontroller Kit includes the following items:

| BASIC Stamp® What's a Microcontroller Kit (#90005) | | |
|---|---|---|
| Parts and quantities subject to change without notice | | |
| **Parallax Part #** | **Description** | **Quantity** |
| 555-28158 | HomeWork Board™ with breadboard | 1 |
| 28123 | What's a Microcontroller Text | 1 |
| 27000 | Parallax CD – includes software | 1 |
| 800-00003 | Serial cable | 1 |
| 28122 | What's a Microcontroller Parts Kit | 1 |
| 700-00037 | Rubber feet – set of 4 | 1 |

**A note to educators:** The HomeWork board is available separately in packs of 10 as an economical solution for classroom use, costing significantly less than the Board of Education + BASIC Stamp 2 module. Please contact the Parallax Sales Team toll free at (888) 512-1024 for quantity pricing.

| BASIC Stamp® HomeWork Board™ Ten-Pack (#28158) | | |
|---|---|---|
| **Parallax Part #** | **Description** | **Quantity** |
| 28158 | BASIC Stamp® HomeWork Board™ (BASIC Stamp 2 is built into the board.) | 10 |

# Appendix C: BASIC Stamp and Carrier Board Components and Functions

## The BASIC STAMP® 2

Figure C-1 shows a close-up of Parallax Inc.'s BASIC Stamp® 2 microcontroller module. Its major components and their functions are indicated by labels.

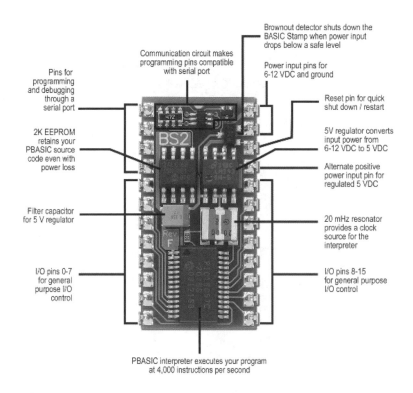

**Figure C-1:** Parallax Inc.'s BASIC Stamp® 2 Microcontroller Module Components and their Functions

## The Board of Education® Rev C

Parallax Inc.'s Board of Education® Rev C carrier board is shown in Figure C-2. Its major components and their functions are indicated by labels.

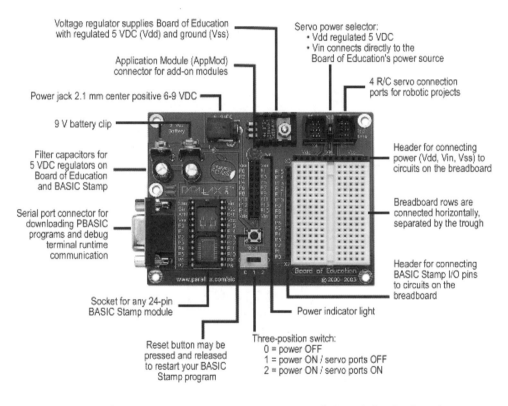

Voltage regulator supplies Board of Education with regulated 5 VDC (Vdd) and ground (Vss)

Servo power selector:
• Vdd regulated 5 VDC
• Vin connects directly to the Board of Education's power source

Application Module (AppMod) connector for add-on modules

4 R/C servo connection ports for robotic projects

Power jack 2.1 mm center positive 6-9 VDC

9 V battery clip

Header for connecting power (Vdd, Vin, Vss) to circuits on the breadboard

Filter capacitors for 5 VDC regulators on Board of Education and BASIC Stamp

Breadboard rows are connected horizontally, separated by the trough

Serial port connector for downloading PBASIC programs and debug terminal runtime communication

Header for connecting BASIC Stamp I/O pins to circuits on the breadboard

Socket for any 24-pin BASIC Stamp module

Power indicator light

Reset button may be pressed and released to restart your BASIC Stamp program

Three-position switch:
0 = power OFF
1 = power ON / servo ports OFF
2 = power ON / servo ports ON

**Figure C-2:** Parallax. Inc.'s Board of Education® Rev C Carrier Board for BASIC Stamp® Microcontroller Modules

## The BASIC Stamp® HomeWork Board™

Parallax Inc.'s BASIC Stamp® HomeWork Board™ project platform is shown in Figure C-3. Its major components and their functions are indicated by labels.

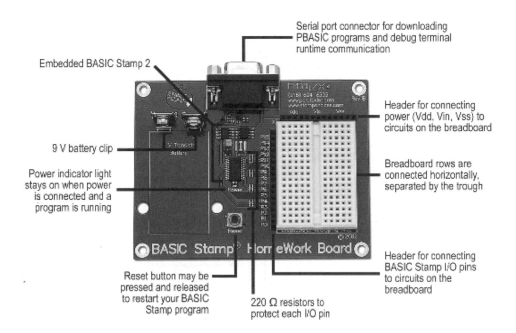

**Figure C-3:** Parallax Inc.'s BASIC Stamp® HomeWork Board™ project platform features a surface-mounted BASIC Stamp® 2 microcontroller module.

## The Board of Education® Rev B

Figure C-4 shows Parallax, Inc.'s Board of Education® Rev B carrier board. Its major components and their functions are indicated by labels.

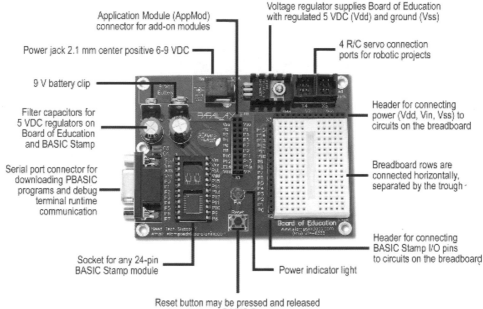

**Figure C-4:** Parallax. Inc.'s Board of Education® Rev B Carrier Board
for BASIC Stamp® modules

# Appendix D: Batteries and Power Supplies

## 9 V BATTERIES

For best results, 9 V batteries are recommended.

---

**9 V battery specifications:** Look for batteries with ratings similar these:

**Not Rechargeable**

- Alkaline

**Rechargeable**

- Ni-Cad (Nickel Cadmium)
- Ni-MH  (Nickel Metal Hydride)

For best results, the battery's milliamp hour (mAh) rating should be 100 or higher.

Not all chargers work for both types of batteries.  Make sure that your charger is recommended for the battery you are using (either Ni-Cad or Ni-MH).

Follow all battery and charger instructions and caution statements.

---

## PARALLAX DC SUPPLIES

Parallax carries several power supplies that can be used with the Board of Education Rev C only.  For the servo experiments in this text, the jumper between the X4 and X5 servo headers should be set to Vdd.  The supplies listed in Table D-1 are designed for AC outlets in the USA, and both have 2.1 mm center-positive barrel plugs that connect to the Board of Education's barrel jack.

| Table D-1: Power Supplies You Can Get from Parallax, Inc. | | | | |
|---|---|---|---|---|
| Parallax Part # | Input | | Output | |
| | VAC | Hz | VDC | mA |
| 750-00008 | 120 | 60 | 9 | 300 |
| 750-00009 | 120 | 60 | 7.5 | 1000 |

## GENERIC DC SUPPLIES

For best results with the BASIC Stamp HomeWork Board or any of the Board of Education Revisions, use a DC supply (also called an AC adapter) with the following ratings:

### Input

This depends on which country you live in and the amplitude and frequency of the AC power at the wall outlets. For the USA and Canada, the input should be 120 VAC, 60 Hz.

### Output

6 VDC, 800 mA
The mA rating can be higher. A 6 V, 1000 mA supply would be acceptable, for example.

### Plug

The Board of Education has both a barrel jack, which can be connected to a barrel plug, and a 9 V battery connector, which can be connected to a 9 V battery extension. The HomeWork Board has only the 9 V battery connector.

### Barrel Plug

Figure D-1 shows DC supply commonly used with the BASIC Stamp and Board of Education. It has a 2.1 mm center-positive barrel plug along with the center positive symbol that is evident on its label.

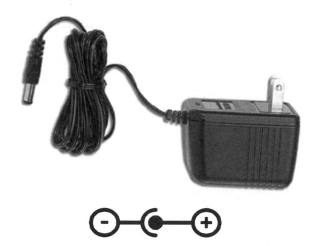

**Figure D-1**
DC Supply with Barrel Plug
and Center Positive Symbol

## 9 V Battery Extension

Figure D-2 shows an AC adapter connected to a 9 V battery extension that can be used with the BASIC Stamp HomeWork Board. See WARNING discussed next.

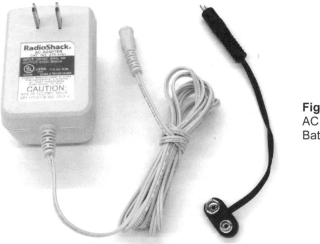

**Figure D-2**
AC Adapter with 9 V
Battery Extension

## WARNING - Beware of Universal AC Adapters and Reversed Supply Terminals

Figure D-3 shows a common mistake that should be avoided with universal adapters. Many of these allow you to reverse the terminals on the 9 V battery extension. Although it cannot hurt the BASIC Stamp, Board of Education or Homework Board, it can destroy the Parallax Standard Servo connected to Vin in a matter of seconds. The only system that can protect the servo from this mistake is the Board of Education Rev C (with jumper set to Vdd).

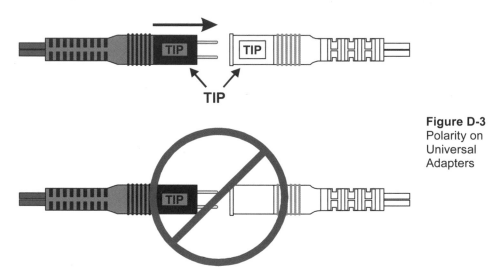

**Figure D-3**
Polarity on
Universal
Adapters

## Beware of "Battery Replacers"

Many battery replacers are designed to supply appliances with low current draw. With current ratings in the neighborhood of 10 mA, their output capacities are insufficient for many of the activities in this text. For example, two LEDs connected to 220 Ω resistors draw a total of 14.5 mA, and the BASIC Stamp takes an additional 3 to 7 mA. A servo draws upwards of 100 mA, and that definitely won't work with a "battery replacer".

NOTE: It's pretty easy to tell when a circuit is drawing more current that the supply can deliver because the Pwr LED on the Board of Education (or HomeWork Board) flickers and/or goes dim.

# Appendix E: Trouble-Shooting

Here is a list of things to try to quickly fix any difficulties getting the BASIC Stamp Editor to communicate with the BASIC Stamp:

√  If you are using a Board of Education Rev C, make sure the power switch is set to position-1.
√  Rule out dead batteries and incorrect or malfunctioning power supplies by using a new 9 V battery.
√  Make sure the serial cable is firmly connected to both the computer's COM port and the DB9 connector on the Board of Education or BASIC Stamp HomeWork Board.
√  Make sure that your serial cable is a normal serial cable.  DO NOT USE A NULL MODEM CABLE.  Most null modem cables are labeled NULL or Null Modem; visually inspect the cable for any such labeling.  If you find that label, do not try to use it to program the BASIC Stamp.
√  Disable any palmtop communication software.

If you are using a BASIC Stamp and Board of Education, also check the following:

√  Make sure the BASIC Stamp was inserted into the socket right-side-up, aligning the reference notch as shown in Figure 1-28 on page 17.
√  If you are using a DC power supply that plugs into the wall, make sure it is plugged in to both the wall and the Board of Education.  Verify that the green Pwr light on the Board of Education emits light when the DC supply is plugged in.
√  Make sure the BASIC Stamp is firmly inserted into the socket.  Visually inspect the BASIC Stamp to make sure that none of the pins folded under the module instead of sinking into their sockets on the Board of Education. Disconnect power first, then press down firmly on the module with your thumb.

If your Identification Window looks similar to Figure E-1, it means that the BASIC Stamp Editor cannot find your BASIC Stamp on any COM port. Note that the Loopback and Echo columns show "No." If you have this problem, try the following:

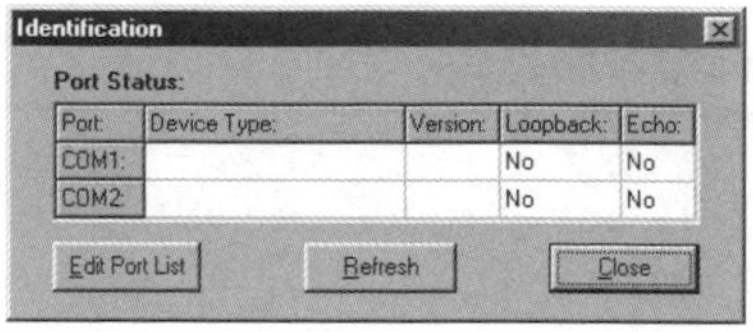

**Figure E-1**
Identification Window

*Example: BASIC Stamp
2 not found on COM
ports.*

√ Close the Identification Window.

√ Make sure the serial cable is properly connected.

√ Try the *Run → Identify* test again.

√ If you know the number of the COM port, but it does not appear in the Identification Window, use the *Edit Port List* button to add that COM port, and then try the *Run → Identify* test again.

√ If you have more than one COM port, try connecting your Board of Education or BASIC Stamp HomeWork Board to a different COM port and see if *Run → Identify* works then.

√ If you have a second computer, try it on the different computer.

If you get the error message "No BASIC Stamp Found" but the *Run → Identify* test shows a "Yes" in both columns for one of the COM ports, you may need to change a setting to your FIFO Buffers. This is happens occasionally with Microsoft Windows® 98 and XP users. Make a note of the COM port with the "Yes" messages, and try this:

Windows® 98:

√ Click on your computer desktop's *Start* button.

√ Select *Settings→ Control Panel → System → Device Manager → Ports (COM & LPT)*.

√ Select the COM port that was noted by the *Run → Identify* test.

√ Select *Properties → Port Settings → Advanced*.

√ Uncheck the box labeled "Use FIFO Buffers" then click *OK*.

√ Click *OK* as needed to close each window and return to the BASIC Stamp Editor.

√ Try downloading a program once more.

Windows® 2000:

√ Click on your computer desktop's *Start* button.

√ Select *Settings → Control Panel → System → Hardware → Device Manager → Ports (COM & LPT)*.
√ Select the COM port that was noted by the *Run → Identify* test.
√ Select *→ Port Settings → Advanced*.
√ Uncheck the box labeled "Use FIFO Buffers" then click *OK*.
√ Click *OK* as needed to close each window and return to the BASIC Stamp Editor.
√ Try downloading a program once more.

Windows® XP:

√ Click on your computer desktop's *Start* button.
√ Select *Control Panel → Printers and Other Hardware*.
√ *In the* "See Also*"* box select *System*.
√ Select *Hardware → Device Manager → Ports*.
√ Enter the COM port number noted by the *Run→ Identify* test.
√ Select *Port Settings → Advanced*.
√ Uncheck the box labeled "Use FIFO Buffers" then click *OK*.
√ Click *OK* to close each window as needed and return to the BASIC Stamp Editor.
√ Try downloading a program once more.

Windows® XP Pro:

√ Click on your computer desktop's *Start* button.
√ Select *Control Panel → System → Hardware → Device Manager → Ports(COM & LPT1)*.
√ Select the Communications Port number noted by the *Run → Identify* test.
√ Select *Properties → Port Settings → Advanced*.
√ Uncheck the box labeled "Use FIFO Buffers" then click *OK*.
√ Click *OK* to close each window as needed and return to the BASIC Stamp Editor.
√ Try downloading a program once more.

If none of these solutions work, you may go to www.parallax.com and follow the Support link. Or, email support@parallax.com or call Tech Support toll free at 1-888-99-STAMP.

# Appendix F: More about Electricity

**What's an Electron?** An electron is one of the three fundamental parts of an atom; the other two are the proton and the neutron. One or more protons and neutrons stick together in the center of the molecule in an area called the nucleus. Electrons are very small in comparison to protons and neutrons, and they orbit around the nucleus. Electrons repel each other, and electrons and protons attract to each other.

**What's Charge?** The tendency for an electron to repel from another electron and attract to a nearby proton is called negative charge. The tendency for a proton to repel from another proton and attract an electron is called positive charge. When a molecule has more electrons than protons, it is said to be negatively charged. If a molecule has fewer electrons than protons, it is said to be positively charged. If a molecule has the same number of protons and electrons, it is called neutrally charged.

**What's Voltage?** Voltage is like electrical pressure. When a negatively charged molecule is near a positively charged molecule, the extra electron on the negatively charged molecule tries to get from the negatively charged molecule to the positively charged molecule. Batteries keep a compound with negatively charged molecules separated from a compound with positively charged molecules. Each of these compounds is connected to one of the battery's terminals; the positively charged compound is connected to the positive (+) terminal, and the negative compound is connected to the negative (-) terminal.

**The volt** is a measurement of electric pressure, and it's abbreviated with a capital V. You may already be familiar with the nine volt (9 V) battery used to supply power to the Board of Education or HomeWork Board. Other common batteries include the 12 V batteries found in cars and the 1.5 V AA batteries used in calculators, handheld games, and other devices.

**What's Current?** Current is a measure of the number of electrons per second passing through a circuit. Sometimes the molecules bond in a chemical reaction that creates a compound (that is neutrally charged). Other times, the electron leaves the negatively charged molecule and joins the positively charged molecule by passing though a circuit like the one you just built and tested. The letter most commonly used to refer to current in schematics and books is capital 'I'.

**What's an amp?** An amp is the basic unit of current, and the notation for the amp is the capital 'A'. Compared to the circuits you are using with the BASIC Stamp, an amp is a very large amount of current. It's a convenient value for describing the amount of current that a car battery supplies to headlights, the fan that cool a car's engine, and other high power devices.

**What's Resistance?** Resistance is the element in a circuit that slows down the flow of electrons (the current) from a battery's negative terminal to its positive terminal.

**The ohm** is the basic measurement of resistance. It has already been introduced and it's abbreviated with the Greek letter omega ($\Omega$).

**What's a Conductor?** Copper wire has almost no resistance, and it's called a conductor.

## BONUS ACTIVITY: OHMS LAW, VOLTAGE, AND CURRENT

This activity applies some of the definitions just discussed.

### Ohm's Law Parts

(1) Resistor – 220 Ω (red-red-brown)
(1) Resistor – 470 Ω (yellow-violet-brown)
(1) Resistor – 1 kΩ   (brown-black-red)
(1) Resistor – 2 kΩ   (red-black-red)
(1) LED – any color

### Test Circuit

The resistance value of $R_i$ in Figure F-1 can be changed.  Lower resistance allows more current through the LED, and it glows more brightly.  Higher resistance values will cause the LED to look dim because they do not allow as much current to pass through the circuit.

√  Disconnect power to your Board of Education or HomeWork Board whenever you modify the circuit.
√  Build the circuit shown starting with a 220 Ω resistor.
√  Modify the circuit by replacing the 220 Ω resistor with a 470 Ω resistor.  Was the LED less bright?
√  Repeat using the 1 kΩ resistor, then the 2 kΩ resistor, checking the change in brightness each time.

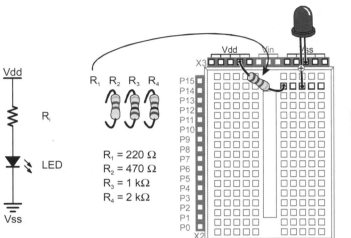

**Figure F-1**
LED Current Monitor

F

If you are using a 9 V battery, you can also compare the brightness of a different voltage source, Vin. Vin is connected directly to the 9 V battery's + terminal, and Vss is connected directly to the battery's negative terminal. Vdd is called regulated 5 V. That's about half the voltage of the 9 V battery.

√ If you are not using a 9 V battery, stop here and skip to the Calculating the Current section below. Otherwise, continue.
√ Start with the circuit shown in Figure F-1, but use a 1 kΩ resistor.
√ Make a note of how bright the LED is.
√ Disconnect power
√ Modify the circuit by disconnecting the resistor lead from Vdd and plugging it into Vin.
√ When you plug the power back in, is the LED brighter? How much brighter?

 **DO NOT** try the Vin experiment with a 220 or 470 Ω resistor, it will supply the LED with more current than it is rated for.

## Calculating the Current

The BASIC Stamp Manual has some rules about how much current it can supply to circuits. If you don't follow these rules, you may end up damaging your BASIC Stamp.

The rules have to do with how much current an I/O pin is allowed to deliver and how much current a group of I/O pins is allowed to deliver.

**Current Rules for BASIC Stamp I/O Pins**

- An I/O pin can "source" 20 mA. In other words, if you send the **HIGH** signal to an I/O pin, it should not supply the LED circuit with more than 20 mA.

- If you rewire the LED circuit so that the BASIC Stamp makes the LED turn on when you send the **LOW** command, an I/O pin can "sink" up to 25 mA.

- P0 through P7 can only source up to 20 mA. Likewise with P8 through P15. If you have lots of LED circuits, you will need larger resistors so that you don't draw too much current.

If you know how to calculate how much current your circuit will use, then you can decide if it's OK to make your LEDs glow that brightly. Every electronic component has rules for what it does with voltage, resistance, and current. For the light emitting diode, the rule is a value called the diode forward voltage. For the resistor, the rule is called Ohm's Law. You need to figure out how much current your LED circuit is using. There are also rules for how current and voltage add up in circuits. These are called Kirchoff's Voltage and Current Laws.

**Vdd – Vss = 5 V** The voltage (electrical pressure) from Vdd to Vss is 5 V. This is called regulated voltage, and it works about the same as a battery that is exactly 5 V.

**Vin – Vss = 9 V** If you are using 9 V battery, the voltage from Vin to Vss is 9 V. Be careful. If you are using a voltage regulator that plugs into the wall, even if it says 9 V, it could go as high as 18 V.

**Ground and/or reference** refer to the negative terminal of a circuit. When it comes to the BASIC Stamp and Board of Education, Vss is considered the ground reference. It is zero volts, and if you are using a 9 V battery, it is that battery's negative terminal. The battery's positive terminal is 9 V. Vdd is 5 V (above the Vss reference of 0 V), and it is a special voltage made by a voltage regulator chip to supply the BASIC Stamp with power.

**Ohm's Law: V = I × R** The voltage measured across a resistor's terminals (V) equals the current passing through the resistor (I) times the resistor's resistance (R).

**Diode Forward Voltage:** When an LED is emitting light, the voltage measured from anode to cathode will be around 1.6 V. Regardless of whether the current passing through it is a large or a small value, the voltage will continue to be approximately 1.6 V.

**Kirchoff's Voltage Law Simplified: voltage used equals voltage supplied.** If you supply a circuit with 5 V, the number of volts all the parts use had better add up to 5 V.

**Kirchoff's Current Law Simplified: current in equals current out.** The current that enters an LED circuit from Vdd is the same amount of current that leaves it through Vss. Also, if you connect three LEDs to the BASIC Stamp, and each LED circuit draws 5 mA, it means the BASIC Stamp has to supply all the circuits with a total of 15 mA.

### Example Calculation: One Circuit, Two Circuits

Calculating how much current an LED circuit draws takes two steps:

1. Figure out the voltage across the resistor
2. Use Ohm's Law to figure out the current through the resistor.

Figure F-2 shows how to figure out the voltage across the resistor. The voltage supplied is on the left; it's 5 V. The voltages used are on the right. The voltage we don't know at the start is $V_R$, the voltage across the resistor. But, we do know that the voltage across the LED is 1.6 V (the diode forward voltage). We also know that the voltage across the parts has to add up to 5 V because of Kirchoff's Voltage Law. The difference between 5 V and 1.6 V is 3.4 V, so that must be the voltage across the resistor $V_R$.

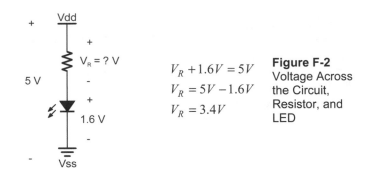

$$V_R + 1.6V = 5V$$
$$V_R = 5V - 1.6V$$
$$V_R = 3.4V$$

**Figure F-2**
Voltage Across
the Circuit,
Resistor, and
LED

**Kilo is metric for 1000.** The metric way of saying 1000 is kilo, and it's abbreviated with the lower-case k. Instead of writing 1000 Ω, you can write 1 kΩ. Either way, it's pronounced one-kilo-ohm. Likewise, 2000 Ω is written 2 kΩ.

**Milli is metric for 1/1000,** and it is abbreviated with a lower-case m. If the BASIC Stamp supplies an LED circuit with 3.4 thousandths of an amp, that's 3.4 milliamps, or 3.4 mA.

**What's a mA?** Pronounced milliamp, it's the notation for one-one-thousandth-of-an-amp. The 'm' in mA is the metric notation for milli, which stands for 1/1000. The 'A' in mA stands for amps. Put the two together, and you have milliamps, and it's very useful for describing the amount of current drawn by the BASIC Stamp and the circuits connected to it.

**How much current is 7.23 mA?** It's the amount of current the LED shown on the right side of Figure F-3 conducts. You can replace the 470 Ω resistor with a 220 Ω resistor, and the circuit will conduct 15.5 mA, and the LED will glow more brightly. If you use a 1000 Ω resistor, the circuit will conduct 3.4 mA, and the LED will glow less brightly. A 2000 Ω resistor will cause the LED to glow less brightly still, and the current will be 1.7 mA.

Figure F-3 shows an example of how to calculate the current the circuit uses if the resistor is 470 Ω. Start with Ohm's Law. You know the answers to V (3.4 V) and R (470 Ω). Now, all you have to do is solve for I (the current).

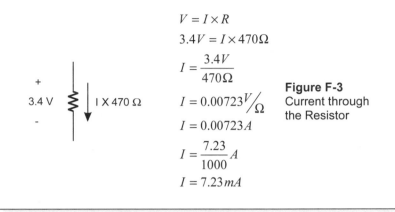

$$V = I \times R$$
$$3.4V = I \times 470\Omega$$
$$I = \frac{3.4V}{470\Omega}$$
$$I = 0.00723 V/\Omega$$
$$I = 0.00723 A$$
$$I = \frac{7.23}{1000} A$$
$$I = 7.23\, mA$$

**Figure F-3**
Current through
the Resistor

 **Yes, it's true !  1 A = 1 V/Ω**  (One amp is one volt per ohm).

Let's say you turned two LEDs on at the same time. That means that inside the BASIC Stamp, it is supplying the circuits as shown in Figure F-4. Have we exceeded the 20 mA limit? Let's find out. Remember that the simplified version of Kirchoff's Current Law says that the total current drawn from the supply equals the current supplied to all the circuits. That means that I in Figure F-4 has to equal the total of the two currents being drawn. Simply add the two current draws, and you'll get an answer of 14.5 mA. You are still under the 20 mA limit, so your circuit is a safe design.

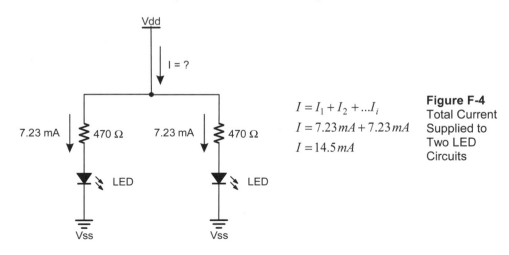

$$I = I_1 + I_2 + ...I_i$$
$$I = 7.23\, mA + 7.23\, mA$$
$$I = 14.5\, mA$$

**Figure F-4**
Total Current
Supplied to
Two LED
Circuits

## Your Turn – Modifying the Circuit

√ Repeat the exercise in Figure F-2, but use Vin – Vss = 9V. The answer is $V_R$ = 7.4 V

√ Repeat the exercise in Figure F-3, but use a 1 kΩ resistor. Answer: I = 3.4 mA.

√ Use $V_R$ = 7.4 V to do the exercise in Figure F-3 with a 1 kΩ resistor. Answer: I = 7.4 mA.

√ Repeat the exercise shown in Figure F-4 with one of the resistors at 470 Ω and the other at 1 kΩ. Answer: I = 7.23 mA + 3.4 mA = 10.63 mA.

# Appendix G: RTTTL Format Summary

This is a summary intended to help make sense out of RTTTL format. The full RTTTL specification can be found published at various web sites. Using any search engine, use the keywords RTTTL specification, to review web pages that include the specification.

Here is an example of an RTTTL format ringtone:

```
TakeMeOutToTheBallgame:d=4,o=7,b=225:2c6,c,a6,g6,e6,2g.6,2d6,p,
2c6,c,a6,g6,e6,2g.6,g6,p,p,a6,g#6,a6,e6,f6,g6,a6,p,f6,2d6,p,2a6
,a6,a6,b6,c, d,b6,a6,g6
```

The text before the first colon is what the cell phone displays as the name of the song. In this case, the ringtone is named:

```
TakeMeOutToTheBallGame:
```

Between the first and second colon, the default settings for the song are entered using d, o, and b. Here is what they mean:

```
d - duration
o - octave
b - beats per minute or tempo.
```

In the TakeMeOutToTheBallGame, the default settings are:

```
d=4,o=7,b=225:
```

The notes in the melody are entered after the second colon, and they are separated by commas. If just the note letter is used, that note will be played for the default duration in the default octave. For example, the second note in TakeMeOutToTheBallGame is:

```
,c,
```

Since it has no other information, it will be played for the default quarter note duration (d=4), in the seventh octave (o=7).

A note could have up to five characters between the commas; here is what each character specifies:

```
,duration  note  sharp  dot  octave,
```

For example:

```
,2g#.6,
```

means play the half note G-sharp for 1 ½ the duration of a half note, and play it in the sixth octave.

Here are a few examples from TakeMeOutToTheBallGame:

> `,2g.6,` – half note, G, dotted, sixth octave
> `,a6,`   – default quarter note duration, A note played in the sixth octave
> `,g#6,`  – quarter duration, g note, sharp (denoted by #), sixth octave

The character:

> `,p,`

stands for pause, and it is used for rests. With no extra information, the p plays for the default quarter-note duration. You could also play a half note's worth of rest by using:

> `,2p,`

Here is an example of a dotted rest:

> `,2p.,`

In this case the rest would last for a half note plus a quarter note's duration.

# Index

- % -

%, 177

- * -

*, 94
**, 243
*/, 95, 243

- 3 -

3-position switch, 16

- 7 -

7-Segment Display, 165–70

- A -

Active-High, 79
Active-Low, 79
AD5220 Digital Potentiometer

Pin Map, 266

Pin Names and Functions, 266

Algorithm, 96
American Standard Code for
Information Interchange, 30
Amp, 317
Anode, 40
Array, 290
ASCII, 30, 252

- B -

Base, 263
BASIC Stamp

BASIC Stamp 2 Module, 1

Components, 305

HomeWork Board, 303

BASIC Stamp Editor

Identification Window, 19

Identify, 314, 315

Memory Map, 261

Software, 5

Trouble-Shooting, 313

BASIC Stamp HomeWork Board, 14
BASIC Stamp HomeWork Board

Components, 307

Battery, 44
Beat, 226
Bi-Color LED, 61
Binary Numbers, 20, 77, 177
Bit, 55, 175, 246
Board of Education, 13

Components, 306

Full Kit, 301

Revision label, 105

Servo Header, 106

Board of Education Rev B

Components, 308

Boe-Bot, 3
Breadboard. See Prototyping Area
Byte, 55, 246

- C -

Cadmium Sulfide, 189
Capacitor, 143–45, 149

Ceramic, 150

Polar – identifying terminals, 143

Carriage return, 25
Cathode, 40
Charge, 317
Circuit, 41
Collector, 263
COM Port, 15, 196
Comment, 24
Comment, 52
Compiler directives, 21, 24
Components

BASIC Stamp, 305

BASIC Stamp HomeWork Board, 307

Board of Education, 306

Board of Education Rev B, 308

Conductor, 317
Counting, 90
CR, 25
Current, 38, 44, 45, 317

Flow, 45

Milliamp, 322

Cycle, 219

- D -

DATA, 230
DEBUG

Command, 25

DEBUG Formatters

CR, 25

DEC, 25

Debug Terminal, 23

Receive Windowpane, 120, 121

Transmit Windowpane, 120, 121

DEBUGIN, 120–23, 290
DEBUGIN Formatters

STR, 290

DEC, 25, 120
Digital Potentiometer, 265–75
Diode Forward Voltage, 321
DIRH, 175–78
Disconnect power, 32
Dot Notes, 238
Duration, 222, 229, 231, 232–37

- E -

Echo, 120, 121
EEPROM, 197–203, 230, 261
Electron, 45, 317
Embedded system, 1
Emitter, 263
END, 25
EXIT, 290

- F -

Fetch and Execute, 261
Flat, 227
FOR…NEXT, 53–56, 114
FREQOUT, 221
Frequency

Duration, 222

Mixing, 222, 225–27

Musical Notes, 227–29

- G -

GOSUB, 206
Ground, 321
Guarantee, 3

- H -

Hertz, 219
HIGH, 49
Hz. See Hertz

- I -

I/O Pins. See Input/Output Pins
IC. See Integrated Circuit
Identification Window, 19
Identify, 314, 315
IF…ELSEIF…ELSE, 85
IF…THEN…ELSE, 81
IN3, 77
IN7, 151
Indicator light, 37
Input/Output Pin

Input, 71

Input/Output Pins, 42

Default Direction, 177

Integer, 243
Integrated Circuit, 262

Pin Map, 266

Reference Notch, 266

Interference, 226

- J -

Jumper, 106

- K -

kB, 199
KB, 199
KCL, 321
Kilo, 322
Kilobyte, 199
Kirchoff's Laws (Simplified)

Current, 321

Voltage, 321

KVL, 321

- L -

Label, 206
Light Emitting Diode, 37–38, 40–41

Anode, 40

Bi-Color, 61

Cathode, 40

Circuit Calculations, 321

Schematic Symbol, 40

Terminals, 40

LOOKDOWN, 182
LOOKUP, 179–81
LOW, 49

- M -

mA, 322
Math Operations, 242
Memory Map, 198, 261
Menu, 285
Metric units of measure, 322
Microcontroller, 1
Microsecond, 114
Milli, 322
Millisecond, 49, 114
Mixing, 222, 225–27
Multiply, 94
Music

Dot, 238

Flat, 227

FREQOUT and Notes, 228

Natural, 227

Note Duration, 229, 231, 232–37

Notes, 227

Piano Keyboard, 227

Rest, 233

Ringtone, 245

RTTTL Format, 325–26

RTTTL Format, 245, 250–56

Sharp, 227

Tempo, 233

- N -

Natural, 227
nc, 167
Nested Loop, 223–25
Neutral, 45
Nib, 55, 246
No-Connect, 167
Notes, 227
NPN, 263

- O -

Offset, 155
Ohm, 38, 317
Ohm's Law, 321
Omega, 38
ON…GOSUB, 285–94
Operator, 95
OUTH \r, 174
Overflow, 247

- P -

Parallax Standard Servo, 103

Caution, 104, 154

Parts, 104

Power Supply Caution, 312

Parallel

Bus, 173

Device, 173

Part Drawing

7-Segment Display, 165

Bi-Color LED, 61

LED, 40

Photoresistor, 190

Piezoelectric Speaker, 219

Potentiometer, 140

Pushbutton – Normally Open, 71

Resistor, 38

Transistor (NPN), 263

PAUSE, 49
PBASIC Commands

DEBUG, 25

DEBUGIN, 120–23, 290

DEC, 120

DO…LOOP, 49

END, 25

EXIT, 290

FOR…NEXT, 53–56, 114

FREQOUT, 221

GOSUB, 206

HIGH, 49

IF…ELSEIF…ELSE, 85

IF…THEN…ELSE, 81

LOOKDOWN, 182

LOOKUP, 179–81

LOW, 49

ON...GOSUB, 285

PAUSE, 49

PULSOUT, 113

RANDOM, 95

RCTIME, 151–52, 152

READ, 202–3, 230

RETURN, 206

SELECT...CASE, 245–50

TOGGLE, 270

UNTIL, 93

WRITE, 199–201, 230

PBASIC Directives

DATA, 230–32

PBASIC, 24

PIN, 285

Stamp, 24

PBASIC I/O Registers

DIRH, 175–78

IN3, 77

OUTH, 175–78

PBASIC Operators

%, 177

*, 94

**, 243

*/, 95, 243

DCD, 243

Order of Execution, 242

Parenthesis, 242

Photoresistor, 189–90

RC-Time Circuit, 190

Piano Keyboard, 227

Piezoelectric

Element, 220

Speaker, 219

Pin Map, 166, 266

Pitch, 219

Polling, 90

Potentiometer, 139–41

Digital, 265–75

Terminals, 140

Prototyping Area

Input/Output Pins, 41

Power Terminals, 41

Prototyping Areas

Socket, 41

Pseudo Random, 96

Pull-Up Resistor, 79

Pulse, 113

PULSOUT, 113

Pushbutton, 71–72

Circuit, 75–77

Normally Open, 72

- R -

Radio Control, 153

RANDOM, 95

RCTIME, 151–52, 152
READ, 199, 230
Receive Windowpane, 120, 121
Reference, 321
Reference Notch, 266
Resistance, 317
Resistor, 38–40, 48

Color Codes, 39–40

Leads, 38

Pull-Down, 79

Pull-Up, 79

Tolerance, 39

Rest, 233
RETURN, 206
Ringtone, 245
Robot, 2–4
RTTTL Format, 245, 250–56, 325–26

- S -

Scaling, 155
Schematic

Dots Indicate Connections, 84

Drawing, 45

Schematic Symbol

7-Segment Display, 166

Bi-Color LED, 61

LED, 40

Photoresistor, 190

Piezoelectric Speaker, 219

Potentiometer, 140

Pushbutton – Normally Open, 71

Resistor, 38

Transistor (NPN), 263

Seed, 96
SELECT...CASE, 245
Sensor, 189
Sensor Array, 279, 285
Servo, 103–4

Cable, 103

Case, 103

Caution Statement, 104, 154

Connecting to BASIC Stamp, 105–13

Header, 106

Horn, 103

Jack, 103

Potentiometer Controlled, 153

Power Supply Caution, 312

Sharp, 227
Speaker, piezoelectric, 220
Stamp Plot Lite, 193–97
Status indicator, 37
STR, 290
Subroutine, 206–13

Label, 206

Subsystem Integration, 279
Superposition, 226
Syntax highlighting, 24

- T -

Tempo, 233
Terminal

Piezoelectric Speaker, 220

TOGGLE, 270
Token, 261
Tolerance, 39
Transistor, 262, 263–65

2N3904, 263

Base, 263

Base Current, 264

Collector, 263

Emitter, 263

NPN, 263

Switching, 264

Transmit Windowpane, 120, 121

- U -

UNTIL, 93
US232B, 299
USB to Serial Adapter, 6, 16, 299

- V -

Variables, 53, 55, 246

Array, 290

Bit, 55, 246

Byte, 55, 246

Nib, 55, 246

Word, 55, 246

Vdd, 41, 46, 321
Vin, 41, 321
Volt, 317
Voltage, 45, 317
Vss, 41, 46, 321

- W -

What's a Microcontroller

Parts Kit, 301

Text, 301

Word, 55, 246
WRITE, 199–201

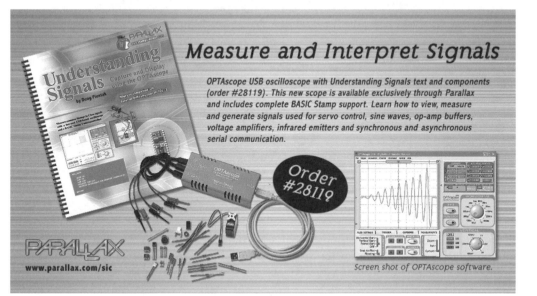

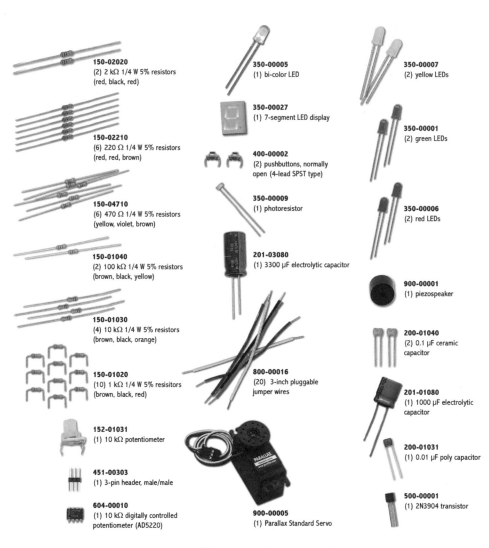

**150-02020**
(2) 2 kΩ 1/4 W 5% resistors
(red, black, red)

**150-02210**
(6) 220 Ω 1/4 W 5% resistors
(red, red, brown)

**150-04710**
(6) 470 Ω 1/4 W 5% resistors
(yellow, violet, brown)

**150-01040**
(2) 100 kΩ 1/4 W 5% resistors
(brown, black, yellow)

**150-01030**
(4) 10 kΩ 1/4 W 5% resistors
(brown, black, orange)

**150-01020**
(10) 1 kΩ 1/4 W 5% resisitors
(brown, black, red)

**152-01031**
(1) 10 kΩ potentiometer

**451-00303**
(1) 3-pin header, male/male

**604-00010**
(1) 10 kΩ digitally controlled
potentiometer (AD5220)

**350-00005**
(1) bi-color LED

**350-00027**
(1) 7-segment LED display

**400-00002**
(2) pushbuttons, normally
open (4-lead SPST type)

**350-00009**
(1) photoresistor

**201-03080**
(1) 3300 µF electrolytic capacitor

**800-00016**
(20) 3-inch pluggable
jumper wires

**900-00005**
(1) Parallax Standard Servo

**350-00007**
(2) yellow LEDs

**350-00001**
(2) green LEDs

**350-00006**
(2) red LEDs

**900-00001**
(1) piezospeaker

**200-01040**
(2) 0.1 µF ceramic
capacitor

**201-01080**
(1) 1000 µF electrolytic
capacitor

**200-01031**
(1) 0.01 µF poly capacitor

**500-00001**
(1) 2N3904 transistor

Parts and quantities in the various What's a Microcontroller kits are subject to change without notice. Parts may differ from what is shown in this picture. Please contact stampsinclass@parallax.com if you have any questions about your kit.

## WHAT'S A MICROCONTROLLER?

Find the answer as you:

- **SEND SIGNALS**
  by blinking LEDs
- **SENSE CONTACT**
  with pushbuttons
- **READ A DIAL**
  using a potentiometer
- **MEASURE LIGHT**
  with a photoresistor

- **CONTROL A MOTOR**
  using a servo
- **MAKE MUSIC**
  to play on a piezo speaker
- **DISPLAY DATA**
  on a 7-segment LED
- **PREPARE YOURSELF**
  for robotics, programming, and inventing!

**Hours to completion: 40**
**Level of Difficulty (out of 10): 3**

## You will need one of the following sets of hardware:

**BS2-IC is built onto the board!**

BASIC Stamp What's a Microcontroller Kit
(#90005 - individual parts not pictured)

Board of Education® Full Kit (#28102) combined with *What's a Microcontroller?* Parts Kit (#28122; not pictured)

**Parallax software CD included with both kits. Requires a PC running Windows® 98 or higher, a 9 V battery (not included) and an available serial port -OR- USB port with USB to Serial Adapter (#800-00030).**

WARNING: This product contains chemicals, including lead, known to the State of California to cause birth defects or other reproductive harm. *Wash hands after handling.*

## The BASIC Stamp® and Stamps in Class™

A BASIC Stamp microcontroller module is like a small computer about the size of a postage stamp. Its clear, easy-to-learn programming language makes the BASIC Stamp module widely popular with hobbyists and artists alongside scientists and engineers. Millions can be found all over the planet on everything from deep-sea submersibles and arctic expeditions to cave explorations and high-altitude balloon flights. These very same BASIC Stamp modules are also found at the core of the Parallax Stamps in Class educational curriculum. *What's a Microcontroller?* is the perfect gateway to *Robotics with the Boe-Bot, Applied Sensors*, and more. Our Stamps in Class program fills the need for affordable electronics and engineering resources for high schools, vocational schools, colleges, and independent inventors. See our full line of Parallax educational products, support services, and applications at www.parallax.com.

This Stamps in Class text features expertly drawn schematics side-by-side with wiring diagrams. Now learning to use the BASIC Stamp is clearer than ever!

## About the Author

This *What's a Microcontroller?* Student Guide was authored by Andy Lindsay after collecting observations and educator feedback while teaching BASIC Stamp Educator's Courses for Parallax, Inc. Andy received his Bachelor of Science degree in Electrical and Electronic Engineering from CSU, Sacramento. Andy is a Product Engineer and Educational Author for Parallax, Inc.

ISBN 1-928982-02-6

9 781928 982029    90000>